GLEAM FLYING ONWARD

Gleam Flying Onward

A Century of Bruton School for Girls

David Parsons

ELSP

Published in 2001 by
ELSP
1 The Shambles
Bradford on Avon
Wiltshire
BA15 1JS

Typesetting and design by Ex Libris Press

Printed by Cromwell Press
Trowbridge, Wiltshire

ISBN 1 903341 69 8

~ To Nicolette ~

CONTENTS

Preface

Having worked in Bruton School for Girls for almost a fifth of its first hundred years, I have grown to love it, and was delighted at Judy Wade's invitation, backed by the Governors, to write its history. The task was a joy, and made easy by the kindness of many people.

Mrs Wade in her years as Headmistress had begun to collect materials about the School, and the Hon. Mrs. Victoria Jolliffe generously lent many papers belonging to her grandfather Sir Arthur Hobhouse covering his years as Chairman of Governors. The school magazine, The Gleam, provided the skeleton of the narrative, fleshed out not only by the papers mentioned but also by letters written, photographs lent and interviews readily given by old girls and former Headmistresses and teaching, administrative and ground staff. Their names (using maiden names for old girls) are recorded in the text of the book. One of my greatest pleasures was to sit listening to a variety of people all speaking with affection, not unmixed with criticism, of times they remembered and people they had known. It is their words that give this book its life.

For the early years my problem was to find out enough information to paint a full and true picture of events and personalities. It was exhilarating to piece together newspaper reports found on micro-fiche in the County Library, reminiscences in speeches given twenty-one or twenty-nine years after the events, and carefully preserved archives, to find out exactly what happened in the year 1900. For the later chapters the problem was what to select from a wealth of material, and how to write honestly of my own contemporaries without causing offence or embarrassment. I have side-stepped the latter issue as far as possible by using the words of others, but no doubt my own prejudices and preferences still show through.

I have been encouraged by the support of the present Principal, Mrs Barbara Bates, who appreciates the importance of history. Judy Wade, Val Floyd and Letitia Holt have done a splendid job in pointing out many errors in my work, but mistakes that remain are entirely my responsibility.

David Parsons
Downend, South Gloucestershire
April 2001

William Knight

Chapter 1

"That very hot July day"

July 1900 was very hot. Hay-making had been actively carried on during the past three or four weeks in Bruton churchyard and, for the first time within living memory, a very fine rick had been made there. One particularly fine day a group of public-spirited local people were meeting to choose the first Headmistress for the new school they were building.

Arriving at Cole Station on the Somerset and Dorset Railway, one of several applicants for the post, Edith Radford, had her first sight of the still unfinished school. She was only 31 years old, brought up in a town. William Knight, headmaster of the recently opened Sexey's Trade School in Bruton (1889), and one of the interviewing panel, had sent three of his children, Ethel, Arthur and Edgar, to Cole Station to meet her. She would have worn a long skirt after the fashion of the day. Bustles and corsets were out in 1900, and the skirt was continuing its relentless rise past the ankle, while the Rational Dress League was calling for women to abandon dresses - for knickerbockers; but MissRadford clearly had no use for such trends. (An early pupil who had trodden on the train of Miss Radford's skirt received a quick reprimand: "You'll never make a lady if you don't look where you're going.") Her hair was probably drawn back severely, with a centre parting. Perhaps she wore a high frilly collar such as we see in a 1909 photo.

As she took the short walk with the Knight children, and possibly with some of the other candidates also, she had little thought, as she confessed later, that the choice would fall on her. She was not, however, coming to interview as a complete unknown.

Early in that year Henry Hobhouse, at one of the many meetings he attended on County business, had bumped into an old friend, the Reverend Doctor Thomas Scott Holmes, Chancellor of Wells Cathedral, and had told him that a school was being built and equipped on Sunny Hill. "We still have to find a Headmistress," he confessed. "It is giving the Governors some anxiety." Chancellor Holmes immediately replied, "The Governors need not be troubled about that. I know someone very suitable." And the name he had suggested was Miss Radford.

Edith was always keenly aware of world events, and commented decisively upon them. As she looked forward to her interview, she might have prepared comments on some recent developments. It was an exciting time. Since the 1870s everything had been in question, opinions, institutions, and conventions. Queen Victoria was still on the throne, but a number of socialist organisations had been emerging in the past 20 years. In February of 1900 trade unionists and socialists had founded a committee under Ramsay MacDonald to work for the election of Labour M. Ps. Of more particular interest to women, Millicent Fawcett's National Union of Women's Suffrage Societies was three years old.

Much else had filled the papers that year. The Prince of Wales had survived an attempt on his life in Belgium in April. In May, Parliament had raised the minimum age at which boys could work in coal mines from 12 to 13 years. The first long-distance bus service was being advertised: London to Leeds in 2 days. Central Railway "Tuppenny Tube" opened in London, connecting Shepherd's Bush with Bank. The first jug of Coca Cola had arrived in Britain.

Abroad, the Boxer Uprising, a violent movement by the Chinese people beginning in 1898 to rid their country of foreigners and foreign influences, was nearing its climax. But the event which had probably excited Edith Radford most, as it had everyone else, had happened a few weeks before the interview. The South African War, also known as the Boer War, had begun the previous year, involving nearly 450,000 British soldiers. After some months of Boer victories they had besieged Mafeking. When British troops under Lord Kitchener and Lord Roberts relieved the beleaguered garrison in May, the nation went wild. A new word entered the language, "to maffick", 'to rejoice with hysterical boisterousness, from the scenes in the streets of London on the news of the relief of the town,' as Chambers Dictionary puts it.

The Knight children were delighted by the way this town-bred lady appreciated the Somerset scenery and surroundings. As they came up from the station, they approached the site of the old Sunny Hill Inn and the children told her, "This hill is called Sunny Hill." She said "What a nice name." That scrap of conversation may have settled the official name of the School for the next 60 years, and its unofficial name for a century.

*   *   *

Edith may have wondered what kind of woman the founders were seeking to set the course of the new school. One role model, Dorothea Beale, was still alive and active, aged 69, as the principal of Cheltenham Ladies' College, where she had been in charge since 1858, and the subject of a well known rhyme:

Miss Buss and Miss Beale
Cupid's darts do not feel.
How different from us,
Miss Beale and Miss Buss.
(Anon, about 1884; Miss Buss was principal
of the North London Collegiate School.)

Miss Beale gave evidence in 1865 to the Endowed Schools Inquiry Commission and gave immense impetus to girls' education. She founded St Hilda's College, Cheltenham, the first English training college for secondary women teachers, in 1885, and St Hilda's Hall in Oxford in 1893, to give teachers in training the benefit of a year at Oxford (Cambridge already had Girton College founded in 1869 and Newnham College in 1871.). There was already a Headmistresses' Association, of which Miss Beale had recently been President. Edith Radford might have studied a book called 'Work and Play in Girls' Schools', which Miss Beale and others had written recently in 1898.

Secondary schools for girls were clearly not a new idea. Readers of nineteenth century novels may recall Charlotte Brontë's heroine in 'The Professor' teaching in such a school in Belgium, and Trollope's Grace Crawley helping at the Miss Prettymans' school in 'Silverbridge'. In real life, Haberdashers' Aske's School, an old foundation for boys, had made provision in 1875 for girls to be educated separately on its Hoxton site. The 1881 census shows a Weston-super-Mare school run by a woman of 63 and her niece, helped by two teachers and four servants, at which there were just nine girl boarders. At a different level, Roedean School was founded in 1885 by three sisters: Dorothy, Penelope, and Millicent Lawrence. They had three aims: "to give physical education [its] due place in every girl's life"; training for "independence and self-reliance"; and "sound and careful intellectual training." Nearer to Somerset, Colston's and Redlands in Bristol, and the Godolphin School in Salisbury, were well established.

What the new Headmistress was being asked to do was perhaps pioneering work of a different kind. Sunny Hill was to be a school for local girls, set in the depths of the countryside, and yet providing a first class education, at least comparable to that available to their brothers. There were indeed local primary schools for both girls and boys, and a couple of years before Miss Radford was born, a college prospectus set out the teachers they required:

Undoubtedly goodness and piety are prime qualifications for a schoolmistress, but they are not the only ones. A schoolmistress must be strong in health, pleasant in her manners, fond of children, sufficiently well-informed, and apt to convey her information in simple and attractive language. It should also be borne in mind that, as country children are generally more dull of comprehension than those who dwell in towns, it needs clearness of head, with patience and tact, to teach them. (1865 College of St. Matthias prospectus, quoted in Jane Miller: School for Women, Virago 1996 p.17-18)

Sunny Hill was to bridge the wide division between the privileged few and the deprived many. One writer put the situation (with boys chiefly in mind) like this: "The minority, destined to become potential leaders, attended the élite secondary schools: the English 'public' schools (such as Harrow, Eton, and Rugby), the French lycees, or the German Gymnasien. The majority, destined to become followers, either went from elementary schooling to vocational training or dropped out of school to go to work." (Compton's Encyclopedia)

*   *   *

The group that Edith faced at her interview consisted of the Governing Body; it was a formidable one. There sat the father of her young companions on the walk, the first Headmaster of Sexey's Trade School, old boy of King's School, Bruton, 33 year old William Albert Knight. That school had been founded by the Trustees of Hugh Sexey (1559-1619), a local boy who had worked himself from stable boy to Auditor at the King's Treasury; the new school was to be supported, though not to the same extent, by the same Trustees. William Knight was a tall, spare figure with dark hair and moustache, and blue-grey eyes that struck one of his pupils as penetrating, another as 'not piercing' but 'calm, reflective and compelling.' His initials W A K led to the nickname 'Wakker', and he had a strong sense of humour, often carefully disguised, so that a boy noted that 'he kept his thoughts to himself. You felt that you could not lie to him.'

Edith was probably introduced to Mr F. Whitelock from Castle Cary, whose daughter Caroline was to be a pupil of the new school, and to four men from Bruton itself: Mr F.E. Stroud, a Town Councillor, Roland T.A. Hughes Esq., a solicitor of great courtesy and charm, who was at that time rehearsing the Bruton Choral Society to sing Mendelssohn's 'Elijah'; Thomas Oatley Bennett Esq., a County Councillor, chairman of the Town Council and generous supporter of the town, whose wife had provided the School with its site, and Mr J. Golledge of Grove House, another "prospective parent" of the school, who acted as Secretary. Margaret Hobhouse was the only woman present. She clearly took the greatest interest in every detail connected with the education of girls and the management of the School, and Edith felt she would be always sure of a patient hearing for any matter she might wish to discuss with her. Her husband, Henry, was Chairman and obviously the leader.

Henry Hobhouse, still only in his mid forties and father of three girls and three boys, their ages ranging from 7 to 19, was a country squire living in Hadspen House, and a nephew of Baron Hobhouse. He had been educated at Eton and Balliol College, Oxford, where he gained first class honours in the Classics (Literae Humaniores) in 1875 at the age of 21. He was called to the bar at Lincoln's Inn, and became a county magistrate when only 26. A pioneer in local government theory, before he was 30 he had written, with Sir Robert Wright, 'An Outline of Local Government and Local Taxation.' He was elected the Liberal Member of Parliament for East Somerset in 1885, becoming Liberal Unionist the following year. In 1902 he would be a Privy Councillor, and two years after that he would begin a 20 year reign as Chairman of Somerset County Council. He was especially interested in agriculture, and, more to the present purpose, in education. When he was only 34 he had started the processes that led to the foundation of the Sexey's Schools at Blackford and Bruton. On his death in 1937, the school magazine wrote:

> As Member of Parliament, as Chairman of the Somerset County Council, as Pro-Chancellor of Bristol University, as Recorder of Wells, as Chairman of the County Councils Association, as an Ecclesiastical Commissioner, as a member of the National Assembly of the Church of England, and as member, and generally Chairman, of many other Boards and Committees, he had scope for his great gifts and wide knowledge; and he used his powers and energies for the welfare and good government of the community in general and for Somerset in particular.

This formidable person may have explained to Edith Radford the background to the school's foundation.

It had all begun when Henry Hobhouse had sprained his ankle in 1898. He was a Governor of Sexey's Trade School, and the Headmaster, William Knight, had come to visit him in Hadspen House. The schoolmaster in Mr Knight could not resist a weak pun about Mr Hobhouse 'hobbling about,' but Henry did not seem to be in the best of tempers. When, however, William Knight spoke of his three daughters, Ethel, Edith and Maud, and of his concern for their education, he forgot all about the sprained ankle. He rose and said "Ah! I was just going to come down and see you. Don't you think we ought to have a girls' school here?" So the idea was born. Mr Knight told him that neighbours like Mr. Golledge also wanted a good secondary school for their daughters. Sexey's School could provide the pattern.

Mr Knight at his own interview in 1889 had offered to start that school with only his wife and himself as teachers, and boarding accommodation for about 50, and since then the school had grown steadily. Mrs. Hobhouse was brought into the discussion, and it became clear that the first step was to gauge the strength of local support for the project. Perhaps Miss Radford had heard about the public meeting held in Sexey's School on Saturday October 15th 1898, at which, so the report stated, it was unanimously resolved: "That in the opinion of this meeting a demand exists for a middle-class Girls' School of a public character in this neighbourhood."

(Miss Chappell, by the way, read this in 1959 when preparations for the Diamond Jubilee were sending people to research the School's origins. She found what follows most interesting because it indicated the breadth of the founders' vision.)

"It would obviously be an advantage for the school to receive recognition and aid from public authorities, and to be eligible for this, it is necessary that it should be established on a public footing and not worked for private profit. It is therefore suggested that the requisite funds be provided by a Limited Liability Company, and that the interest shall not exceed a fixed maximum rate of, say 4 per cent per annum. The capital required will be at least a sum of £3,000. It was announced at the above meeting that more than half the required capital had been promised, in sums of not less than £50."

(As Miss Chappell was busy in 1959 with new buildings, she was in a good position to comment: "The capital expenditure [£3,000] compared with what we need today, even for our gym and classrooms, is fantastic.") The document approved by the 1898 public meeting concluded:

"The curriculum of the school will, it is hoped, correspond to that of the Sexey's Trade School for Boys, with any modifications which may be desirable for girls, and provision will be made for a fair proportion of boarders. If you are willing to take shares in such a company, when formed, you are requested to fill up the enclosed form and return it to W. A. Knight, Sexey's Trade School, Bruton, at your earliest convenience.

(Signed) Henry Hobhouse, T.O. Bennett, F. Whitelock,
R.B. Drewett, Wm. A. Knight."

Had Miss Radford seen the prospectus that had been issued in April 1899 by the Bruton Girls' School Company Limited, advertising the School and inviting new investors? It would be "a thoroughly efficient middle-class School for Girls, (both day pupils and boarders,) giving a modern education".

We can imagine Miss Radford reading the prospectus, perhaps as she sat with others in an anteroom before the interview:

The Bruton Girls' School Company Limited

REGISTERED UNDER THE COMPANIES' ACTS

DIRECTORS: -
H. HOBHOUSE, Esq., M.P., HADSPEN HOUSE, CASTLE CARY
(CHAIRMAN)
T.O. BENNETT, Esq., C.C., TOLBURY, BRUTON
MRS. HOBHOUSE, HADSPEN HOUSE.
R.T.A. HUGHES, Esq., M.A., BRUTON
MR. W.A.KNIGHT, HEAD MASTER OF SEXEY'S TRADE SCHOOL,
BRUTON
MR. F.E. STROUD, BRUTON
MR. F. WHITELOCK, CASTLE CARY.

Secretary :   *Offices :*
Mr. J. Golledge   High Street, Bruton

This Company has been formed to establish in South-East Somerset a thoroughly efficient middle-class School for Girls, (both day pupils and boarders,) giving a modern education corresponding as far as possible to that given at the very successful Sexey's Trade School for Boys in the same neighbourhood.* In the absence of endowments a sum of £2,600 has been raised by private subscription, but an additional sum of at least £400 is still required.

Each subscriber of £25 will be allotted one £5 Ordinary Share and one Debenture of £20. As the School is to be conducted on a public footing and not for private profit, and is to be qualified to receive aid from the public authorities, no interest will be payable on the share capital. The Debentures will bear £5 per cent interest accruing from the date of the opening of the School Buildings; but this interest will be only payable if in the opinion of the Directors the accounts for the year justify such payment.

The Directors have secured a suitable** site for the School Buildings at Sunny Hill, on the main road, half-a-mile distant from Bruton and three minutes' walk from Cole Station on the Somerset and Dorset Railway. The buildings will be

---

commenced this summer, and will (it is hoped) be ready for occupation in the summer*** of 1900.

Any person willing to subscribe is requested to fill up the enclosed form and return it to the Secretary of the Company. £3 per share is payable on allotment, and £2 on the 1st July 1899. The money subscribed for Debentures will be called up in instalments as required for building expenses.

Dated April 20th, 1899.

N.B. The Memorandum and Articles of Association can be obtained from the Secretary on application.

A later version of this brochure, with a drawing of the first building by the architect, Arthur J. Pictor, A.R.I.B.A., of Bruton, whose daughter Madge was among the early pupils, was issued when the amount subscribed had reached £3,000, but still asked for an additional £400. By that time the founders' ideas had become a little clearer, as additions to the earlier version show.

*   The later version added: "Such an education, practical, good in quality, and moderate in cost, is keenly felt by parents to be a great want in this part of the County, where so few educational advantages are open to girls."

**   Second version: "a healthy, elevated and convenient site"

***   By the time of the second version: "Buildings are in course of erection which will afford accommodation for about 70 girls, (including 20 boarders) and which will, it is hoped, be ready for occupation in the summer or autumn, of 1900." The founders had discovered that building completion dates are not always reliable. They also had to deal with a practical problem: "A continuous supply of good water will be laid on from Bruton."

The Bruton Girls' School Company Limited,

REGISTERED UNDER THE COMPANIES' ACTS.

DIRECTORS:—

H. HOBHOUSE, ESQ., M.P., HADSPEN HOUSE, CASTLE CARY *Chairman*.
T. O. BENNETT, Esq., C.C., TOLBURY, BRUTON.
MRS. HOBHOUSE, HADSPEN HOUSE.
R. T. A. HUGHES, Esq., M.A., BRUTON.
W. A. KNIGHT, Esq·, HEAD MASTER, SEXEY'S TRADE SCHOOL, BRUTON.
F. E. STROUD, Esq., BRUTON,
F. WHITELOCK, Esq, CASTLE CARY.

Secretary :
J. GOLLEDGE Esq.

Offices :
High Street, Bruton.

"The curriculum will include the ordinary English subjects, (viz.: Grammar, History, Geography, Handwriting and Composition), French, Arithmetic, Drawing, Needlework and Singing. Cookery, Laundry-work and Science will be taught in well-fitted rooms, specially built and equipped. Great importance will be attached to the Physical Education of the girls by means of exercises, Drill, and organised Games. Instruction will be given, to the older girls at least, in the important subjects of Hygiene and Physiology. Opportunities will be afforded for individual instruction in Instrumental Music.

Well-qualified and experienced Teachers will be appointed, who will be expected to exercise proper supervision over the physical and moral, as well as the intellectual, welfare of the pupils."

*　　*　　*

When Miss Radford was asked about her education and experience, she told them of the London private school she attended from age 11 to 16, and the Burton-on-Trent school where she was a pupil teacher for 4 years, before her training at Whitelands College in Chelsea. She gained a first class certificate and after a probationary period in Peterborough, she had taught girls since 1892 in Carmarthen. We can guess at the drift of Edith Radford's other answers to this daunting panel of interviewers, because years later she summed up her aims:

"So far as in me lay, I have striven, beyond and above all else, to give the girls a sense of duty to the community - a true appreciation of beauty in all its many forms - and a desire for some spiritual sanction to give life a meaning and a purpose."

If Miss Radford put forward aims like these, which are evident in everything she wrote, we can also guess the impression she made on her interviewers. On her retirement, Mr Knight said,

"I venture to say Miss Radford's success has been due first to her unbounded enthusiasm, which she imparted to everyone who came in contact with her. Another characteristic was her wonderful generosity of effort and time, which she has always been ready to devote not only to the School as a whole, but to individual pupils. She has succeeded in producing what a school should be, and that is a happy family. The happiness of the Staff and teachers, I should not think, can be surpassed anywhere."

Enthusiasm and the fostering of happiness were two of the qualities that the interviewing panel saw in her, and a member of her staff in later years pointed out others, most necessary in a headmistress:

> "She was not the type to encourage familiarity at school; in fact, she inspired a very respectful awe, sometimes even terror. But however wrathful she might be at laziness, or impatient of stupidity, she was always human, and would confide in and co-operate with those whom she had previously reviled as cumberers of the earth, and a misfortune to their parents. There was no Olympian detachment about 'Raddy'. She had strong likes and dislikes, even prejudices, but could always see another person's point of view, and could laugh at herself; she moved with the times."

It would be pleasant to think that she and William Knight discovered on that first day their common love of nature and enthusiasm for botany. Mr Knight often led pupils on botany walks through local lanes and woods and inspired them with his own enthusiasm for all natural things. Before the building of the school began, so he told his grand daughter in later years, Mr Hobhouse and he had stood in the field where it was to be and looked down towards Glastonbury Tor and the setting sun. Miss Radford's similar enthusiasm for nature influenced generations of Sunny Hill girls.

Of details of the momentous interview we know nothing. We do know that, out of several candidates that very hot July day, the Governors chose Miss Radford and offered her the post on the spot. She immediately accepted. This is how she finished her recollections, as she spoke to the School in 1925:

> "I little thought the choice would fall on me, and when the post had been offered to, and accepted by me, and I was once more on Cole Station waiting for my return train, I remember regretting my decision and wondering how long it would be before the Governors regretted it too!"

*   *   *

Postcard of School, 1904, before it was covered in creeper

Chapter 2

"White Elephant on Sunny Hill"

In July, when Miss Radford first saw the School building, it was still in the hands of Mr. T. Hobbs, the Bruton builder.

It was built in local stone with Bath stone dressings, and roofed in plain red tiles. Henry Hobhouse had wanted to find a site a little nearer Bruton, but the owners of likely land either would not sell or demanded too high a price. The site finally chosen had belonged to Mrs T.O. Bennett, who had let the management committee have it on very reasonable terms. Mr. Hobhouse was quick to see the advantages, once it was chosen. It was close to Cole Station, and the new buildings were, as the local paper put it, 'delightfully situated on a commanding eminence, from which the surrounding country is spread out like a panorama.'

Albert Hill the plumber and decorator had installed pipes for the new mains water of which Bruton was so proud. Thomas Bennett had given a spring at Gilcombe for the use of the town some three years previously, and with a huge £5,000 loan Bruton had achieved their water supply just a few months before the school opened. Gas for lighting had also been laid on in the school, and a sewage tank installed. Mains sewage was not provided until after the Second World War. Now Mr. Hill was preparing to paint the windows a creamy white, and the buildings were forming 'a very pleasing and effective, if simple, group.' A visitor entering today by the main school gate will see largely that original building, although it did not then extend so far either along the road or to one's right. The back of the building had two parts extending, between which was the space mentioned below.

Arthur J. Pictor, the architect, had done his work well so far. The project had cost more than expected, because of rising costs of building materials and wages. The grounds were still to be finished. Paths were being formed round the building. Land had already been levelled, and was being sown to make tennis courts. More was ploughed up to make the kitchen garden. Part of the land was reserved as a playground, and a space 'up the back' nearly surrounded by buildings, and well sheltered, was going to be asphalted for recreation in hot weather, but by the end of

October the job still remained undone. Whether the gales at the beginning of August slowed work down we do not know. There were trees and shrubs also yet to be planted.

The plan was to register the first pupils on 2nd October. Understandably, as Edith Radford said: "After that first Governors' meeting there followed some weeks of busy preparation," during which she celebrated her 32nd birthday on September 19th. There was not a large teaching staff to appoint, at this stage just one assistant, Miss Sides the music mistress, but many practical arrangements to be made.

*   *   *

On Tuesday 2nd October Ethel Knight sat on the doorstep at the Bruton end of the building in expectancy of the opening door. Miss Radford, clearly with a sense of history in the making, opened the door and Ethel and the other waiting girls entered the corridor and saw the school for the first time. On the ground floor was a large schoolroom 44 feet long by 20 feet wide with space for 60 or more scholars, and which could be divided into two by means of a sliding partition. There were also two roomy classrooms for cooking and laundry work; a dining hall to seat 50 girls, large kitchen, with pantry and servery, cloakroom, lavatory, store, scullery, wash house, and 'usual offices'. The new pupils would not have seen the teachers' study and the Headmistress's dining and drawing rooms beyond. These were smaller rooms along the corridor. The present Principal's dining and drawing room were built on later.

Upstairs, Mrs Thick, a young woman of twenty-five, was making up the beds for the first five boarders. Mrs Thick at 80 was still active in the service of the School, which marked her birthday in February 1955 with gifts, a cake whose 80 candles had to be hastily blown out for safety's sake, and a bouquet from her great granddaughter; she died shortly after her 90th birthday. Lent to help her was Mrs. Humphries, the Hobhouses' cook from Hadspen House, who prepared meals not only for Henry Hobhouse the founder, but also for his 14 year old son Arthur who as Sir Arthur would be the School's third Chairman.

The upper floor of the building was reached by two staircases, the one from the school being 'in broad and easy flights of stone steps.' Upstairs there were not only 'three large and airy dormitories for 20 to 30 beds, sick ward for four beds, six other bedrooms, bathrooms, linen-room, &c.' but also 'a spacious and lofty room for science and art work with store room attached.' The first five boarders were certainly not cramped.

As Ethel Knight recalled the scene, "School opened with eight girls; the younger ones wore white starched pinafores - and the others black satin aprons - and we all wore black woollen stockings useful for wiping inky fingers on. This was not uniform but the usual dress at that time." As they lined up, Miss Radford herself entered their names in her register, and from that moment regarded them, as she did the thousand and more that she personally enrolled during her 29 years as Head, as permanent members of her School family, not only during their time as pupils, but into later life. These were the Sunny Hill pioneers:

• Ethel F. Knight was the first name in the book. She went in 1907 from Sunny Hill to Manchester University, suffered a long illness, taught in a school for the deaf in 1911, and married in 1924 Fred K. Makins, the brother of another early Sunny Hill pupil, Edith. She was living in India in 1925, and had two sons, Jim and Hugh.
• Two sisters, Flora and Annie Neil, came to board, as their parents lived in Alexandria in Egypt. They both married in 1908, becoming Flora Polity and Annie Wallace.
• Another pair of sisters, Dorothy M. and Evelyn E. Laver, whose brother was at Sexey's, were temporary residents in the Dower House in Cole, and did not stay long at the school.
• Winifred A. Golledge, daughter of the Secretary to the Governors, walked up from Bruton. She left school for a life at home.
• Alice C. S. White came from Castle Cary. She later went into business, first in millinery and then in ironmongery.
• Bessie Sealey came from Evercreech, and Dorothy Faulkener, whose mother was Head of the village school, from nearby Milton Clevedon. Dorothy later went to Whitelands Teacher Training College in Bristol and proved herself 'a born teacher', good at explaining difficulties.
• Finally, on that first day, came a delicate-looking child from Batcombe, Beatrice Butler. She married Mr James during the Great War, at the beginning of 1916, but did not live to enjoy the peace. The very day after the Armistice came into effect she died a victim of the great 'flu epidemic, leaving a baby just one month old.

The following Monday Caroline Whitelock, the Governor's daughter, and Amy Elliott came from Castle Cary. Amy was an honoured guest at the 1925 prizegiving. Caroline's marriage is mentioned below. On October 24th May Creed joined Bessie Sealey from Evercreech. They both settled later into home life. They came by train - over 20 trains a day stopped at Cole Station - and "out of compliment to some Sexey's boys," as Ethel Knight put it, "were escorted to the station by Miss Radford herself or her first assistant, Miss Sides."

First pupil register

Once the School was in action, an advertisement appeared in the local paper to announce the official opening, and adding, 'In view of the obvious advantages to Pupils of entering the School at once, the Committee of Management requests parents of intending pupils to call and INSPECT THE SCHOOL PREMISES without delay. The First Term has just commenced, and Girls can be admitted at any time. For Prospectus and further information apply to the Head Mistress.'

It is interesting to see what other girls' schools were advertised in the same newspaper, and how different Sunny Hill aimed to be. At Girton House, Yeovil, Mr and Mrs Nosworthy were assisted by six certified 'governesses', a term that seems strange to us. Buckland House, Axminster, claimed to be a long established Home School for Girls. The Principal Miss Pope, was assisted by an efficient staff of certificated resident and visiting teachers, inclusive of a French master. (It was not until 1950 that Sunny Hill had male staff.) In Bournemouth there was a vacancy in a high class Ladies' School for a PUPIL at half fees (£30 per annum). 'Offer includes board and tuition in English, literature, science, mathematics, French, German, music and drawing. Large staff of English and foreign governesses. Visiting professors. Home comforts. Sea bathing, tennis, cycling.' Another school would not divulge its location, but advertised 'Vacancies for one or two BOARDERS in good GIRLS'

SCHOOL, 14 guineas yearly, including thorough English, Music, French and drawing.' For comparison, Sunny Hill's fees for tuition, as noted below, were 8 guineas a year, and for boarding 18 guineas - it was not being run for profit, although compared with the heavily subsidised Sexey's School the fees were high. Its curriculum was broader than those advertised by its rivals.

* * *

So the great day came. On Friday October 26th eleven girls sat on a platform in the schoolroom, wearing white frocks for the official opening ceremony. The room had been "nicely decorated for the occasion", and was filled with a large number of local people, including four clergymen and their families, a couple from Castle Cary, and the wives of Committee members. The platform party included Mrs Hobhouse and other members of the Management Committee, Miss Radford, Mr Pictor the architect, Mr Hill the plumber-decorator, W. S. Clark of the Street shoemaking family, representatives of the County Education Committee, and the President of the School, the Marquis of Bath, who was to open the School. Henry Hobhouse took the chair at 2.30 p.m.

There is no need to reproduce the many speeches reported by The Western Gazette. Henry Hobhouse's was the most informative, William Knight's the most amusing, Lord Bath's the most predictable, Mr Clark's apparently not worth reporting. When another speaker hoped that Sexey's would one day produce a Plato or an Aristotle, and Sunny Hill a Jane Austen or a George Eliot, the audience greeted the suggestion with laughter, even though Sexey's was already outgrowing its 'trade school' role and becoming the school of choice for the brightest Somerset junior scholarship winners. Miss Radford's contribution was to say that she believed in the higher education of girls, but not the higher education which neglected the domestic arts.

When Lord Bath formally declared the School open, Miss Radford looked around the room thoughtfully. As she remembered in later years, "There were then but 11 girls to receive that announcement, and only one assistant mistress to support me, and I wondered where the girls were to come from to fill the many empty rooms, and whether any degree of success awaited me..."

At the end of the proceedings Miss Radford entertained the company to tea, thus starting a long tradition of Sunny Hill hospitality.

Ethel Knight in later years remembered another early occasion when the 71 year old Earl of Cork (who was not present at the opening) made two pronouncements that would raise a storm of protest from today's pupils for their male chauvinism, and that stuck in people's memory. First, aware of nearby Cole Station, he said he hoped the girls would learn to use a railway timetable, as he had never met a woman who could. Even then Ethel, seated on the platform, silently disagreed. As she said, "I felt sure Miss Radford could, as she could do anything." Secondly, the Earl promised a prize to the first Sunny Hill girl to marry a Sexey's boy. This was in fact Caroline Whitelock, who married Cornelius Martin in 1908, but the old Earl had died in 1904, and the prize was never given.

*　*　*

With the ceremonial over, work continued. From Miss Radford's perspective, the first three years were "years of uphill work, and there were many false prophets in the neighbourhood who foretold a sad and sudden end to what they chose to call 'the white elephant on Sunny Hill.'"

In addition to the School's noble President, The Most Hon. the Marquis of Bath, it now had nine Vice-presidents including three Justices of the Peace, two clergy, one County Councillor, a Captain, and The Right Hon. Lord Hobhouse, K.C.S.I., uncle to Henry. The Directors of the Company were the Committee of Management, having recruited Mrs J.O. Cash to their number.

The curriculum (previously advertised as Grammar, History, Geography, Handwriting and Composition, French, Arithmetic, Drawing, Needlework and Singing, Cookery, Laundry-work and Science) now also included Religious Instruction, English Literature and Mathematics (not just Arithmetic). Boarders were expected to make their own beds and keep their 'own personal belongings in perfect order,' a requirement that appeared in subsequent prospectuses and was found to need all the sticks and carrots that staff ingenuity could devise.

Tuition fees were now eight guineas a year [£8.40] (14 guineas for two sisters, 20 for three), and boarding 24 guineas a year [£25.20]. Pupils bought their own books and drawing materials, but stationery was provided free.

Day girls could buy 3-month railway season tickets from Templecombe to Cole for 17 shillings [85p], for example, or from Evercreech Junction for only nine shillings and sixpence [47p]. Their cloak room 'is provided with a heavy rack on which to dry their boots, which they are expected to change every day.' This was very necessary. Mary Queen for example walked from other side of Creech Hill daily. Her long black hair was sometimes dripping wet, and she would have to change not only her boots, but also her skirt and stockings.

Day girls could join the boarders for lunch at sixpence [$2\frac{1}{2}$p] a day or a guinea [£1.05] a term. They did not have to begin school until 9.30 and could leave at 3.45, with a lunch break from 12.30 to 1.45.

* * *

Pupils remembered their Head as "certainly versatile. At the beginning she had to teach most subjects, including cookery." She herself recalled that "Miss Sides and I had to share the subjects and the classes between us, as well as all the out of school duties. I remember teaching English, History, Geography, French, Arithmetic, Geometry, Drawing, Science and Cookery; doing all the Housekeeping and sick nursing, carving the joint for dinner and taking the boarders' walk!" Miss Radford's chief subjects were Art and English and she gradually dropped the others, but Edith Makins remembered Geography lessons she gave on her return from a course at Cambridge. "She came back loaded with isobars and isotherms, which did not appeal to us much. Her geography lessons became known as 'the roaring forties'." Gladys Maud Court's mapping book. containing beautifully drawn maps of England (awarded 9 out of 10), Scotland (8 / 10), Palestine in Old Testament (6 / 10) and New Testament (8 / 10) times, and Australia (unmarked), still exists. "In Art and Literature, however, Miss Radford's enthusiasm was catching and she gave us a wonderful start. Bertha White, who left in 1902, and Ida King who left the following year, were the first two girls to take and pass the Senior Oxford Exam, and Ida later went to Girton. She was the eldest of three West Indian girls who came as boarders and gave Miss Radford a shock at Bruton Station. Having an English father and English names she had expected them to be white." [Edith Makins in 1960]

Science teaching concentrated largely on Botany. Each girl was allotted a certain patch on which they were to cultivate plants for study. Laura Ganden, who came as a fifteen year old in January 1904, felt peeved that she was assigned to the dandelion patch.

Laura, a teacher's daughter, had learned Cookery and Needlework already, and found it almost an insult to be instructed. In a cookery lesson she had been so quick in making her cake that her teacher thought she had not made it properly. "You've done it jolly quickly. I hope you've put all the ingredients in." Laura could not help retorting with indignation. "This isn't the first cake I've made."

Parents had been told that the timetable "will be taught in well-fitted rooms, specially built and equipped." In fact, in those first years, rooms changed function or were multipurpose. Edith Makins well remembered dishing up school dinner in what became the hobbies room and carrying a dish of vegetables along to the dining room, later 'the cosy'. The cookery room was also the Gym and opening out of it was a scullery which later became the library and then Garrett Anderson sitting room.

"Great importance" the prospectus said, "will be attached to the Physical Education of the girls by means of exercises, Drill, and organised Games." As a pupil remembered it, the only sports they played were tennis and gym. It was quite all right to be rather a tomboy. They played 'hare and hounds' when the hare often had to dash across the fields leaping stiles. Miss Radford told members of the School in later years that they would have felt deprived in the first years because there was no hockey.

"Opportunities will be afforded for individual instruction in Instrumental Music." This was certainly so. All girls, it seemed to an old lady looking back, were required to study the piano.

One of those early boarders said she simply loved the School and Miss Radford. She made the School a happy place where staff and girls all felt at home, like a large family. Laura Ganden called her "sweet, charming, but strict." Ethel Knight claimed: "I never came across a girl who did not wholeheartedly admire Miss Radford and some of us still think that there was never anyone like her. Bertha White, said she felt the same. 'She was wonderful,' she said." A 1913 pupil, Norah Clacee, called her "a brilliant teacher."

"Instruction will be given, to the older girls at least, in the important subjects of Hygiene and Physiology." "Boarders are taken for daily walks." So the prospectus. Naturally, even in that age of careful chaperones, girls did their best to make contact with boys. Laura Ganden found this possible, because she had a day girl friend and could visit her for tea and meet her brothers. Sexey's was a focus of the girls' attention and Laura still remembered 80 years later the daily walks which took them past Sexey's, when some girls (not, she claimed, including her!) winked at the Sexey's boys.

*   *   *

The three years of uphill work to which Miss Radford alluded brought their reward. "In spite of all difficulties and hindrances," Miss Radford said, "1904 saw us recognised by both County Education Committee and Board of Education." This meant that from 1904 onwards capitation grants were received from the County Council, and that finances, with no endowment or state aid, were not so precarious.

In 1904 also came problems with the addition of the Pupil Teacher Centre to the School. A Balfour education act of 1902 had abolished the school boards, transferred educational responsibilities to the all-purpose local authorities, and laid the foundations of a national system of secondary education. So in 1904 the Somerset County Education Committee decided to give a secondary school education to all the pupil teachers in the elementary schools. Sunny Hill had the sudden influx of 36 fully grown young women sent to school in most cases much against their will. Although Miss Radford in 1921 looked back quite cheerfully, saying, "They were soon absorbed, and many of them are now faithful members of the Old Girls' Association," this was not the whole story. These women taught in an elementary school for one week, and came to Sunny Hill the next, so that they could not easily be fitted in to ordinary classes without missing half the syllabus or else disrupting the education of ordinary pupils. A School Inspection held in 1906 pointed this out as a major problem, and the Report of the Second Inspection in 1910 returned to the same theme, but without being able to suggest an answer.

By then, however, much else had happened. Let us first try to gather together some details of school life in these early years.

Miss Radford in frilly collar, 1909

Yellow House in 1911

Chapter 3

"Clean, Vigorous and Loyal"

The ideal Sunny Hill girl was to Miss Radford, 'a healthy, honest, bright, generous,"open air" creature; clean, vigorous, and loyal; a lover of beauty in art and nature, literature and music; quick to rise to the occasion, able to turn her hand to anything; a sportswoman; a hostess; a homemaker.'

By 1902 a Prospectus was able to show photographs of the first school building, and a couple of classes in progress, one with 20 pupils sitting at individual desks facing two dumpy-looking teachers and two blackboards and easels, in the room that recent lower sixthformers will recognise as their Centre, and the other at a cookery lesson. The last picture shows the dining hall set out with two long tables holding 14 places, great white tablecloths, table napkins and, for the teacher at the head of the table at least, a full set of three knives and three forks.

Sunny Hill girls were not altogether healthy in 1902, because there was an epidemic, but of what disease we do not know. Until the coming of antibiotics almost any illness could be a danger to life, and when one girl, let alone a number of them, went down with a disease the whole school would be disrupted by precautions to isolate the sufferers.

One or two Sunny Hill girls have left their memories of the early days, and of their friends. 'Gander' as Laura Ganden was known, took great pride in her school. Girls who came in 1904 with fees paid by the County were known as "scholarship girls", and 'Gander' was keen to improve the manners and speech of the "scholarship girls" in her last terms.

*   *   *

We can get some flavour of lessons at that time in this tribute to one lively pupil: "In May, 1904, Edie Makins came to the school. She gave her fellow pupils an impression of intense vitality and health which expressed themselves in irrepressible mirth and humour. She had a genius for mimicry and a most eager wit which often got her into trouble because she could not suppress it even in the most serious situations. Always in trouble with her mistresses for petty offences, such as being late or noisy, she was a constant source of joy to her class mates in her amazing intrepidity in retorting to a rebuke with such successful humour that more often than not she was readily forgiven. She never seemed to take life seriously yet she took a normal place in school work and excelled in games and physical activities."

It may be of interest to know that Edie spent her later life devoted to gardening, but in 1942 was in the West Cornwall Hospital. A friend went to visit her: "I was amazed to find her so unchanged. She joked with the patients and plagued the nurses in exactly the same way as she had exasperated her mistresses with her refusal to take life seriously. And I could see that those around her in the hospital, as we at school, loved her and felt her strength and courage an inspiration." She died on November 15th.

*   *   *

The year Edie Makins arrived, the first building expansion took place, as music rooms, cloakrooms and bicycle house were added, and the rooms for cookery and science were enlarged. Miss Radford in 1929 remembered: "Only four years later [after the school's opening] not only were those [first] rooms full, but the Governors were compelled to begin enlarging the premises to accommodate the increasing numbers." The staff also grew. Miss Sides had come in 1900 to teach music, and stayed until 1906, when Miss Birkett took over for the next 6 years. Miss Underhill came fresh from Chelsea P. T. College to teach Physical Education in 1907, one of the country's first P. E. specialist teachers. In September 1908 Miss C. M. Gibson took over Science teaching. She, Miss Underhill and another P. E. teacher from Chelsea who came in 1909, Miss Bentham, all left in 1913.

*   *   *

The Inspectors' report of the first School Inspection, which took place in 1906, is lost, but some facts can be deduced from the second report of 1910. There were approximately 66 ordinary pupils, including more than 34 boarders, and more than 80% of the pupils were 14 or older. We have seen the considerable problems posed by the large number of pupil teachers. Another problem that the Inspectors noted was that "the organisation of the Curriculum suffered from the want of effective classification in the lower division of the School." Evidently girls of widely different ages and abilities were being taught together. Certainly the progress of some girls up the school was erratic, to say the least. Financially, the school in 1906 was quite sound. Boarding and tuition fees amounted to £1,826. The inspectors, however, recommended that the school buildings should be extended.

As a result of this first full inspection, on 1st August 1907 Sunny Hill was included in the Board of Education's List of Efficient Schools. Unfortunately the number of boarders began to fall, and the school's finances grew less healthy, fees falling by almost a sixth to £1,533 in 1907 and to £1,456 in 1908. At the same time there was 'a substantial increase in the sum expended on salaries' leading to a net loss for 1908 of £62. 19. 4. The generous investors who financed the school's foundation received no interest on their debentures in 1908 or 1909.

* * *

Frances Everett came in 1906, having celebrated her 11th birthday on 6th April. This was the year the Liberals had a landslide electoral victory, and when 29 Labour MPs entered parliament, and Keir Hardie introduced a bill for female emancipation. Frances Broster, as she became, lived well beyond her 100th birthday, and in May 1996 was able to tell Mrs Wade about her schooldays between 1906 and 1911.

She remembered the people best. Among the staff she well remembered Miss Birkett, Miss Gibson, Miss Underhill and Miss Bentham, and of course Miss Radford. Miss Sarah Blotchie came for the year 1908-09, her duties including the teaching of Latin out of school hours. Among her friends were Margery Brooks (Madge) who later married and settled down in Glastonbury High Street, and Maggie and Freda Barton who moved from Wells to Pitcombe. Maggie left in 1912 and went on to gain a Bristol degree and to work at St Bartholomew's and Garrett Anderson Hospitals in London, before her early death in November 1925. There were also Ella Raikes, Evelyn Proctor (Pictor?), and Sybil Carver from Shapwick. She mentioned Spider (Edie) and Babs (Maud) Knight, daughters of the Sexey's Headmaster. She remembers only 5 boarders. Pamela Knight (Mrs Richards) was able to fill in some details about the last two: "My eldest aunt was among the first pupils. The other two, Edith and Maud , soon followed Ethel. Edie, or Teddy, as she was known, died in 1995, within three weeks of her ninety ninth year. She was a great character, wore trousers and rode a motor bike before the first World War, when it was considered outrageous and was the first woman to qualify as a vet."

Among Frances' memories was looking towards Bruton on a Saturday morning from the window at School End, with nothing then standing between the school and the town. The high point of the day was when the chocolate boy came into view, his tray of sweets and chocolates slung round his neck. She and her friends were allowed to spend 2d each on a Fry's chocolate cream, and also to buy boiled sweets, which came wrapped in a twist of paper. On some Sundays they all trooped down to Pitcombe church in crocodile, wearing hats and gloves. Afterwards, in the afternoon, they would have toast with beef dripping. They had no sitting room to eat in, but sat in the cookery room. Their spare time was largely taken up with arts and crafts - painting furniture, seating stools and so on, and of course they played hockey, tennis and netball with fervour.

Frances remembered also the early outings which were such an innovative part of Miss Radford's education. There was a science expedition to Shapwick to look for bog cotton. There were also unauthorised outings, limited to walks round the school grounds after the time when girls should have been confined to the house. These illicit excursions seemed very daring at the time, but probably took place at about 6 p.m.!

* * *

On 10th and 11th February 1910, Mr E.M. Battiscombe and Mr T.W. Phillips, His Majesty's Inspectors, visited Sunny Hill for a second Inspection. Their report is full of useful detail, but parts of it must have made uncomfortable reading.

Miss Radford had 6 full time and one part time assistant teachers. One teacher devoted all her time to Music, and another to Physical Exercises, leaving only $4\frac{1}{2}$ to cover the main academic curriculum.

Of the 83 pupils, 17 were pupil teachers and 49 were day girls. Only two were aged under 11, and only one over 18. The largest group, 30 in all, were aged 13 or 14. No class was larger than 24, and the top class contained only 3 girls. The two upper classes consisted almost entirely of girls who intended to become teachers.

Among the uncomfortable observations were these: "The age range in Form IV is exceedingly wide and the classification is hardly adequate to provide a duly graded course." More generally, "the unevenness of the pupils' attainments within each Form is the most serious obstacle to effective class instruction." The organisation of the Pupil Teacher Classes was still a difficulty. It was, however, in the teaching of History, and to some extent French, that the Inspectors found most to criticise.

On History: "The work in this subject is not in a satisfactory condition. The lessons seem to consist, for the most part, of the teacher merely reading the text book to the Class, with a running commentary upon the incidents as they arise. It is rare for a girl's voice to be heard, and there is no evidence that the class takes any active part in the work. The girls may get a vague and general impression of the subject, but they possess no exact knowledge of it. This was clear from the complete break-down of Form IV when they were asked some quite elementary and straightforward questions on work that they had quite recently done. The written exercises are usually unsatisfactory, for although girls may write several pages for home work, it is quite evident that they do so immediately after reading the portion of the text book bearing upon the subject in hand."

The French teaching was not given quite so hard a ride. After praising the qualifications of the recently appointed Mistress the Inspectors wrote:

"An excellent beginning on purely oral lines is made in Form II, but in the Forms above this the attainments of the girls are so varied that effective classification is hardly possible. This is a grave hindrance to progress, and it is not surprising therefore that the standard in the upper Forms is not as high as might be expected. In Form III many of the girls have been learning for a considerable time but they are still doing the elementary picture work which is suitable to girls who have recently joined the School. In Form IV the case is even worse. The Class contained girls at all stages (the length of time during which they had been learning varied from $1\frac{1}{2}$ to over 5 years) but the work has necessarily to be kept down to the level of the lowest. A fair number of girls in this Form are preparing for the Junior Oxford Local Examinations, but the text book used is of quite an elementary description."

Fortunately there was nothing but praise for Miss Radford's favourite subjects, Art and Botany: "Art: Excellent work is being done in this subject in accordance with a well planned and properly graded Scheme. The course is based upon natural form and common object drawing and leads to very good work in design and light and shade. The excellence of the work is all the more notable inasmuch as, in the absence of a proper Art room, it has to be done in the class-rooms on ordinary desks."

Almost certainly Miss Radford still herself taught Art. She was an educator of wide vision, determined that Art, Craft, Music, Home Economics should all be part of the full and rounded education which the school was to offer. She was herself a painter and a crafts woman, and she inspired a love of beauty in her girls. She said in 1927, "I have for many years now based my Art teaching upon design, the designs being in almost every case at once applied to some craft. In every way I find my system justified. We always get good results in examinations."

"Science: This subject is in charge of a keen and well qualified teacher who has specialised in Botany and who has succeeded in communicating some of her enthusiasm to the girls. The course of work is carefully arranged and properly graded, the importance of a knowledge of chemistry for a correct understanding of it not being overlooked."

Miss Gibson (1908-13) had been the 'keen and well qualified teacher' of Science

The First Brownie – Miss Radford as photographer

The Cottage, Stourton

for the two years before this second Inspection, but she had inherited the legacy of Miss Radford's teaching. Long before Geography and Biology Field Courses were heard of, Miss Radford introduced her botany expeditions. She sometimes took girls to a Cottage, known as the Convent, in Stourton Woods near Alfred's Tower. One pupil remembered spending "some happy days at the Cottage on Kingsettle Hill, and on long botany excursions with Miss Gibson on chalk downs, peat moors and salt marshes."

In their conclusions, the Inspectors gave a mainly favourable picture of the school. True, there had been frequent changes in the Staff during the last few years, which were "perhaps inseparable from a country School such as this" but "at the present moment the School is very fortunate in its Staff and much sterling work is being done... The School has done creditably in external examinations... The social side of School life is active and vigorous, and owes much to the readiness with which Staff throw themselves into the interests of their pupils... Every attention is paid to the health and happiness of the girls, and the tone and discipline continues to be excellent."

These final comments could have been made about the school at almost any time between 1910 and the present.

*   *   *

When we reach 1910 we are no longer dependent on people's long memories, or chance references, for in time for Christmas the first issue of *The Gleam* was published, a 64-page publication (8 + x 5 3/8 inches) printed by Shepherd's Printing Works, Wincanton, and with an olive-green wrap-around cover decorated in art nouveau style by two pupils: Sybil Carver designed the sweet-pea border (the white sweet-pea is the school flower) and the lettering and rising sun motif were by Kathleen Phillips.

By 1910 Sunny Hill had been provided with several attributes that helped to give it identity: - a school uniform, naturally (on Prize Day in 1910 the girls looked 'very nice in their white frocks'), a motto (Follow the Gleam), a flower (the white sweet-pea), a school song, (see below), and of course a school magazine. Judging by its cover, the school colour was already green.

The contents of that first Gleam were surprisingly like those of recent editions: Editor's letter, account of Prize Day, reports on the sports teams, diaries of expeditions (one entirely in French), letters from old girls, and a complete list of Old Girls' Association members, all 106 of them. There was also a formal essay on 'Time' and a few poems.

September 29th 1910 heard the first of the four settings that have been made of the school song. Dr Edward Woodall Naylor, organist, composer, and musicologist who at the age of 43 was at the height of his powers, having just had his opera 'The Angelus' performed at Covent Garden, provided a full-bodied setting of Tennyson's words for a chorus dividing at times into two parts, momentarily into three, with a demanding piano part suggesting an orchestra, and ending in great excitement with the voices singing faster and imitating trumpets (Poco piu mosso Quasi Tromba). Miss Radford wrote:

"'The Motto (Follow the Gleam) we have had for nearly four years, but we only just succeeded in getting the Song; Dr. Naylor has set it to music for us, and it was sung for the first time publicly on Prize Day this year.

"The words of the Song are taken from Tennyson's 'Merlin and the Gleam.' In that poem, Tennyson is reviewing his own life as a poet, and his struggles to follow true inspiration. He imagines his genius to have been given to him by Merlin, that magician of old, who, when inspiring him with the poetic gift, promised that a 'Gleam' should always go before him to guide him on his way......

"We, too, must 'Follow the Gleam,' and it will not always lead us through smiling valleys; we must expect sometimes to be led into difficult places and to be confronted with the choice between what is easy and pleasant, but wrong, and what is difficult and unpleasant, but right. But if we 'Follow the Gleam' it will lead us safely past all rough places, and as the light gets broader and brighter we shall come to our 'haven under the hill,' and with happy conviction give evidence of the true guiding light to young mariners just launching their vessels for their first voyage o'er 'life's unresting sea.'"

Of the 78 pupils in 1910, 26 came from Frome, 19 from Bruton, 10 from Radstock, 7 each from Castle Cary and Wincanton, 4 from Bridgwater, and only one or two from any other place. There was only one overseas pupil, from Hong Kong.

The one group of people who may have been dissatisfied with the school's progress, according to the Chairman of Governors, was the shareholders, who had never received a dividend.

*   *   *

What kind of life did girls look forward to in 1910? Clues come from Old Girls' news in The Gleam. Some were married, which in those days meant an end to their careers. The vast majority who kept in touch with the school were teachers, one, May Dauncey, the Head Mistress of North Barrow Elementary School, and another, Amy Doble, in Hong Kong with the Church Missionary Society. Bertha White had a drapery business in Wincanton. Winnie Cross was a secretary. Betty Harrold was a governess, and Ethel Hedges a nurse. Many were at colleges (Truro, Cheltenham etc.) or universities (Girton College Cambridge, Manchester, Bristol). Women at Oxford and Cambridge, it should be noted, could complete a degree course, but were not allowed to proceed to a degree until 1920 in Oxford, 1948 in Cambridge. This explains why Ida King, despite leaving in 1903 and going to Girton, was not the first Sunny Hill graduate.

Five old girls had died.

*   *   *

Chapter 4

"It is still the School"

The three years before the Great War were a time of important changes to the school. By July 1913 the Old Girls who visited Sunny Hill had to admit: "It is still the School, though it is nearly twice as large as the one we used to know, and has rooms of which we never even dreamed. Did we ever imagine a dormitory with cubicles, or a huge dining hall with French windows opening into the garden?" Each cubicle was a white tent for dressing and washing, formed by two curtains hung from the ceiling, and was beside the owner's bed.

There were invisible changes, too. Henry Hobhouse, who could always be relied upon to keep school and parents up to date with the school's affairs, stood up at the 1911 Prizegiving and made this announcement:

> "This school has for 11 years been the property of the Bruton Girls' School Company. It has been a public school from many points of view, having been several times inspected by the Board of Education and pronounced efficient, but, in law, it has been till now a private concern."

Many local people had indeed paid out good money to get the school started, and had in all £4,000 tied up in it. 41 people had contributed on average about £75 each, and there were two larger shareholders, Mr Bailward who paid £275, and Henry Hobhouse himself who contributed £675. As for the Inspectors, we have seen that they had their reservations about some of the teaching, but had been impressed enough to issue a certificate of efficiency. One of them, Mr. Battiscombe, kept in close touch and visited Sunny Hill each term afterwards. Mr Hobhouse at any rate felt confident enough to claim: "During these 11 years I believe that the object of the original founders has been attained, and that the neighbourhood has been supplied with a thoroughly good girls' secondary school; over 200 girls have received their education here, and have had an excellent training, and most of them have been drawn from the district around."

Then came the news. "A change is now about to take place in the legal position of the school, and in a few months' time it will become a public secondary school under the control of the Board of Education." What then of the money invested by those public spirited individuals? With the help of Sexey's Charity part at least of their investment would be repaid. Mr Hobhouse explained: "The Trustees of the Hugh Sexey Charity are about to divert some of that money to form an endowment for this school, and thanks to that and the liberality of the shareholders, the Governors of the school have been enabled to draw up a scheme which has received the assent of the Board of Education and which will put the school upon a permanent footing."

What had happened was this. In 1877 Hugh Sexey's Trustees stopped educating boys and began training girls "in domestic duties". These girls, 15 at a time, were educated and "were then placed out at service with a bonus to supplement their first year's earnings." In 1911 it was decided "to give up the training of the servant girls and to devote the money to the education of girls in another manner. £200 a year now comes to Sunny Hill, which has enabled us to raise a sum of money for our buildings."

Most investors agreed to have just 60% of their money back. Some were content with half, one with 40%. The major benefactors, Henry Hobhouse and Mr Bailward, along with the Marquis of Bath and one or two more, generously surrendered their complete holdings and received nothing. A dry solicitor's letter notes that "The school buildings were conveyed by the Bruton Girls' School Company to Sunny Hill Girls' School in 1912 and the property was vested in the Official Trustee by an order dated the 10th December 1912."

Mr Hobhouse went on to reassure parents: "There will be no difference in the internal management of the school, which will continue, I hope, to instil knowledge - both moral and intellectual, to cultivate artistic ability and interest in nature, and to turn out useful members of society."

* * *

So much for the business side of the school. Pupils and staff were more concerned with other exciting innovations like the House system. In 1911 pupils and staff were divided into four Houses, Blue, Brown, Red and Yellow (The names of famous women were not added until 1943). Miss Radford had made it all as fair as she could. "As far as possible each Form is equally represented in each House, and each House has its share of Mistresses. Endeavours have also been made to keep the Houses fairly equal as to ability in games by giving to each House some members of the First Eleven. Each House has a prefect, sub-prefect, games' captain, secretary, and selection committee for the election of house teams." All this at a time when there were 70 girls and 14 pupil teachers in the school, so that there would be only 21 girls per House.

Once the system was in place, a great deal of the school's life revolved round Houses. "Three times during each term marks are added up, and class lists published; then the secretaries collect the information from those lists which contain their own houses, and lists are drawn up, showing the percentage of good and bad marks won by each house." 86 years later, House totals of Honourables and Detentions were still being read out at each end of term to a silent and eager school. "Each house" of just 21 girls "has a hockey team, first and second net ball teams, and four tennis champions." Every girl must have had a good chance to play for her House. The system had moral advantages, too. "The stronger members of each house have helped the weak, for the honour of their house. A girl who did not mind how many disorder marks she got as far as she herself was concerned, shrank from swelling the bad mark list for her house."

As a matter of record, Red House won the hockey and tennis that year. Netball ran into snags: "We started Net Ball last winter, and began to play a round of house matches, but were unable to finish because of the wet weather at the end of the Easter Term. We tried to finish them at the beginning of the Summer Term; but the heat was so great that we had to give it up."

While on the subject of sport we may note that in 1911 the school hockey team had a good season, winning 8 of their 11 matches against Wells Blue School, Bishop Fox's, Ilminster, and even Lord Digby's near Basingstoke. Team members had to face public comment on their progress in 'The Gleam', all right if you were D. Amor: "Good and quick, and, on the whole, shot well," but embarrassing for M. Barton: "Not nearly so good as last season. She did not use enough judgement in guarding her goal, and did not clear nearly hard enough." Such reports continued until the Twenties.

The school also had its first Sports Day. "On Thursday April 18th, 1912, some sports were held in the School Hockey Field" from 2-5 p.m. Events included standards like the 100 yards, high jump and long jump, but also Catching the Train Race, Skipping race, potato race, flag team race, slow bicycle race, egg-and-spoon race, hopping race, obstacle race, Sum Race, blindfold driving race, throwing the hockey ball (156 ft), three-legged race, sack race, tug of war (a 7-strong team from each house), lady visitors' race and gentlemen's race.

*   *   *

School expeditions continued. Expeditions by 1911 were not only botanical but also historical. Botanical trips that year were to Cheddar, Weymouth, Burnham and Ashcott (two expeditions to the peat levels). Photographs of 'A Group of Botanists, at Ashcott' and 'Refreshment after toil' show the uniform of the time, straw hats with dark and light striped ribbon adorned with badge; white blouses with large floppy collars; gym-slips (described in the write-up as holland dresses) reaching well below the knee; brown stockings and long boots. Some girls had school badges on their gym-slips.

The first historical expedition was to Bath, to see houses where 'Jane Austen, Fanny Burney, Lord Clive, Lord Lytton and the two Pitts' had stayed, and 'Roman curiosities' at the Pump Room, to attend Matins in the Abbey, to walk about the streets and take photographs (a more serious business then than now), to have lunch in Cafe Theobald, see 'the museum', particularly the geology section, tour the Roman Baths, and attend a concert in the Pump Room. After tea in the Cafe Theobald they took the train back to Cole. The second historical expedition was to excavations of the Glastonbury Lake Village, then taking place in Meare. Two girls reported that "Some fine specimens of ornamental pottery were shewn us, but most of it had been put into brown paper bags, ready for the Taunton museum." A third expedition, to Cadbury Camp, called out the romantic in the girls: "One legend says that on the night of the full moon Arthur and his knights ride round the camp. Arthur's horse was supposed to be shod with silver, and once, a silver horseshoe was found there!"

Girls travelled either by train or by horse-drawn carriages or brakes. Botany expeditions in 1913 to Kelway's Gardens in Langport, and to Burnham on Sea were by train; those to Chalk Downs and Stourton were by carriage. Incidental references to this evoke a world far remote from our busy life: "About half past nine the carriages drove up to Sunny Hill School ... About a quarter to eleven the carriages stopped at the foot of the downs." Expeditions, naturally, were not all work. In Burnham girls were shown various biological specimens, and then "When all this had been explained to us we were allowed to take off our boots and stockings and wade along by the shore till we got to the other end of the Promenade, when we made ourselves as tidy as possible under the circumstances and went to have tea. After tea we amused ourselves as we liked, some having donkey rides." In the days before the First World War the consumer society had not yet forced young people to believe that nothing is of interest that does not include shopping and recorded music.

* * *

The Old Girls who admired the finished new buildings in 1913, had made wry comments the previous year. At the Old Girls' Reunion, Saturday July 20th 1912, "there were great alterations being made in the School and we were horrified to see the state of the place; in our day such untidiness would not have been allowed. So much has the School degenerated since we left that there were bricks and mortar all over the place. Miss Radford, warning us to avoid the bricks, leads us into a walled enclosure through a gap she called a 'beautiful big window.' The floor is bumpy earth and the only furniture a bucket and a pile of mortar. 'This is the drawing room,' she announces with pride which we do not share. We had tea together in the dining hall (which is going to be knocked into the schoolroom)."

Mrs Cash, the speaker at the December 1913 prizegiving, who said she had known the School from the beginning, endorsed this view of Miss Radford's carefree attitude towards buildings: "I can remember when the roof was blown off, and I can remember, too, that Miss Radford did not seem at all upset. She seemed to think things would go on equally well with or without a roof, perhaps because of her strong belief in fresh air." This belief, incidentally, meant that breakfast in summer was taken with the French windows open to the breezes.

Sunny Hill Girls' School, Bruton.

School and play-field

The alterations had been designed by the original architect, Arthur Pictor, and were carried out by Messrs. Hobbs & Hill, of Bruton. The foreman was Mr Jacobs, and Miss Radford paid tribute to the extraordinarily pleasant behaviour of the workmen. Academic work was not interrupted, and "what unavoidable inconvenience" the girls and staff suffered during the course of the work was "wonderfully counterbalanced" by the real joy in seeing the buildings grow. The building was extended to provide a dining hall, drawing room, staff room, dormitories, staff bedrooms, bathrooms, cloakrooms, pantries, larder, coal cellar, and alterations in the main School Room. The Old Girls were right in saying that the school was now almost twice its original size. There was now accommodation for at least 36 boarders, and MissRadford was keen to recruit girls to fill the places. At the same time the school "play-fields" as Mr Hobhouse called them "had been added to very considerably by the purchase of the field opposite at the sale of Lord Ilchester's Redlynch Estate."

*   *   *

Amid all the changes the girls had a full and busy life. In 1912 we first read of the Social Evenings which remained a feature of Sunny Hill into the Sixties. "On one or two evenings of each winter term we have all home work excused, and proceed to amuse ourselves with great heartiness. On one night some of the younger boarders gave us a little play of their own, on another we had quite a long programme. consisting of tableaux, scenes from 'Henry V,' and from Dickens' 'Our Mutual Friend.' On this occasion Miss Radford invited the members of the Pitcombe 'Mothers' Meeting' to come and see our plays. They enjoyed it thoroughly." Next year the Third Form, which with 33 members was the largest in the school, produced a play "of home manufacture" about Robin Hood. The Remove, a form between Form III and Form IV with 16 girls, offered 'Alice in Wonderland'. Forms IV, Vb and Va, which had only 17 girls between them, acted three short plays in one evening, and the Prefects organised a General Social on October 22nd, which was reported vividly thus:

"After coming out of school at 3.30 p.m., the desks all had to be moved from three form-rooms. There were many eager helpers, and the room was cleared at lightning speed, and the partitions folded back, so making one huge room. After the Charade everyone was eager to begin dancing. M. A. Marsh struck up a waltz, and this made everything go with a swing for the rest of the evening. Thanks to the kindness of Miss Radford supper was put off until 8.30 p.m., so giving us an extra half-hour. We all felt we had spent a very pleasant evening."

Girls performed Goldsmith's play, 'She Stoops to Conquer' twice, once to parents on Prizegiving day, and again for the Old Girls. Nearly all the costumes were made by the girls. Most of the upper forms went to Bath one Saturday to see 'Hamlet' and 'As You Like It' directed by Francis Robert Benson, who had been producing a Shakespeare season at Stratford on Avon each year since 1886.

A School Orchestra was started in 1913, but its six members, three girls and three staff, were not sufficiently advanced to perform in public at the opening of the New Wing on April 4th. By December they had summoned the courage to accompany Elgar's song 'Fly, Singing Bird' and gave, so their hearers politely insisted, much pleasure.

* * *

Despite any problems that Inspectors may have noted, Sunny Hill could boast solid academic achievements. In June 1912, "the Upper Fourths had an examination conducted for the Somerset County Council by the Oxford Local Delegacy, while the Lower Forms were examined by the staff. A good number of the Upper Form girls also sat for the Oxford Local Examination in July; 12 of them passed in the Senior, and 6 in the Junior."

One can sense Miss Radford's pride as she lists the triumphs of her beloved girls: "Of the Seniors, Mary Ward and Gertrude Moody gained First Class Honours, Mary Ward also having distinction in English; Maggie Barton (could she be the unfortunate goalkeeper so publicly criticised in the school magazine?) took Second Class Honours, with distinction in French; Kathleen Nutley and Pearl Ashman gained Third Class Honours, and the other six passed in the First Division. Of the Juniors, Marjorie Marsh had Second Class Honours, Dorothy Towse and Elsie Wheeler, Third Class Honours, and the others passed in the First Division."

The school could also be pleased at the girls who went on to college and university, no common thing in those days. "During the last year four girls held Board of Education Bursaries; they were Mary Ward, Gertrude Moody, Maggie Barton, and Elinor Gee. They all qualified for admission to College, and are now training at Bristol College and University, three of them doing degree work. This year there are two Bursars, Kathleen Nutley and Elsie Dobb; they both qualified for admission to Training College before taking up their Bursaries. The County Secondary Scholarship last year was won by Lorna Dyke."

The Old Girls in Bristol made sure they were not forgotten. They wrote in The Gleam:

"In view of the fact that there are seven Sunnyhillians now at Bristol University, two just left, and several more who have been here, we think ourselves justified in appearing before the public in the pages of the Magazine. Only a few weeks ago, in October, Mildred Longman went up the middle of a crowded hall to be admitted to the degree of Bachelor of Science, by the Vice-Chancellor. She has also become a trained certified teacher."

Miss Radford was delighted that Mildred. "by gaining her B.Sc. this year, has secured the first Degree for Sunny Hill Girls." There were more graduates in the making. In December 1913 Miss Radford could report: "Maggie Barton passed Inter. Arts and Mary Ward and Gertrude Moody, Inter. Sc.. Mary Ward is now taking an Honours Course in Botany."

Unfortunately the Bristol students had a grave complaint against their former Headmistress: "In past times we have been cheered on our laborious way by visits from Miss Radford, but lately she has neglected us. We beg to announce that we are deeply hurt."

To balance these academic successes it is only right to point out that in 1913 the expectations of women were, for better or worse, rather different from today's. The school's good friend and co-founder, William Knight, had this to say at Prizegiving:

"We have travelled far from the Mid-Victorian Academy, where education for girls consisted chiefly of deportment, and the use of the globes; but I am not sure that there is not, perhaps, a tendency to go too far in the other direction, and girls' education tends to approximate too closely to the education of boys. I may be old-fashioned, but I believe, rightly or wrongly, that a knowledge of the organisation of a household is as important as the ability to solve a quadratic equation. Domestic economy has been developed at Sunny Hill, and I hope that it will be developed farther, as it is very important."

*   *   *

In the same speech William Knight reflected on what has, through the years, been one of the major strengths of Sunny Hill: "I have compared the School with other schools, both in regard to organisation and fees. There is no school in England with the same advantages offered here, educational, mental, moral, and social, at such a low fee. This applies especially to the Day Girls."

Mr Hobhouse had put figures to this, just a few months previously: "The fees are moderate, and the education and boarding accommodation both excellent; the boarding fees only just cover the cost of maintenance, and the Tuition fees (only 9 guineas a year), do not nearly cover the cost of the education given. A good deal has been heard in certain quarters about 9d. for 4d. We do not quite do that at Sunny Hill, but we do give an education for 9 guineas, which actually costs 14. Some parents get off even lighter than that, because there are a substantial number of scholarship holders in the School."

In case there should be any snobs among the parents, Henry Hobhouse felt bound to add: "The scholarship or 'free place' system, I am glad to say, has not tended to lower the School in any way, either intellectually or morally. The girls who obtain scholarships are selected for their special attainments, and very soon adapt themselves to the tone of the School. I hope that any parents who have any misgiving on that point, will rest assured that an excellent tone and discipline prevails throughout the School."

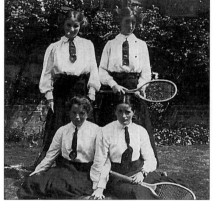

Tennis Champions

The Old Girls opened this chapter. We return to them at its close. Miss Radford knew them all and kept in touch with many or most of them. "One of the things of which I am most proud," she said, "is the evidence of continued affection for Sunny Hill on the part of those who have left, shown by the fact that they come and see us whenever the opportunity occurs; not only once but again and again. Many have finished their College course and have become successful teachers in various parts of the country and some abroad. Some are training as nurses, some are doing secretarial work, others are at home, several have married, and Sunny Hill has now several grandchildren."

One Old Girl who had gone on to a school in Lindau, Bodensee in Germany, wrote some lines of verse which she called "Farewell, Sunny Hill." It is poor stuff, no doubt, but through the conventional phrases and false rhyme we sense a genuine affection for the old school. Coming from Germany on the eve of Word War I it has an added poignancy. Here is the first stanza:

> The sun was set, and twilight mists were creeping down the glen,
> The clinging vapour wreathed the slopes and swathed the grassy hills,
> The train was slowly moving thro' the twilight vale; and then
> I saw it last, and seemed to take my leave of Sunny Hill.

Above: Mistresses, summer term, 1916,
surrounding Miss Radford

Right: Miss Edwards, who brought
Eurhythmics to Sunny Hill

Chapter 5

"Living in Wonderful Times"

The next four years were lived in the shadow of the Great War, and school life changed in many ways. The months before Britain's declaration of war on Germany, however, were filled with their own local excitements.

In February 1914 suffragettes, to demonstrate their political maturity and fitness to be granted the right to vote, burned down Redlynch House. [Source: Colin Clark, *Tales from Old Bruton*]

'On April 15th, eight Sunny Hillites set out from different places to join Miss Radford, who was to take us to London for a long-arranged week of gaiety and sight-seeing.' They visited all the usual tourist attractions, and went to the theatre each evening, including George Bernard Shaw's new play 'Pygmalion' at His Majesty's with Sir Herbert Tree and Mrs Patrick Campbell, and 'Midsummer Night's Dream' at the Savoy Theatre. They clearly enjoyed Selfridge's, and even caught sight of King George V and Queen Mary at Victoria Station.

At the beginning of the summer term the school gave two very successful performances of Gilbert and Sullivan's "The Mikado," the first of many G & S performances recorded in The Gleam over the next forty years or more. It made a profit of £12 which was handed over to Miss Radford, towards buying instruments for the new School Orchestra. The Headmistress herself had put up the money for the orchestra, and the £12 did not repay her fully.

Games enlivened the summer term. In the House tennis competition each House had four champions, and played 12 matches against each opposing couple (evidently doubles only). Mistresses played on equal terms with girls, 2 each for Yellow and Red house, 1 each for Blue and Brown. Having 2 teachers playing did not automatically bring success, Yellow House winning and Red House being last. The Third Annual Sports were held in the Hockey Field on Saturday, May 9th. The under 14 High Jump was won by B. Feltham of Form III with a jump of 3 ft 7 inches. D. Tobbs of Form Vb won the Hat Trimming Race.

Later in the year Katherine Makins scored a notable first for the school. This Wincanton girl, who had left from the VIth form in 1910, and who stayed on at the school to assist before going up to Bristol University, gained the first ever Sunny Hill BA. She went to teach in Norwich for a while, before catching the great 1918 'flu which killed 30 million people world-wide, three times more than died in the Great War. Happily Katherine survived to join the Sunny Hill staff, which she left in 1934.

*   *   *

On 28th June, which must have been just when Katherine was graduating, the Archduke Rudolph was assassinated in Sarajevo, and from then on Europe stumbled almost by accident towards the horrors of warfare. From midnight on Tuesday 4 August 1914 Britain and Germany were at war. Miss Radford poured out her thoughts and feelings in a five page article in The Gleam. "We are living in wonderful times; we are witnessing a world war - and the remaking of the map of Europe. But all this mighty work is being done by men, and we, the women and girls of our great British Empire, must do what we can to help."

This is no empty generalisation, for she goes on, "We are, I believe, all knitting and sewing; we are perhaps helping to find homes for Belgians; many are working with the Red Cross and other organizations." The Gleam prints an article on 'The Destruction of Malines. An eyewitness's account, given in French to E. Barnes, and taken down and translated by her.' Elise Barnes was then in the Remove. The article begins, "Our little town of Malines, which is so pretty, with its cathedral and bells, is now in ruins - and why? - for the only reason that the Germans delight in the destruction of beautiful places." There follows a harrowing description of destruction and mutilations. The family eventually escaped to England, one of those who needed help in finding a home.

Perhaps remembering the arson attack in Redlynch, Miss Radford cautioned: "It is no time for women to struggle against men for political freedom; men and women must work together for the common good of all, and surely whatever sacrifice that may entail will make women more not less fit for any wider duties and privileges the future may bring." Commenting on Edie Knight's enthusiastic letters about her year on a farm where "we have six horses, nine cows, two calves, four pigs, two dogs, three cats, and twenty-two chickens," she wrote: "I think many girls fond of animals and outdoor life might well follow Edie's example. Men will be scarce after the war, and women will have many chances of doing their work for them."

Sunny Hill girls, past and present, were caught up in the solemn yet, at that stage, exultant mood of the nation. Kathleen Phillips, who had left in 1911 and was living in Frome, wrote a poem on November 7th which she entitled 'An Englishman.'

The third stanza reads:

> Forgotten is the football field,
> Relinquished "footer" game; -
> His strength and courage he has steeled
> For a far nobler game...
> Stern Duty's call he has obeyed -
> For active service, unafraid,
> He's sailed across the foam...
> For King and Country dear he fights -
> For Honour, and for Freedom's rights,
> And the loved ones at home!

Girls were aware of the enemy point of view also. Madeleine Mundy, who had left Sunny Hill in 1909 and gone to a school in Lindau, wrote from Leeds University: "I had a letter from a German school friend the other day, via Switzerland. It had been opened by our Censor, and one passage was pencilled through, but was still legible. It ran, 'The only reward for so many sacrifices will be the final victory of the German army, and we know that we'll get it!'"

Among present pupils K. Coles, in Form IV, also wrote in solemn mood. I quote a few lines:

> ..."Tell me," the young man cried, impatient then,
> "What is of all life's many treasures best?
> Love, Beauty, Strength?" the sage but shook his head,
> And said, "Life's fullest, rarest gift is Rest." ...

> Brooding above, the awful form of Death
> Hung, like the guardian angel of that place....
> It raised its arm - it touched him on the brow
> His life was over; he had found his rest.

By the end of the war 65 old boys of Sexey's and 55 of King's had been killed in action or had died of wounds. Many Sunny Hill girls must have lost members of their family, or friends.

*   *   *

Despite the war, most school activities continued almost as usual. A Prize Day was held on October 9th, 1914, but this was the last with prizes. From 1915 to the end of the war the girls agreed to give up such luxuries. At the 1914 Prize Day Miss Radford was able to report many cheering facts.

"Once again we have escaped all epidemics. The numbers continue to go up. This time last year there were 97 girls in the school; last term for the first time the total reached 100, and now there are 109 altogether. Of these 88 are full-time pupils and 21 are pupil teachers attending during alternate weeks. In spite of the increased boarding accommodation, every room in the house is now fully occupied, staff, children and maids making a household of 52 residents. As very few of the day girls can go home at noon, there are over 100 people every day for midday dinner in our new dining hall."

No wonder Mr Hughes, one of the governors "caused some amusement by referring to Miss Radford's ambition to enlarge her borders still further by building a Gymnasium and Studio, adding that the combined efforts of the whole committee were necessary to keep her from immediately embarking on this scheme."

Miss Radford did not merely have growth in numbers to report, but also exam successes, and that the school orchestra had grown to 20 players, "though all are not yet sufficiently advanced to play to you this afternoon." The teachers were now better qualified academically. Miss Odling was a B Sc. and Miss Stoodley a BA, and Miss Carey (Maths) and Miss Harvey (Modern Languages) could point out that they had taken Honours in the Tripos at Cambridge. Only the teachers of the youngest girls, Miss Underhill and Miss Ward, had not been to university.

Who chose the books which were given as prizes we are not told, but Miss Radford was lavish with prizes as a way of getting books into the hands of the girls. The choice seems to us uncompromisingly adult. There were novels by Dickens (David Copperfield, Oliver Twist, Pickwick Papers, Tale of Two Cities, Barnaby Rudge, Dombey and Son), Charles Kingsley (Westward Ho, Hereward the Wake), Walter Scott (Heart of Midlothian, Old Mortality, Ivanhoe), Ballantyne (Coral Island, Gorilla Hunters). Tom Brown's Schooldays featured in the list, along with Pride and Prejudice. Then there were books of romance and magic: Scottish Chiefs, Tales of King Arthur, The Arabian Nights, Hans Andersen. There was poetry: Palgrave's Golden Treasury, Tennyson, Wordsworth, Newbolt, Milton, Shakespeare, Longfellow, Arnold, Keats. And there were books on wild life: Bird-folk at Home, Wood-folk at Home, The Story of a Red Deer. The novels of Dickens and Scott, and the poetry of Shakespeare, Milton and co. represent Miss Radford's determination that her girls should have the best. The tales of magic and romance were to stir their imaginations. And the nature books reflect her own passionate desire to share with them her love of the living world.

Girls were indeed encouraged to know the countryside that lay around them. Botany expeditions continued. They heard a lecture on the River Brue, illustrated by lantern slides. These were the days before electricity was installed, and the pictures may well have been thrown on the screen by a carbide lamp. The difficulties of the operation would have made for an exciting evening. Visits to Pitcombe Church on Sundays were enlivened by the arrival of the Reverend Francis Peter Synge as Priest in Charge. It was not Mr Synge himself that was the focus of interest, so much as his wife and six strapping sons, who together formed the church choir. His departure ten years later, with his large and musical brood, to be Vicar of Wookey caused considerable sadness.

Pupils heard in 1914 about a 'Slum School' in Walworth, "one of the slummiest parts of slummy London." Their imaginations were fired by tales like this: "The first time Miss N. took charge of the dinner room she was horrified to find children emptying their plates on to the floor. When asked why, they said they 'didn't like' something or other among the things provided; what they did like was fried fish and chips off street barrows well soused in vinegar!" Later, the school formed a lasting link with a poor area of London.

✳　✳　✳

By 1915 the mood of the school had altered. The first flush of exhilaration, that caused Rupert Brooke to feel that with the outbreak of war "we have come into our heritage," faded. The Germans were demonised. Shortages were felt. Everyone had to be part of the war effort.

Miss Radford was now quite clear in her own mind. This war was "a war of civilization against barbarism." She listed German 'atrocities' - "the Armenian massacres, the sinking of the Lusitania, the murder of Miss Cavell, the inhuman treatment of conquered Belgium and Servia, the use of asphyxiating gas and liquid fire in battle, and the bombardment of peaceful towns - atrocities which have horrified the world." Her sentiments were supported by a poem by a Sixth Former, E.H. Noble, called Unknown Heroes. Verse 3 reads:

> There on the lonely field our soldiers die,
> And no one knows where now their bodies lie,
> No stone was raised whereon to carve their name,

No friends to deck their graves with flowers came;
They died amid the thickest of the fight,
Saying "Thank God that we die for the Right!"

Miss Radford called for economy and self-sacrifice: "England is a wealthy nation, but even England cannot go on for ever spending five millions or more a day without risking national bankruptcy unless her citizens nobly help in every way to reduce the national bill for food, clothing, travelling, building, &c. Every penny saved from our own pleasure is a penny ready for a nobler use." The school was quick to respond.

Botanical and other expeditions, like many other things, were considerably curtailed, and limited to expeditions to Cogley Woods, and other places within cycling and walking distance. The Inter-Schools Tennis Cup Tournament, due to take place that year at Sunny Hill, was given up and no netball matches took place. The money thus saved on railway and driving fares was given to the Red Cross Society. Prize Day was a Day without Prizes, for by the girls' own request the money that would have been spent on books was given to the British Red Cross, and certificates were presented instead.

The girls buckled down to practical work for the troops. Social evenings that winter developed into war working parties, enlivened by some music. During those evenings and at other spare times, flannel shirts were made and hundreds of knitted things, the wool for which was subscribed or collected by the girls. Indeed knitting was described as 'Another Epidemic!' in a special article which includes the wry observation: "It is obvious from the various sizes of the socks that attempts have been made to provide for 'Life Guards' and 'Bantams;' it is rather unfortunate that enthusiastic knitters sometimes make one sock to fit a giant and the other for a dwarf."

Money collected in the school in the first 16 months of war supplied material for the following garments, exclusive of those made by girls of wool of their own: -

> 10 shirts
> 133 pairs of socks
> 126 pairs of mittens
> 17 pairs of gloves
> 18 pairs of cuffs
> 5 pairs of bed-socks
> 40 scarves
> 20 body belts
> 5 helmets
> 85 swabs.

Parcels were sent to: - 7th Somersets, 8th Wiltshires, 11th Cornwalls, 25th General Hospital in France, and to numerous friends and relations of individual girls.

The school could still combine war work with pleasure. 'The Rose and the Ring' was performed by staff and girls on December 2nd 1915. Proceeds of £18.9s.7d. were given to the Pitcombe Belgian Relief Fund.

*   *   *

In March 1915 the school went through another full inspection. For the first time the inspection team included women. Miss Barrett joined Mr. Battiscombe, the regular local Inspector, and Mr. Dufton, for two whole days, and Miss Preece came for just one day. Unfortunately we do not have a copy of their report, and when Mr Hughes, who represented the Governors at the 1915 Prize Day, mentioned the inspection, he explained: "Though the Board of Education forbid the reading of the Report, I feel justified, in fact constrained, to quote some of the concluding remarks of it." We have seen how the 1910 report, having made some harsh criticisms, left the compliments to the end, so it is no surprise that "the general organisation, discipline and tone of the school, and the staff were highly praised."

Perhaps, however, there is no need to be suspicious or cynical. Sunny Hill was a flourishing school, improving all the time. It had 113 pupils. There was no room for more, except in one form. Form II, the lowest form, had consisted the previous year of just two girls, and had not qualified for its own form mistress. This year there were 23 girls, with Miss Underhill in charge. The quality of education, judged by results, was rising too. Miss Radford was able to report: "Nearly all Form IV took the junior Oxford examination, and all but a very few in Forms V b, V a and VI took the senior."

It may be interesting to see the standard of exam question which girls had to answer. The author's mother in 1917 sat a similar Junior exam at the age of 15, just the average age of Form IV, and the Arithmetic paper included the following:

1.   Find the prime factors of 66528.
What is the smallest number which has all of the numbers 24, 28, 32, 36, and 40 as factors?

2.   Simplify $\dfrac{\frac{19}{5} - \frac{14}{10}}{\frac{21}{15} - \frac{11}{9}}$

Find the value of 6.971 x 1.732 correct to two places of decimals.

3.   Find the price of 351 articles at 6s. $9\frac{1}{4}$ d each

These were the easy ones. Towards the end of the paper we find:

B4. Two men, A and B, each own £10,000 of American 4 per cent. railway stock. A retains his stock and pays 7s. in the £1 income tax. B sells his stock at 90, and invests the proceeds in a British 5 per cent. railway stock at par, and pays 5s. in the £1 income tax. What is the difference between their net incomes? [Brokerage is to be neglected.]

Remember that all these were worked without pocket calculators. Here is just one question each from two other papers:

Geography: On the map of North America and the West Indies insert (where necessary) and name the Selkirk Range, Great Slave Lake, Santa Cruz Island, the river Mississippi with its tributaries the Missouri and Ohio; mark and name Havana, New Orleans, Louisville, Winnipeg, and against the names of these towns indicate the chief crop or vegetable product of the surrounding district; draw the 70 degree and 80 degree mean isothermals for July.

English: Punctuate: Pray why am I to do this enquired the child bewildered as she put down Robinson Crusoe never question your nurse at any time I do it for your good my good indeed well said Elaine I will come this time whereupon she rose and in tripping across the room upset the goldfish bowl a dire disaster.

G.C.S.E. pupils of today should not feel superior about the achievements of these 15 year old girls. Miss Radford had still greater achievements to report:

"This year, for the first time, the Somerset County Council awarded an Intermediate Scholarship to a girl candidate, and it was won by a Sunny Hill girl, Katherine Coles, who entered the school three years ago as a Junior County scholar. Gertrude Moody, a former Bursar in this school, who left three years ago, is now a B.Sc.. of Bristol University. Another old girl (Winnie Morgan) has recently gained an Honours L.L.A. Diploma of St. Andrew's University."

*   *   *

The remaining years of the war saw slow but steady growth in numbers, more scholarship places and some new building, but also signs of a coming financial crisis.

There were 100 pupils when war broke out, 113 the next year, 116 in 1916, 126 in 1917 and 132 in the term before the Armistice was signed. Some parents who wanted places for their daughters had to be refused for lack of accommodation. 'Scholarship girls' had come to the school since 1904, when Laura Ganden had, as we have seen, taught them what she considered 'proper' speech and manners. In 1917 the County Council increased their number from four to ten a year, with the promise of more to come.

The new building, put up in 1916, was at a little distance from the main school and was designed as a Sanatorium. It was too late for the scarlet fever outbreak of 1914 and the German measles in 1915 which had not only interrupted school work, but had caused the school sports to be postponed (they were in fact cancelled, because "then the weather became too hot"!). The building was scarcely used for its original purpose, but as 'New House', with several rebuildings and extensions, became invaluable for staff accommodation, girls' boarding, a house for the youngest pupils, and most recently Sunny Hill Preparatory School.

An old account book carries the signs of looming crisis. Miss Radford used to calculate each term the average cost of feeding each pupil for a week. In the autumn of 1915 it was 5s. 5d. (27p). The following term it was 6s. 7d. (33p). By the autumn of 1917 the cost had soared to an inflationary 9s. 3d. (46p). That term expenditure exceeded income by almost £2, not indeed a large sum out of a total termly expenditure of £1,228, but a cause for concern. Worse was to come in the post-war years.

*   *   *

Our story of the school in wartime shall not end in gloom, for during the war two people joined Sunny Hill who in different pleasant ways are important to the school's history. The first was Miss Edwards, who came on to the staff in September 1917 and stayed until 1931, and who brought with her the modern subject, Eurhythmics. The second was a small girl of 11, Vera Walker, who came with her 12 year old sister Molly in January 1918, on Miss Edwards' recommendation. In 1987 Vera published her reminiscences in a gentle and delightful book called 'Wayfaring.' The chapters on her time at Sunny Hill will be plundered shamelessly in the following pages.

And in 1918 the hopes of those who burned down Redlynch House in February 1914 were partially fulfilled. The Parliament (Qualification of Women) Act gave the vote to women householders over 30.

Left Dick and Yeo;

Above: Sainsbury and Mrs Sainsbury;

Below: Girls of Sunny Hill, 1919

Chapter 6

Competition, Crisis & Coming of Age

In 1919 the school acquired a hut which saw many uses in its overlong life – gymnasium, music school, geography room, junior department, exam room, scenery store and workshop, before being demolished to make way for "Hobhouse," the present drama and domestic science building. When it was on its last legs the author had permission from the bursar to use it on winter evenings to make stage scenery. The bursar said: "Don't forget to turn off the electric fire when you leave; on second thoughts, leave it on, and then the hut may burn down!" When it was new, however, it was a fine addition to the school's facilities. Alice Yeo, a pupil from 1917 to 1920, wrote: "I so well remember when the old Gym was put on that grass tennis court. When the first load arrived we all rushed about saying 'Gym has come,' and of course some people said, 'Jim who?'" The girls were thrilled to use that Gym after the one in the old Cookery Room.

* * *

When Henry Hobhouse rose to give his Prize Day speech in 1921 he had a grave message to deliver. During and after the war prices had risen greatly. Miss Radford's account book shows the trend.. We have noted the rise of weekly food cost per pupil from the autumn of 1915, admittedly the lowest figure in those years, when it was 5s. 5d. (27p). By the autumn of 1920 it had more than doubled to 11s. 7d. (58p). The Governors were reluctant to raise the fees, wanting the school to continue to serve the whole local community. The account book charts the post-war slide into the red.

	Receipts	Expenditure	Surplus
Spring term 1919	£1724	£1481	£ 243
Summer term 1919	£1809	£1696	£ 113
Autumn term 1919	£1911	£1948	£ 37 deficit

Spring term 1920	£1877	£2027	£ 150 deficit
Summer term 1920	£1891	£2084	£ 193 deficit
Autumn term 1920	£2119	No total given	
Spring term 1921	£1504	No total given	
Summer term 1921	£1930	£2252	£ 322 deficit
Autumn term 1921	£1685	£2302	£ 617 deficit

To realise how deep the descent was by Autumn 1921, it is better not to try to translate the figures into present day values (though to multiply by 40 or 50 might give some idea) but to look at proportions, and see that receipts covered less than 75% of expenses.

Pupil numbers dropped during the school year 1920-21, from 165 to 143. Mr Hobhouse put it down to two causes: first, the opening of a new school in Frome, which competed for potential pupils, and secondly, Sunny Hill's own stricter entrance requirements. Two problems had been identified in earlier years, classes containing girls of widely differing ages and abilities, and the short stay at the school of the average girl. Now candidates had to pass an entrance test suitable to their age: elementary English and Arithmetic for the under 12s, and in addition French, Maths and Science for older entrants. Parents were given the choice of sending their daughters at an early age, or else seeing that they were taught well enough elsewhere to be "fit to take their place on a higher rung." The problem of the short average school life was tackled by an insistence that parents make a legally binding undertaking to keep their daughters at the school until the age of 16, unless the school governors released them earlier.

To add to the crisis, the school was given notice to quit "Sunfield." This house, now the working home of the Bursar's staff, had been rented for three years as an extra boarding house. Once the crisis was over, Mr Hobhouse revealed that "as no other house was available it seemed probable that fifteen boarders and two mistresses would be turned out into the street."

The governors tackled the financial crisis by raising the fees, a step which needed the approval of the Board of Education, and by seeking, and receiving, a further gift from Sexey's School Foundation to wipe out the debit balance in the accounts. For the first time the school accounts show a charge for board and lodging paid by resident staff. The crisis of accommodation remained. Miss Radford refused to be daunted. She appealed to the parents of old girls and present pupils to subscribe to her building fund, put on School performances including a staff concert, and ran a sale of work. Henry Hobhouse contributed

£50 in memory of his wife who had recently died. Miss Radford herself undertook to make up any shortfall in the fund, as her Twenty-first Birthday present to her beloved school. With the £565 raised from these various sources she bought two huts, each 66 by 20 feet and had them erected in the field behind the school and joined to the main building by a covered way. The classrooms so formed freed two rooms in the main building to become dormitories again, to make up for the loss of Sunfield. Since these huts have long gone, we have to rely on the careful description in The Gleam:

> "One Hut is divided by a partition (which can be removed) into two equal portions, which when separated make two large class rooms, and when thrown together make an excellent assembly room and auditorium. The other Hut is put up at right angles to the first one and is raised three feet higher. Where the end of the first hut joins on to the side of the second, there is another moveable partition, and about two-thirds of the second hut constitutes a stage with roomy 'wings.' This stage, when partitioned off, forms a splendid room for Art and Eurhythmics. The smaller portion of this second hut makes another class room. Under the raised hut there is capital storage space."

This cunning arrangement of huts was the scene of many of the best remembered events of the next decade.

Miss Radford summed up the position at the end of 1921: "Only those connected with the inner workings of the School's administration know what an anxious time this year has been; but there is now good reason to believe that our chief difficulties have been, or will be, overcome and that we may hope to avoid the rocks in the future."

*　　*　　*

As far as the pupils were concerned, these weighty matters were for others to worry about. Vera and Molly Walker, arriving on the Bristol train via Bath and Radstock, found themselves on Cole Station among a turmoil of arrivals from other places. Vera's observant eye noted that among the 60 boarders that term there were two from London, one from Sheffield and one from Devon; apart from them, and a handful from Bristol, most came from the more distant towns and villages of Somerset, Wiltshire and Dorset.

Immediately the new arrivals had to become accustomed to the school uniform, white cotton blouse with long sleeves, and a dark green serge tunic, without pleats or girdle, cut with a slight 'A' line below a shaped yoke. The regulation hemline was "fourteen inches above the ground when wearing low heeled shoes." When out of doors a navy blue coat was worn, and a green serge cap with the school badge, a rising sun and the motto, 'Follow the Gleam'. This was long before the school obtained an official coat of arms.

Mondays to Fridays brought the day girls, some from Bruton and local farms, and many arriving by train from Wincanton, Castle Cary, Shepton Mallet or Frome, to make up the full pupil roll of 148. There were still 21 pupil teachers at the school, four of whom were boarders. Lessons taken by a variety of teachers were a novelty to Vera and Molly after their primary school - as they are to Year 7 girls still. So was homework, for which boarders were given two hours a day, although each of the two subjects set was intended to take 40 minutes; the remaining 40 minutes was for girls to use as they chose, whether for revision as exams loomed, or for writing letters. After school girls crowded to look at the games lists for hockey and netball. Those whose names did not appear went for a walk with a mistress. Organised walks, which continued to be part of Sunny Hill life until the Sixties, were not universally popular, either with pupils or the staff who had to accompany them, but Vera had a passion for wild flowers and small creatures, and loved the fact that she could step out of the school gate directly into a country lane.

It was at weekends that the boarders most felt themselves a special community. On Saturdays Vera at least was glad that they could go for a longer walk. Two favourites were to Jack White's Gibbet on the Wincanton - Cary road near the road to Bratton Seymour, and the walk to Wyke Champflower with its haunted house all boarded up. Vera loved to walk the lanes strewn with windfalls from the cider orchards, red and gold.

Sundays meant the walk in crocodile to Pitcombe church, twice every Sunday by that time, wearing galoshes in wet weather, waterproof overshoes for the muddy lane. Some of the sheep on the hill by the church used in those days to wear bells, and the gentle ringing that she heard on the way to church stayed long in Vera's memory. The Synge family choir must have made churchgoing quite an attractive proposition, but even more memorable was the walk back in the dark after evensong to the dining room, decorated with Miss Radford's water colours of spring wild flowers and woodland scenes, where a peat fire was burning in the hearth. Vera recalled: "Our supper, thick slices of bread and margarine which we called 'butch' and cups of cocoa, was set out on one table. Sometimes we toasted our butch over the glowing peat, then switched off the lights and sat there telling ghost stories until the signal for bed."

Revd. Francis Synge ran a Catechism class for about ten Sunny Hill girls to prepare them for Confirmation by Bishop Charles Fane de Salis of Bath and Wells in March 1919. The classes were held one evening each week in the Vicarage, now Old Vicarage boarding house. The girls knelt to pray round the vicarage dining table, which was covered with a green chenille cloth with a border of chenille bobbles. Vera confesses that one night as she and her sister left the Vicarage "Molly pressed into my hand a collection of bobbles that she had pulled off while supposedly kneeling in prayer." She wonders if that was the reason that next term's classes were held in school. Molly, who did not like going to church twice on a Sunday, and tried several ruses to avoid the evening service, caused something of a sensation on her confirmation day also, as we shall see.

* * *

That winter came the terrible world-wide flu epidemic. Children at other West Country schools died. In the spring term of 1919 the epidemic of influenza reached Sunny Hill. Day pupils stayed at home for some time. Miss Radford with the help of Mrs Sainsbury, who lived with her husband, the school gardener, in the San building and cared for sick pupils, did all she could to avoid the infection spreading. Some boarders were moved downstairs to use the four corners of each form room, leaving the beds more spaced out in the dormitories. Their temperatures were taken three times a day and as long as they were fit they went on walks or played games. The policy worked, and although some girls caught and recovered from the flu, the term ended with the beds returned to the dormitories and the day pupils back at school.

The mischievous Molly was one of those who succumbed and was sent to the San. There she was bored, and got hold of a pair of scissors with which she "bobbed" her own hair in what she hoped was the latest fashion. Her sister saw the result when Molly had recovered and was allowed down to school tea, but their parents knew nothing about it. Their mother was to come to their Confirmation and would have to see the damage, but not until the last possible moment. As Vera wrote: "Before and during the service we wore veils but when mother took us out to tea, the awful truth became known to her. Both Molly and I had naturally curly hair and mother was quite upset."

Let Vera herself tell another story from that spring term:

"I remember a Sunday afternoon walk in February when we found frog spawn in a ditch at the foot of Ridge Hill. On the hill there was a climbing post similar to the post in the bears' pit in a zoo. The hill was out of bounds to us because the boys from both King's and Sexey's schools walked there. We carried some of the spawn back to school in our caps and obtained empty jam jars from the kitchen. These we placed on the window sills outside our dormitories, where they were soon noticed by the Head Mistress, Miss Radford. The culprits were reprimanded at morning assembly and told to remove them."

Half term holidays were very short, and some boarders stayed in school. They were taken on an outing by the member of staff in charge, who must have been less than delighted at missing her own half term break.

*   *   *

The summer term meant a change of uniform. The tunics, of the same pattern, were made of fadeless cotton 'Sundour' fabric in an apple green shade, and cream straw boaters (which the girls called 'brimmers') were worn; these had a striped ribbon band, green/white/green and the rising sun badge.

Since there was only one court, only a few girls could play tennis each day, while the majority went on walks. There was informal swimming in a River Brue pool, near Cole, called Black Hole. Between tea time and the bell for prep at six, Mr Sainsbury used to allow some of the older girls to ride the school's horse on the back drive between the gymnasium and the sanatorium. Mr Sainsbury was not only gardener, but also groundsman and handyman, and looked after the horse and trap, which he drove when required.

On several Saturday mornings in the summer term Mr Sainsbury loaded up the trap with overnight bags and provisions for a group of senior girls who were to stay at the "Convent" in Stourton Woods. A few hardy younger girls were allowed to walk with the seniors, and all set out at around ten o'clock to follow the trap, which went slowly so that they could keep up. Walking to South Brewham by way of Lusty, trap and walkers turned off onto a turf track once a coaching road, and now grazed short by rabbits, towards the woods. Here Vera takes up the tale:

"The Convent at first sight could have been Hansel and Gretel's cottage. The outside walls looked as if large pebbles had been flung at wet mortar or cement and had stayed. There were stained glass windows and in one of them a fly was embalmed in amber. In the sleeping quarters upstairs, hammocks were hung. After unloading the provisions and checking the safety of the hammocks, Mr Sainsbury returned to the school. We were hungry by that time; it had been a seven mile walk. The senior girls boiled a kettle and we had tea with our packed lunches. Between lunch and teatime we all walked up through the woods and explored the area around King Alfred's Tower. The tower was unusual in that it had three sides. We returned to the Convent for tea and in the early evening Mr Sainsbury came back for us younger girls and we rode home, via Kingsettle Hill, Hardway and Redlynch Park."

Another Saturday, early in May, Miss Radford allowed girls to walk with her to Yarlington Woods, then beautiful with late primroses and wood anemones, where she was going to paint. When she had settled to her painting the girls with the mistress on duty walked back to school by way of Yarlington village, passing God's Way and Hadspen.

*   *   *

We have followed Vera Walker through her first year at Sunny Hill. Interested readers will find a fuller story in her book, *Wayfaring*, if they are lucky enough to come across a copy. She was in many ways a girl after Miss Radford's heart, a lover of the living world, of healthy sport and walking, and of learning, even though she found it necessary to work very hard to keep up with her sister's apparently effortless progress. Before we leave her, here is one more paragraph from her writing, and a bittersweet coda.

First, the paragraph, conjuring up idyllic memories:

"A favourite Sunday afternoon walk in early summer was to Holy Water Copse; once I brought back a dark brown woolly caterpillar from there. I put it in a specially constructed box in the Science Room and fed it until it turned into a Chrysalis. When it hatched a Cream Spot Tiger moth appeared. During that summer half term holiday we were taken to Cogley Woods, just beyond Bruton. We walked through Lusty, and passing the Dovecote came to Durslade Farm. Here a footpath led right into the woods and down to the River Brue. We ate our lunch beside the river and paddled where the water was shallow. Later we explored the woods and I saw two very special wild flowers: Herb Paris and Solomon's Seal."

And the bittersweet coda: "In our fourth year it was made known to Molly and me that father had failed to pay our school bills and he was asked to withdraw us. We left part way through the Spring Term 1921." Years later, the Bursar had a letter from Miss Walker with a cheque for £1,000 or £2,000. An uncle had recently died and left her money, and the first call on this money was to pay off the school fees.

What Vera gained from the school she kept to the end of her life. In her old age she could write: "As for the Gleam, I seek and follow it still."

*　　*　　*

Vera and Molly missed the coming of age celebrations in October 1921. Hard as it must have been for governors and headmistress to turn from the recent deep financial crisis to the school's great achievements in its first 21 years, Miss Radford stood up at the celebration Prize Day to look back to the school's foundation and say: 'The years that have passed since that day have held their anxieties and their disappointments, of course, but the prevailing memories are very happy ones - of the girls who have laid the foundations of useful lives, of a procession of mistresses who have worked with me ungrudgingly in the service of those girls, and of Governors, those first ones, and others who have joined them since, all of whom have given me that strong and never failing support which has made all the work here possible.

"Not least among the happy memories has been the satisfaction in the really wonderful good health we have enjoyed. During all these years we have had but few epidemics and none of them severe; here on the premises we have had but 3 cases of really severe illness, and only one death."

She had particular cause for pride in the school's academic advances that year, including success in the newly introduced subject, Latin, once considered something only boys could attempt: "The Senior Oxford Examination is now taken by a whole Form, according to Board of Education rules, and not by picked girls. We are rather proud of our Senior Oxford distinction in Latin, gained by M. Dunford, as that is a subject which has to be taken as an optional and extra one, and therefore is studied at much sacrifice of spare time by the girls who join the classes for it. Mr. Knight has most kindly offered a special prize in honour of it." Latin made its first appearance in the school account book with the following entry for Summer 1920:

Latin lessons   £4. 0. 0

and in the Autumn Term:

Extra lessons etc. Dancing, Latin etc..   £18. 15. 4

Sunny Hill could certainly hold its head up among the schools of Somerset: "We are also very pleased to have won 2 out of the 3 Intermediate Scholarships awarded this year by the Somerset County Council."

Miss Edwards, as I have mentioned, brought Eurhythmics to Sunny Hill. Émile Jaques-Dalcroze, (1865-1950), a Swiss composer and teacher whose pupils included Frank Martin and Ernest Bloch, while professor of harmony at the Geneva Conservatory between 1892 and 1910, developed a system of musical training designed to "create by the help of rhythm a rapid and regular current of communication between brain and body, and to make feeling for rhythm a physical experience". In 1915 he founded the Institut Jaques-Dalcroze in Geneva to teach and further develop this system, which became known as Dalcroze eurhythmics. It has since been taught in schools and colleges all over the world and has influenced modern dancers from Dame Marie Rambert and Nijinsky onwards. Miss Edwards used the techniques at Sunny Hill to produce "rhythmic mimes." One of the earliest was "Hiawatha" which was given several performances, some in the summer of 1920 and the others in April 1921. Miss Radford reported: "Fortunately some members of the former cast who left last July, were able to return and take their old parts; other characters had to be taken by new performers. In fact, in the short interval of two terms, nearly every girl had outgrown her former part! So 'birds' had to be transformed into 'spirits' and 'spirits' into 'Indians,' and new 'birds' brought on from among the School's littlest ones." She concluded that "Sunny Hill has never produced anything more charming."

The stage in the new huts, "fitted up by Miss Radford," was a boon for eurhythmics, although one summer term Miss Edwards arranged a eurhythmics display in the Italian Garden of Hadspen. It was also good for more conventional music and drama. As part of the 1921 celebrations it was reported that after tea "guests proceeded to "The Theatre" in the New Hut, where they witnessed a very charming performance of a Fairy Play by Miles Malleson, called 'Paddly Pools.' The music was played by Miss Cox, at the piano behind the scenes, with 'humming voices' as an accompaniment. The effect was quite charming."

*　　*　　*

To return to academic matters, we have a glimpse of the staff and the classrooms as described in light-hearted verse. The first refers to the staff room:

SUNNY HILL "STAVES!"

There is a room at Sunny Hill
The terrors of Olympus fill
Our minds, when all we've come to say
Before the portal flies away,
Our feet upon the threshold freeze
Although we do our best to please,
You dare not call at dinner time
Before you hear the second chime,
For if you chance to call before
Their looks will send you through the floor ...

Cryptic descriptions of teachers follow, including a reference to Katherine Makins who had been Sunny Hill's first BA, leaving the sixth form in 1910, and returning to the staff after teaching in Norwich and catching the 1918-19 flu:

The tallest one's been here before,
She knows of little tricks in store.

The second poem is self-explanatory, and shows some technical skill as well as observation and humour:

THE FORM CUP - A SONNET

How hard we tried to gain that silver cup
From which the Genie Tidiness doth peep
With laughing mocking eyes: yet will not leap
To us, who wait so long with hand held up
To clasp the longed for prize. Va, rise up
Rub well your brass, and from your corners deep
With pan and brush awake the dust from sleep
And clear it all away. Yes, like the cup
Itself, so clean we will our formroom make
That when the prize we do most proudly take
Our room will be a fit abode for it
Where any happy sprite might like to sit:
And Tidiness we will so charmed make
That she will never Form Va forsake.

Margery Mann Form Va

Finally let Miss Radford announce some of her pupils' finest achievements to date:

"At the Royal Academy of Music, Constance Loxton and Stella Maloney who went there on leaving school last year have won 3 bronze medals, each having one for Pianoforte Playing, and Constance Loxton having another one for aural Training, only one other being awarded. Edith Knight has distinguished herself and her school by being the first woman to pass the 1st Examination in veterinary surgery gaining honours and beating the men. She has two more years' training to go through and if successful at the end she will most certainly be the first woman Veterinary Surgeon in the country."

She was.

*   *   *

Above: The Forsaken Merman;
Below: Persephone

Chapter 7

Worry, Work and Plays

Sunny Hill was not out of the wood yet. Although Sexey's Trustees had stepped in to deal with the financial crisis (the accumulated balance and the yearly income from the Sexey's Domestic School Foundation was transferred to Sunny Hill School, to be applied to the reduction of liabilities still outstanding, and when the debt was settled, to the provision of school scholarships), the newer schools in Somerset were still taking potential pupils away, and while Henry Hobhouse insisted that competition was welcome, nevertheless he and the Governors had to plan to stem the reduction in numbers. The statistics for 1 October each year tell their own worrying tale:

	1919	1920	1921	1922	1923
Boarders	76	69	58	56	48
Day Scholars	69	84	74	74	69
Total	**145**	**153**	**132**	**130**	**117**

Up to 1920 there had been steadily increasing demands upon Sunny Hill accommodation, which had led to the school catchment area becoming more and more local. Now it was to be extended over the county, and there was a drive to draw pupils from more distant areas. At the time of the General Inspection in October 1924 the picture was this:

Pupils from Bruton	6
Rest of Somerset	78
Rest of England	14
Places outside England	2

Miss Radford said: "I think it is a thousand pities that the boarding accommodation should not be taken advantage of to the fullest extent." The School had excellent accommodation for about 60 boarders. Mr Hobhouse thought that perhaps the time had come for some reduction of fees. Some judicious advertising might make the School more widely known. Miss Radford agreed, but pointed out that the very best advertisements of any school are its old pupils. She appealed to the Old Girls of Sunny Hill to help the school to reach the target of 1,000 admissions by 1928. Up to September 1924 there had been 880.

With the help of the Sexey's Foundation, scholarships were offered for girls who had been at Sunny Hill for at least three years, to help them with university or training college. £100 a year was set aside for providing maintenance allowances at Sunny Hill School for "free placers or other Scholars who were already in the School." There were 31 free places in 1924, 13 awarded by the governors and 18 by the County Council. This was at a time when boarding fees had been raised from the wartime 24 guineas (£25.20), which we have seen led to a large deficit, to £45, still a very moderate charge. The Inspectors were moved to comment on "the excellent and economical management of the boarding house."

Everyone concerned with the school was convinced that they had a fine product to offer. Miss Radford put it like this: "Without boasting I think I may safely say that parents would find it hard to discover a healthier, happier, school in more pleasant surroundings for such moderate fees." His Majesty's Inspectors from their impartial viewpoint concluded: "The wide general education given by the School, and the cultivation of interests other than purely academic, make an excellent preparation either for a future career or for home life. Freedom and enterprise in the individual are encouraged without loss of the orderliness and consideration for others, which are essential to happiness in community life. The spirit of the School seemed to be wholly admirable."

The governors did what they could to improve facilities at a time of financial stringency. A hard tennis court was laid down. Miss Radford looked at the main school building and comparing it with the 1900 building she noticed: "Although the doors are the same, every wall except the one facing the road has been extended and new wings added." With ingenuity she ensured that the girls would not suffer as a result of the forced economies. When the salary bill had to be cut, two mistresses, Miss Feaver (PE) and Miss de Ville (Domestic Science), were shared with other schools at Frome and Yeovil. A classroom which had been built with so much pride so recently in the new huts was now turned into a sitting-room for the girls. Miss Radford was genuinely positive about it. It was, she told her guests assembled for Prize Giving, "a want that had always been felt. This is the room now known as the

Blue Room which I hope you will all visit before you go. This room was specially praised by the Inspectors, for the work of painting and decorating the furniture, making cushions and curtains, staining the floor, etc., has all been done by the girls themselves in their Art and Housewifery classes in the first three weeks of the term; and I quite expect to find that in future some Sunny Hill girls will take up artistic house furnishing and decorating as a profession." One girl clearly remembered Miss Radford herself working with the girls on "painted flowers and fruit on a blue background on tables and chairs."

By 1928 the worst was over. Miss Radford was able to rejoice: "There are now 126 in school as against 115 at this time last year; this number includes 64 boarders, an increase of 10. It has needed the greatest exercise of my ingenuity to find room for everyone, especially all the boarders; and although, for the first week of term, I felt like the old woman who lived in a shoe, I think we are now comfortably settled in. I am beginning to compile a waiting list of candidates who are still too young to be admitted. This is a promising sign." At last there was to be some increase of staff from the five full time and three part time assistants that the Inspectors in 1924 judged "just adequate to the needs of the school."

*　　*　　*

With the aid of the Inspectors' report - there were four women and two men on the team this time - we can look through the windows into the classrooms on three days in late October 1924. There are seven 40 minute periods in the school day, and much to see before 3.15 p.m.

First, then, we see the Class Music lesson taken by a teacher full of quiet enthusiasm, who has chosen songs well and trained the girls to enunciate clearly and produce a good tone, but who is sitting with her back to her pupils as she plays the piano. No wonder some members of the class are making "less effort that should fairly be expected of them," as the Inspector gently comments.

In the English classroom a graduate with teaching experience is trying to follow the latest teaching methods, but has obviously only read about them and not seen them in practice. She is not strong on classroom management, and when a girl stands up to read aloud it is difficult to understand her, so hurried and indistinct is she. We long for the teacher to help her analyse what she is reading. The lesson ends, and the teacher sets prep, as usual a piece of imaginative writing, when what is needed is probably something that includes exact description. A glance at the exercise books shows elementary mistakes, although the girls of Form V have reached a reasonably satisfactory level.

In the History lesson classes have returned to normal after last year's special work in connection with the British Empire Exhibition at Wembley. Miss Howells is telling a story clearly, and the girls are interested, as she emphasises the salient points. This is a class of younger girls, who are covering a wide general syllabus, and the teacher is keeping in mind the danger of the girls getting a vague and confused impression. She has various means to combat this. In this lesson the girls are being set to do independent group work. Each girl has her own record of her reading and individual work, which she will keep all up the school. Everything we see in this class shows us a well qualified and experienced teacher at work. She is the Second Mistress - a teacher of distinction! [We have suffered another loss in the resignation of Miss Howells. She was Second Mistress and the teacher of History - The Gleam, 1927]

The Geography classroom is empty when we look in, because the girls are out of doors with Miss Radford doing surveying. There used to be a Geography specialist, but Miss Radford has taken over the advanced work. There seems to be sound teaching all along the line, particularly in physical geography. The only worry is whether the Headmistress should really take on this teaching on top of all her other work.

Things are rather different in the French class. The teacher obviously knows French well, but whether she knows how to teach is more doubtful. She does not know how to get the girls to make an independent effort. The teacher's accent is fine - she has lived in France for some time - but that of the pupils is poor. They cannot speak real French at all. How many periods a week do they have? Five? They should be much better than they are. Strangely enough, there is a pupil from France in the school. Let us ask her for her impressions. "There is not so much work as in France. I have never been overworked at Sunny Hill, and no one else seems to be. We are not overworked either during school hours or in the evening. We have only a limited time for homework and if it is not finished, it must be left. In France, the pupils work till all the lessons are finished, and as there are ever so many, it results in their sitting up very late at night."

Now here is a young teacher, new to the school this term, with a Liverpool B. Sc.. degree. She is teaching a botany lesson to girls who seem to have been well grounded by their previous teacher. They have followed a course in elementary general science to prepare them for botany and for geography. That is all the science that is taught, except for elementary hygiene taught by the Domestic Science Mistress. This botany class is working for the Oxford School Certificate, and the new teacher is certainly very promising.

Next we visit a mathematics lesson. The Mistress in charge is a graduate of

Manchester and is an experienced teacher. She is teaching a point in algebra. Her expositions are clear and her methods are good. She is able to build on previous work, showing that the course has been mapped out with care.

Across the path now, to the gym, where a group of 15 girls is enjoying a lesson on Swedish style equipment. The Inspector at our elbow is scribbling something. "It is suggested that a wider outlook is desirable of the results to be obtained from modern lessons in this subject." That seems to be meaningless official gobbledegook! The important thing is that the pupils are having healthy exercise which they enjoy.

> Into the gym Vb girls march
>   With well pressed tunics, stockings straight,
> And shoulders all as stiff as starch,
>   Not one too early, not one too late.
>
> Upon the ribs they do the "star,"
>   Back straining exercises try,
> Climb the rope and walk the bar,
>   Under Miss Notcutt's careful eye.
>
> The lesson o'er and in a bunch
>   With heads erect, away they go
> To well earned rest, and welcome lunch
>   Trying to keep themselves just so!

- as Phyllis Pittard, who joined the school in 1924, put it three years later.

Back in the main school, we inspect with interest the Domestic Science room. Really, the School is to be congratulated on the admirable facilities which it offers for the teaching of Housecraft and the way in which they are utilised. This teacher is another newcomer this term, well qualified. Now, the class is beginning some practical work. Why doesn't the teacher demonstrate? That is such a valuable means of teaching. But there is an excellent spirit in this class. There is some artistic needlework on display. Take a glance at the girls' notebooks. They seem to be filled with recipes, and nothing about general principles. No doubt the teacher will correct these faults when she has had more experience.

Now it is the lunch hour, quite short, because nearly all the girls take school lunch, but with just enough time to look in on the one Sixth Former who is studying Latin with the English teacher. She has been well grounded, and could shoot ahead now with reading some literature. It is a pity that so few girls have the chance to learn Latin, but it means that the other subjects can have adequate time.

We have kept the best to the end. After lunch we visit the art room, where Miss Radford's teaching influences many of the other school subjects also. At this point we shall drop the pretence of watching lessons, and simply quote the enthusiastic Inspector:

"The Head Mistress herself undertakes the direction and guidance of the Art work throughout the School, and nothing could be more convincing of the profit, satisfaction and delight that the girls derive from it, than to watch them at work and to see the things which they have done. They have realised that artistic achievement is within the reach of all and by their own efforts they have learned to understand and appreciate the work of those specially gifted. The interest of the work to be done and the desire to succeed furnish the motive for effort, and the ability is thus acquired which mere formal exercises would never have produced.

"That design is the essence of Art is the principle underlying this Mistress's teaching and is implicit in all the work done. If a study is made of a flower, insect or ornament, it almost invariably becomes the material or motive for some definite decorative purpose, perhaps a box or a bowl, a cushion cover or a leather bag. The most recent and successful achievement of this kind has been the entire decoration of the walls and furniture of the girls' day room by the collective effort of most of the girls in the School. It is something of which the Head Mistress and the girls themselves may be rightly proud and which it is to be hoped many will see.

"The characteristics of all the work seen were bold, strong, vigorous form, colour and execution."

We end our survey of the classrooms of the Twenties with two brief quotations.

The first is from the visitor from France whom we have already met. "In English schools, there is time for everything. Games are included in school life. On the Continent, English people have the reputation of always being very calm. Well, they are not like that at Sunny Hill. Everybody seems to be very lively here. The pupils are always cheerful, and any one would say so too if they could see us dancing or during meals or even during lesson time."

The second comes from Marjorie Thomas (née Chambers) who arrived in 1922. "Miss Edwards was my Form Mistress when I was a new girl. She always had lovely clothes and I still remember a Bois de Rose jumper suit she used to wear. I remember being upset because someone had called me, probably with perfect justice, a 'Cry baby' and she took me on her knee and gave me a Marie biscuit."

* * *

What happens in the classroom does not make a school. Performances, dramatic and musical, are important in Sunny Hill life.

Eurhythmics were the basis of several dramas in these years. In 1923 one person reported:

"The lucky visitors who were able to stay, and all the lucky girls who were able to squeeze in or peep, as I did, through the wings, enjoyed a real Eurhythmic treat on Prize Day. I meant to stay for half an hour and then slip out, but it was far too entertaining for that. I stayed to the end and then could have seen more with pleasure. It is hard to say what was most pleasing, but 'London Bridge' was a special joy to watch partly because it was evidently such fun to do. An interesting innovation was the rhythmic acting of a poem, 'The Fiddler of Dooney.' The lines were simply and well said, and the children moved suggestively to the rhythm of the words."

In 1924 it was 'The Forsaken Merman,' a rhythmic mime. Miss E. M. Edwards aimed to express from music, which she had carefully selected, the meaning of Matthew Arnold's poem of the same name. This was "a beautiful phantasy", a study in eurhythmics, "an excellent example of poetry in motion," "of the stuff that dreams are made of." Forty eight girls were involved. Before the coming of mains electricity, "electric lighting effects by Mr C.F. Hancock, Sparkford", added to the charm of the spectacle. Marjorie Thomas remembered one "terrible black wig which Vera Loxton wore in the Eurhythmic Play, 'The Forsaken Merman' which made even her pretty face look peculiar but this was only a slight flaw in a really beautiful production."

Later in the year Sunny Hill girls were invited down the hill to a Sexey's School concert. The part which most delighted them was a burlesque of 'The Forsaken Merman.' The Sexey boys wishing to demonstrate that they also could move gracefully to music and cast a romantic glamour over the audience, produced a Eurhythmic play of their own, entitled 'The Mistaken Batsman' based on the well-known poem "There's a breathless hush in the Close tonight" and set to Mendelssohn's music.

In 1926 Miss Radford reported another mime and expressed her support for Eurhythmics: "We have produced two plays during the year; quite the best things of their kind that we have ever done. One was 'The Fall of Troy', a rhythmic mime with a Greek chorus, the work of Miss Edwards and her Rhythmic pupils. I am more and more convinced of the educational value of Eurhythmics, and for that reason I include classes in that subject in the regular school curriculum of Forms II and III; above Form III, however, we cannot spare school time for it, but I ask all parents who can manage it (and the fees are very small) to give their daughters, especially the musical ones, the opportunity of joining one of the extra classes which Miss Edwards is organising, out of school hours, for their benefit." "Two years later," Marjorie Thomas recalled, "Miss Edwards did 'The Siege of Troy' which was also a great success." Henry Hobhouse, who, it will be remembered, gained a first in Greats at Oxford, hoped "it would recommend a study of the classics to minds hitherto unfamiliar with them."

These and other dramas were helped by an enlarged stage in the new hut. The back wall had been taken out and a wing extended out over the path to Vb. This wing was 20 feet wide, the width of the curtain arch, and had a depth of 10 feet. This extension was raised one step above the level of the original stage.

To raise money for the cost of extra lighting, new fittings, extra curtains, as well as costume material, a Nativity Play was produced, the first of several such productions. It did, in fact, pay all but £6 of the money outstanding. The Nativity Play given just before Christmas 1925 was the same one produced 2 years previously, but with some additional features made possible by the increase in the size of the stage. In 1927 it was based on the old Coventry Nativity Play. Miss Radford adapted it, adding here, curtailing there. The result was such that a visiting clergyman, Rev A. H. Peppin, wrote: "I think it is a public service of great value to present such a performance; - moving, refining, and elevating; and I thank you accordingly." In 1929 the Play was performed for the third time, but in a modified form, Herod's court scene being left out altogether, and the play acted without words to the accompaniment of carols. The play thus became a religious service, in which the congregation took an important part by joining in carols between the scenes. The other carols were sung by the choir, and one especially beautiful one,'How far is it to Bethlehem?' by the children in the Annunciation scene, crossing the stage with lanterns.

Plays or excerpts were habitually performed as part of the normal syllabus. "The most interesting event at the end of last term (summer 1923) was the performance of two plays in the Hut, 'Comus' by Vb and 'Christabel' by the Fourth. They were simply the outcome of ordinary school work. Milton's lines were so spoken that they were a joy to hear. The Fourth Form dramatised 'Christabel' and added two entirely new scenes." On Wednesday evening, April 9th 1924, "the day before the Easter holidays started, the Fourth Form entertained the rest of the school with two French plays, 'La Farce du Pâté et la Tarte' and 'La Farce du Cuvier.'" The second showed the liberation of a hen-pecked husband from his household chores. The use of acting had Miss Radford's hearty approval: "Dramatic Literature is learnt far more forcibly by being acted than by merely being read. Much of the time given to English is now spent upon our school stage." At the end of the Christmas term 1924 the Fourth Form gave three scenes from Macbeth, the first scene in which Macbeth visits the witches, the scene after the murder (acted in almost total darkness), whilst in the last in which Lady Macbeth sleepwalks, a candle lit up the wondering faces of the doctor and gentlewoman, and the tense face of the Queen. There was practically no scenery, yet the result "was one of the best performances of Shakespeare that the school has ever seen."

In July 1927, Form IV and Miss Makins produced a Greek play for the entertainment of the Old Girls' Association at the Annual Meeting. It was the Alcestis of Euripides, in the distorting mirror of Gilbert Murray's translation. One result was this parody, on the topic of confiscated property (I quote a sample):

FRAGMENT OF GREEK TRAGEDY

I will undo the dragon-guarded chest.
These treasures at a price may ransomed be,
One obol each is the ordained fee.

Chorus severally:
Where is my fountain pen
O guardian of the goods of men?

Where is my tunic green
On the wrong peg last seen?

Someone my headdress wore
Fashioned of black velour.

I have lost one galosh.

Where is my mackintosh?

Not though we ask in sorrow
Are we allowed to borrow.

Looking back in 1960 Marjorie Thomas told a good anecdote concerning a school play: "Miss Makins used to produce the form and school plays, and how we used to enjoy them! I wonder if she knew, though, that in the production of 'As You Like It' we hid in the basket that was carried on in one of the scenes in the Forest of Arden, a cold chicken and other items destined for a four course dinner at a midnight feast to end all midnight feasts. This we had in Vb form room, or the Green Room, which led off the stage, or the Art Room. I was deputed to ask William, the Gardener, to leave the stove well fuelled so that we could warm up the soup. Turning round I saw Miss Radford a few yards behind me and I never knew whether she heard or not." Katharine Makins, Old Girl and first Sunny Hill B.A., continued to supervise the drama until 1934. Marjorie adds: "I should like to pay a tribute to Miss Makins. She had a wonderful sense of humour and tolerance and also the knack of taking in her stride all the more outspoken passages of Shakespeare. She was one of the major figures in my school days and it was through her that I first began to get a glimpse of understanding what a mature personality is."

Chapter 8

An End and a Beginning

T he Annual Prize Distribution on Friday, 26th July, 1929, was a memorable one. It marked the close of the twenty-nine year reign of Miss Radford as first and only Headmistress.

The platform was a living history lesson, with people who had seen the opening of the school in October 1900. The Marquis of Bath, Lord Lieutenant of the County and the school's President in its early days, presented the prizes. He had invested - and surrendered - £100 in the original school company, a handsome sum, but nothing compared with the £675 invested and surrendered by the day's chairman, the Right Hon. Henry Hobhouse. He, now aged 75, was accompanied by his second wife Anne, his first, Margaret, who had so impressed Edith Radford with her care and sympathy, having died in 1921. Of the other original Directors only Roland Hughes the musical solicitor and William Knight the Sexey's headmaster were present, with Mr J. Golledge, their then Secretary. Other were Mrs J. O. Cash, who had joined the Managers in 1901, Mr T. Salisbury Donne, whose name is remembered by an annual award, Mrs Hugh Mackie, Mr and Mrs W.F. Pepper, and Henry Hobhouse's son Arthur, on whose able shoulders much of Sunny Hill's future would rest. There were also County Education Committee representatives.

Miss Radford had given warning of her departure. She was out of the school the greater part of the autumn term, 1926, evidently ill. Then at the end of 1928 she broke the news in her letter in The Gleam:

"I have decided to retire from my labours at Sunny Hill at the end of the Summer Term 1929. I had hoped to complete 30 years of service by staying till 1930; but my energies are not what they were, and I think it is wiser to pass my work on to someone younger. I have bought part of an old orchard at West Quantoxhead, with the hills behind and the sea in front. Sunny Hillocks must be sold."

Sunny Hillocks was a plot of land between Berrow and Brean which she had bought in 1923, and on which she had built a little holiday Bungalow. She described charmingly how "It is on the main road from Burnham to Brean Down, and extends from the road to the Beach. A green and white flag flies from the gate post when I am 'in residence' and I hope no Sunny Hillite will ever pass that way without coming to see me."

* * *

Miss Radford's last years as Headmistress were lively and creative ones for Sunny Hill. Music revived at several levels. In 1922 what was recorded in The Gleam showed more enthusiasm than expertise. On December 12th "a most interesting and amusing programme was provided by the members of the hockey team. The programme was thoroughly appreciated, as was evident by the hearty and prolonged applause which greeted the various items, and which mingled with the many discordant sounds proceeding from the diverse instruments employed by the staff, instruments such as mouth-organs, tins and the big gong, the latter banged lustily by Miss Radford." These Hockey Concerts remained a feature for many years. The following year the Old Girls subscribed to a piano fund, a project that had been faltering for some time, and with that and the proceeds of the sale of two old pianos a full size grand piano was bought. Though sadly battered, it survived into the next century to be replaced by 'Stanley' the Steinway, the result of energetic fund-raising and a very generous donation from an Old Girl in memory of Joy Howard, a long serving secretary of the Old Girls' Association.

In 1924 Sunny Hill junior and senior choirs took part in the Mid Somerset Music festival in Bath after a three years' gap. Miss Radford was there to see each choir take first prize in its class. Unfortunately an inconvenient train service meant that the choirs could not stay to sing in the prize-winners concert that evening, and had to leave just one representative to receive the silver cup.

* * *

Social Evenings for boarders were revived in 1923. Twice a week after supper older girls met in the Art Room to play table tennis, to read, and on special occasions such as Halloween to organise entertainments. On colder evenings they had dancing, which became the most popular form of amusement. Before going to bed they would sing a hymn or the school song. After a few terms more ambitious programmes were put on. For instance, in November 1924 two forms, Vb and III, dressed as men to host the evening, and had Miss Rutter act as Town Crier and Mistress of

Ceremonies. The highlight was the performance of a new school song composed by Miss Makins and Miss Rutter:

"SUNNY HILL"

One road my homing fancies follow;
   Road leading up to Sunny Hill.
Still re-echo, long years after,
Shouts of triumph, happy laughter,
Rain or sun by hill or hollow
   May the gleam shine o'er us still.

On every side grow grass and green tree,
   Roses and jasmine at the door,
Soft rain falling, west wind blowing
And at evening, red sun glowing
Making dream clouds in the valley
   Over Glastonbury Tor.

There work and play are subtly blended,
   There in our houses we win fame,
On the field, our lessons ended,
Goals clean shot, and well defended,
Play up Brown, Blue, Red, or Yellow,
   Play up all and play the game.

So through my days will I remember
   All that you gave me, Sunny Hill:
Colour, booklore, song and story,
I'll be mindful of your glory,
I'll be loyal now and ever,
   To the school set on a hill.

Such lofty sentiments were all very well at the end of a jolly evening. Early next morning it was rather different:

GETTING UP

The second bell is clanging and we rub our sleepy eyes,
And we snuggle down in bed although we know it's time to rise;
And bed is oh so cosy, and the outside world so cold,
But being girls of SHS, we do as we are told.
Gingerly our captain puts her big toe out of bed,
She yawns, and she stretches, and she shakes her weary head;
She runs along the corridor to say from bed we're leaping,
Though we know that in her cosy nest our mistress still is sleeping.

We wash in chilly water, and we scrub and brush so well,
That we're waiting, clean and eager, for the clanging breakfast bell;
But we sometimes have a sneaking wish, (we cannot help confessing),
That we could lie and snooze, while everybody else was dressing!

J. Stapleton and M. Heginbothom Form III

Even a girl like Marjorie Thomas who stayed on to become a member of the Tennis Six, Treasurer of the History Society and Captain of Hockey, and who could stand up in later years and proclaim herself "very proud to have been a Sunny Hill girl," had her difficult times as a new girl in Form II. She found she had a trustworthy mother figure in the Matron, 'Thompsie.' She remembered sorting laundry with her in the Gym on a Saturday morning and her saying, "Time and tide wait for no man", and she had this confession to share: "In my first year, when School got too much, I used to knock my head against the iron bed rail in the hope that I'd get a wonderful headache and a day in bed. Miss Thompson was never taken in by this malingering but she had the gift of understanding, and by her comforting presence making one feel a whole person again."

And there were magic moments too, in a boarder's life, like a carol singing party in 1928, when Sixth and Fifth Formers with Miss Edwards visited the two founders of the school. "We were a very merry party, accompanied by Miss Hubbard and some other violinists - and bearers of old-fashioned lanterns which held lively flickering candles. The first night we all packed into two cars and went to Ditcheat. After singing lustily we visited Mr Knight's, where we were regaled in the true Christmas spirit with hot mince pies and ginger wine! From there we went to Hadspen House. After having sung several carols outside we were invited in and Mrs Hobhouse kindly gave us more Christmas cheer! The next evening we made a circuit of the houses around Sunny Hill. It was freezingly cold and as we went singing, from door to door, our lanterns casting weird shadows on our faces and the roads and hedges, we felt like true old-time Waits."

* * *

This was a time for new clubs. Apart from the choirs, the two chief clubs were the (indoor) Debating Society and the (outdoor) Field Club.

The energetic Debating Society, formed (for the third time) in September 1923, has died and been revived at intervals ever since. Lists of topics for debate, and voting results, are social documents of some interest.

> **In 1923-24:**
> 'Architecture is a profession more suitable to women than men' (won).
> 'Meat-eating is a relic of Barbarism and should no longer be indulged in by civilised people.' (lost)
> 'School rewards and punishments should be abolished' (lost);
> 'Boys and girls should be educated together' (won).
> In 1924-25:
> 'Day girls have a better time than Boarders' (lost);
> 'Skirts should be abolished';
> 'Boys should learn Housework';
> 'The nation should be governed entirely by women.'
> (The results of these 'sharp practice' debates were not recorded.)
> In 1928-29 girls were invited to look to world events:
> 'The only hope of world peace is complete disarmament within the next two years'
> (won 15 - 12).

We shall notice other interesting propositions in later chapters.

In the absence of a Literary Society, the Debating Society varied its weekly programme with occasional play readings such as Barrie's 'The Admirable Crichton' and Euripides'The Trojan Women'.

Taking advantage of girls' enthusiasm for clubs, one year the 4th Form 'organised itself', no doubt with staff help and encouragement, into a special Historical Society for the Summer Term.

Most successful, its membership including almost the whole school, staff included, was the Field Club. Formed in 1922, it embodied Miss Radford's love of nature and of the Somerset countryside and her hope that the Sunny Hill girl would be "an 'open air' creature; clean, vigorous, and loyal; a lover of beauty in art and nature." Its activities were very varied. There were monthly nature calendars, designed by the Houses in turn, and pronounced very effective.

Expeditions must have been a great incentive to belong to the Field Club. On 21st June 1927 the whole school including the Staff went to Burrington Combe, then to Cheddar, for a Field Club Expedition. No longer dependent on horse-drawn carriages, a pupil reports: "We started from the School at nine o'clock in four large Charabancs. Unfortunately, however, the weather was inclined to be rainy, and so the hoods of the Charabancs were up."

There were competitions, such as these, in Miss Radford's last year:

Winter Term: Collection of lichens; 'The Wind' - poetry or prose
Easter Term: Bulbs in three stages - drawings; snaps of trees in winter.
Summer term: flower gathering and arranging competition.

In 1928 a Geological section was added. Miss Radford's only regret was that the specimens that she herself brought along were not allowed to count in competitions.

To show how some girls responded to nature, we need only look at the careful pencil drawing of a conifer done by Daphne Edwards, one of Miss Radford's best Art pupils, on June 6th 1926, and this poem by Joan Grey from 1929 which clearly shows first hand observation and a visual imagination. Joan went on to Art School in Bristol:

TREES
Green buds nodding to green buds
As tree sways to tree
In light spring wind;
New leaves fluttering to and fro
With rustle slow and soft
And sun glinting through.
Bent branch and gnarled sturdy trunk,
Wych elms scattered petals,
Green on greener grass.
Catkins silvering o'er the willow
Yellow gleaming dust
On the swaying hazel,
Of such beauty are the trees of England.

It was fitting that on her retirement Miss Radford was presented with a bedspread, worked by members of the Field Club. It was made of squares of linen hemstitched together; on each square different wild flowers were embroidered in their natural colours.

*　　*　　*

Visiting lecturers brought a wide range of interests into Sunny Hill. A pupil said, "We were such a happy and enclosed community that to our immature minds the [1926] General Strike meant primarily that we were afraid the Frome and Wincanton day girls would have a holiday and we shouldn't." Miss Radford was very conscious of the "fact that we carry on our work here in considerable isolation from the great centres of light and learning." It sometimes made her fear that the school might be falling behind the times. Experts from outside could ensure that it did not. To show the variety of subject, here are some of the lectures delivered in 1928:

Balance and Greek Art by Mrs Diana Watts.
The League of Nations (on Armistice Day) by Dr Rutter.
Present Day Poets by Canon Yeats. These were W.H. Davies, Walter de la Mare, Kipling, Bridges, and Masefield (whom he considered "our best modern poet").
Australia the Wonderland, a lantern lecture by Mr Harris.
South Africa (including the Victoria Falls [sic!]), a lantern lecture by Mr Dunning.

Horizons were broadened also by expeditions, whether a local visit to Sexey's Hospital in Bruton, or to Masbury Camp & Wells Cathedral, all undertaken by fourth forms. Sometimes the expedition was to a lecture, especially if the speaker was a famous poet. Miss Makins recalled that on October 15th 1923 "some of us went to Wincanton to hear a lecture by Mr Walter de la Mare on 'Craftsmanship in Poetry.' As there was no train we had to walk the five miles back. Luckily it was a fine night and the walk proved an added attraction to a very interesting evening."

*　　*　　*

Miss Radford was proud of her girls. She must have taken satisfaction in this paragraph in the 1924 Inspectors' report:

"The number of girls who go on to places of higher education, and the variety of the careers for which they train, are striking evidence of the wide and stimulating education given in the School. There are old pupils at present at Oxford, Birmingham,

Bristol and Reading working for degrees, at Physical Training Colleges in Denmark, at Chelsea and at Liverpool, and at Training Colleges for Art, Domestic Science and Agriculture. A satisfactory proportion enter the teaching profession."

One can almost hear the pride in her voice as she announced in 1926:

"Gwen Knapman has won her BA degree at Bristol University, and Margaret Neville, (Head Girl of a few years ago) has taken a 2nd class Honours Degree in Maths at Manchester University. Edith Knight, who a short time ago was the first woman in England to gain a Veterinary Diploma, has now taken her B.Sc.. Degree in Vet. Science at Liverpool University, being the first woman to do so."

She must also have been glad that of her little staff of eight in 1924, four were graduates, and the others had suitable qualifications for their special posts.

She could not have been unaware of the love and respect in which she herself was held, nor of her own excellence as teacher and Headmistress. She was the Art teacher and could announce in 1926 "We have the satisfaction of being told by an inspector, that Sunny Hill is one of the most distinguished schools, for art work, in the South of England." The 1924 Inspectors had become almost lyrical in her praises:

"The School is fortunate in having still the services of the Head Mistress who has directed its growth since its opening in 1900. It has passed through many changes and difficulties; these, as well as the every day emergencies of school life, she meets with unfailing resourcefulness and courage. She has organising ability above the ordinary and is an inspiring teacher. The School owes everything to her, and her influence on the lives of the many girls who have passed through her hands cannot be too highly estimated."

But she was not a graduate.

Finally in 1927 the University of Bristol put that right, and invited her to receive an Honorary Master of Arts degree. On Saturday July 2nd she stood before Viscount Haldane as the Vice-Chancellor said:

"My Lord and Chancellor, I present to you Miss Edith Radford as worthy of the Degree of Master of Arts honoris causa. She has done important service to Education in Somerset by her successful conduct of Sunny Hill Girls' School, Bruton, of which she has been Head Mistress since its foundation in 1900. Her devoted care and wisdom have raised this school to a position of high repute among girls' schools in the Western

Counties, and made it a powerful instrument of moral and intellectual improvement."

At the Prize Giving later that year Henry Hobhouse turned to her and said: "We congratulate you upon your restoration to health, and on the Honour recently conferred. I am glad to see you, at last, appropriately clad in academic robes."

If you will take up Miss Radford's invitation and visit her, not in Sunny Hillocks with a green and white flag on the gate post, but in the nearby Berrow churchyard, her grave marked by a holly tree and lovingly tended by the Old Girls' Association, you will see, along with her dates of birth and death, and the fact that she was First Head Mistress Sunny Hill School Bruton Somerset, this inscription on the kerb stone:

EDITH JANE RADFORD M. A.

*　　*　　*

As she approached retirement, Miss Radford considered "her" girls. That the girls of the Twenties were not like her first pupils was obvious, and yet there were unchanging ideals to be passed on to them. Ruminating on the 1924 Inspection she wrote:

> "Education" gets to be a more and more difficult problem as the years pass. The last 10 years especially have brought such a different mental atmosphere, and its instinctive reactions to it have produced young people with an outlook upon life which is quite different from that of the pre-war days."

Indeed, it would have been surprising to find a Limerick like this one, about the weight problem of one of the prefects, in the Sunny Hill of 1914:

> The crown of this company's Targe,
> Who thought she was just a bit large,
>   So she tried with all haste
>   to get her a waist,
> Now she's 'waisting' away upon 'marge.'

Miss Radford was determined to understand the modern girl. "The chief problem for us teachers, and parents, has been, I consider, to educate ourselves so that we can have a sympathetic understanding of the new aspirations to personal liberty, and the newer modes of self-expression, while endeavouring to build up character upon what to me are the essential foundation, namely habits of hard work, self-discipline, and realisation of one's duty to the community."

It is characteristic of Miss Radford that after nearly a quarter of a century as Headmistress she still felt the need to educate herself in the new world view of her pupils, and to learn from them.

"I firmly believe that each new generation has much that is new and good to give to the world, and that each passing generation has many "broken potsherds of the past" to throw upon the rubbish heap, else how can the world advance? But unless the rising youth can learn to recognise, to reverence, and to build upon the best of what the past has to give, he will but raise a top heavy superstructure which will inevitably fall about his ears in ruin."

In 1925 she analysed some of the changes:

"The present day girl is very different from her predecessors of 25 years ago: she is more detached and independent; slower, I think, to react to human influences; more critical, and quicker to absorb and assimilate the spirit of the time in which she lives, but this I believe is common to all young people of the day - and a Sunny Hill girl who stays long enough in the school to absorb its spirit, has I believe, something about her - a combination of qualities - which is the outcome of that spirit."

*   *   *

When the moment came to retire, Miss Radford could feel great satisfaction. After all the struggles, World War, financial crisis, falling rolls, the school was on the way up. "Both last year and this the difficulty has been to find room for the best qualified of the candidates for admission, and there have been as many refusals as admissions."

Surveying her 29 years she could see that "Good traditions have been founded, and the very name of 'a Sunny Hill Girl' is now a passport in itself. The names of 1,022 such girls have been entered by me on the rolls of the school, and I have had strong personal relations with all of them."

The inevitable presentations followed. Lord Bath presented Miss Radford with a cheque for £100 from friends, including the Governors, and a leather-bound album containing the names of the subscribers. The parting gift of the girls of Sunny Hill took the form of a portable wireless set, which was presented to her on the last Tuesday of term by the Head Girl, Peggy Stephenson. The Old Girls Association

Miss Radford and Kim

got Mrs F.K. Makins (Ethel Knight), the first pupil admitted to Sunny Hill School, to present her with a cheque for £216 10s. A book was also given, written and illuminated by Miss Radford's star artist, Daphne Edwards, with names of Old Girls, past and present Staff, domestic staff, and present girls from the school's foundation in 1900. Other gifts included garden furniture from the Staff and a clock from the domestic staff.

An Old Girl hearing of Miss Radford's retirement wrote from abroad:

"She has been a real mother to many of us. Her wisdom has guided us in the choice of a career. The two ideas she always kept before us were love of beauty and the dignity of labour. Her interest reached far beyond our schooldays. Those who travelled to the far corners of the world could always depend upon it. Others who were more accessible found that counsel and guidance were never asked in vain; affectionate interest never wanting.

The creation of such a school as Sunny Hill is indeed a life work of which anyone might be proud. Often it must have seemed a dream impossible to realise. But Miss Radford's faith was infectious, and her courage in the face of difficulties; and members of the Staff took a willing part in the great work. Her aim was to create a school with a character of its own, a school where girls should be prepared for the adventure of life in such a way that they would make the best of their opportunities; where no one should be forced into a groove; but where girls should develop naturally in a sunny atmosphere."

It was a hard act to follow. Enter Jane Wells.

* * *

Left: Dressed for the occasion: Jean Notley, tennis champion

Right: Dressed for the occasion: Actresses from the 1933 production of 'Hamlet', the first to be lit by electricity

Chapter 9

Miss Wells Digs In

At forty-four years of age, "a straight ramrod of a woman with feet at ten to two," with twenty years' teaching experience in Beverley High School, Yorkshire, Howell's School, Denbigh, and Twickenham County School, Jane Wells had much to offer. At once she struck Henry Hobhouse as capable and sympathetic. "From the first moment that she came she has mothered the School, giving her most considered attention to everything from our spiritual welfare to a gas-bracket."

To the girls this Irish woman appeared more formidable than motherly, very autocratic, with the highest intellectual standards. Marjorie Thomas (later Mrs. Chambers), Miss Wells' first Head Girl, felt a little trepidation about meeting her. After reading the first French essay she set Marjorie, Miss Wells said "It is quite beyond my power to imagine how you got into the Sixth form." Instead of being resentful, Marjorie formed at once a respect for her perspicacity and judgement which stayed with her ever after. Miss Wells was a specialist in French and, as a team of School Inspectors found, "an exceptionally effective teacher." Staff and girls, Miss Allen noted, soon became aware that in every activity and in every department Miss Wells required of them the finest achievement and the greatest thoroughness of which they were capable; and that nothing slipshod or shoddy would pass unnoticed.

Some examples: "A piece of needlework should be a thing of beauty and perfectly finished off." "Use intelligence in games, as well as physical prowess." "Legible handwriting is simply good manners; beautiful handwriting is an art we can all acquire." And a principle that all could see she herself practised: "We cannot all have beautiful faces but we can all have beauty of body, i.e. good deportment." It was one of the Second Form who said, "I think Miss Wells should have a Deportment Badge."

Another girl said that she and her friends feared Miss Wells, "but in the way we are meant to fear God." One of the smallest members of the school wrote: "Her bright eyes twinkle at you when you're good, but when you've been naughty they seem to see right inside you." One method to which some girls resorted when about to face Miss Wells' displeasure was to stare at her feet, which were large; they believed that she then became self-conscious and did not administer such a severe rebuke.

Despite her strict manner, she inspired affection in her girls. "She liked to present herself as very fierce. She was such a tartar," said one, "that we used to say 'I hate Jane!' But we didn't. We loved her. She was very fair, and set clear boundaries so that you knew where you were with her; that gave us a sense of security." The same girl first met Miss Wells when she came with her mother for interview. The mother found Miss Wells a frightening person, but the little girl did not; she was determined that she wanted to come to Sunny Hill. As a new, rather homesick boarder she treasured Sunday evenings in the Headmistress's drawing room when, gathered comfortably round a blazing fire, the only one in the school, they would listen to Jane reading tales like "The Secret Garden." The trace of Irish accent with which Miss Wells pronounced the name "Dickon" is a warm memory still.

A slightly different view of Miss Wells' strictness comes in some verses about getting up in the morning which end:

> Away o'er the san path we stream -
> A herd of mad bulls isn't in it!
> "Miss Wells will say Grace" we all scream -
> "In very much less than a minute!"

> In very much less than a minute
> We again hear the sound of the bells.
> A whirl - and a rush - and we're in it -
> Just a second in front of Miss Wells!

Phyllis Holman

Miss Allen, who served with Miss Wells for all but her first two years, wrote that she held constantly before the school the duty of service. Many years before J.F. Kennedy's inaugural address (Ask not what your country can do for you ...) she said: 'It isn't what you can get out of life, but what you can put in.' "Every girl was expected to do her share for her group - perhaps a small group at first - form, or dormitory, or House, and then for the whole community. It was significant that Miss Wells altered 'prizes for school subjects' to 'awards for service.' She was deeply concerned, too, that our service should not end with the school community: 'We who are so lucky - what are we doing for those who are less well off?' And she took the degree of our interest and our achievement for those others, as a kind of index of our own well-being."

*   *   *

Miss Wells did not wait long before beginning a quiet revolution in school government and discipline. Half way through her first term a boarders' committee was formed, consisting of Miss Wells, the second Mistress, the House Mistress, Prefects, and a representative from each dormitory, to discuss the Boarders' rules and anything else to do with the House part of the School. This continued at least until 1947, and its Minutes book gives a reliable, if unexciting, view of boarding life. Could boarders be allowed to practise psalms as well as the hymns for Sunday service? No. Could the Houses exchange Cosies? Yes. Two years later the Head proposed, first to the staff and then to a Prefects' Meeting, a system of democracy and devolution of responsibility. Her ideas were welcomed, and once a fortnight a meeting of Prefects, Form-Captains and Vice-Form-Captains was held, to receive any complaints from Form-Captains, and to discuss matters of school interest.

New arrangements for discipline were explained: "All Disorder Marks and punishments resulting from them were to be abolished, and instead of this, Form - and Dormitory - Captains were made entirely responsible for those under their charge. Meetings of the Forms, with the Form Mistress presiding were to be held regularly; and complaints were to be presented and offenders dealt with. The Form Captains were authorised to give suitable punishments - each Form having its own method of dealing with unruly members."

After a month's trial this became permanent. It was not, however, a complete novelty to Sunny Hill. In 1917 Miss Radford had tried what she called 'Federal Home Rule,' in which each Form had had its elected committee, responsible for maintaining order within its own ranks, and had sent two members to join the prefects and sub-prefects in a Central Council which had 'control of matters that lie outside the province of the individual Forms.' Any suggested revision of rules had to be suggested to the Head, "who reserves to herself the 'Crown' prerogative of the veto."

This earlier experiment faded away in a couple of years, but Miss Wells' arrangements had a longer life. Soon the report went that "The result of that larger share in the government of the School had been a marked improvement in keeping the rules, a keener form spirit, and a sense of form responsibility, and that, in turn, had had its effect on the work of the School. A form which was capable of maintaining good discipline had the privilege of doing preparation in School unsupervised, and it was the rule rather than the exception for the forms to win that privilege."

*   *   *

Miss Wells' high intellectual standards were made very clear to the whole school.

Parents also were encouraged to do their part in making their daughters' school life as beneficial as possible. One Speech Day they faced some plain speaking from Miss Wells. First, she mentioned punctuality.

"A late start from home in the morning is a very bad beginning for a good day's work. The first lesson, and sometimes the whole morning is lost because the child is getting over the rush.

"Secondly, I do not think that you realise how much a late bed hour affects the work at school. Children sleep during class to make up for the hours lost the night before, and so waste not only their own time, but often other girls' as well. This is especially noticeable among the weekly boarders and day girls on Monday mornings, and I can say that less good work is done on Mondays that on any other school day because girls go to bed so late on Sundays.

"My next point is home work. As we aim at getting really good work done in school, the time allotted to home work is not great. We do expect the best possible work in that time from each girl, and that can only be obtained if you parents provide the right conditions. No girl can do her work late at night, or when there is talking in the room. To help you co-operate with us in the matter of time spent on home work, duplicate copies of each girl's home work timetable will be made in future at the beginning of the year, one of which we shall ask you to sign and return.

"Again, I don't think that you realise how unsettling it is to the girls to hear their leaving discussed in advance, especially when it is a case of withdrawing them before they reach the School certificate form. In many cases it takes away the incentive to work. If every girl coming here is given to understand by her home people that she has to get her School certificate before she leaves it will undoubtedly help that girl's attitude to her work and her school life in general."

That was telling them.

In 1931 Miss Wells introduced a new method of awarding prizes. She persuaded the Governors that it was unfair to give prizes on a competitive basis; they agreed instead to give them to leaving girls for their service to the School. No longer were girls of all ages to stagger from the stage with arms full of the books that Miss Radford had delighted to present. In 1934 a type of academic competition was reintroduced, but no longer individual, with House Trophies for French and Latin, English and History, Arts, Crafts, Domestic Science, Mathematics, Geography and Science, and Music, as well as for Netball, Rounders, Games, the Field Club, Hockey, and Tennis.

* * *

"One aspect of her thoroughness was more visible, perhaps," wrote Miss Allen, "to the Staff than to the girls themselves. That was her intense interest in, and the detailed knowledge of, each individual child. When a form mistress went to consult her about some problem she invariably came away knowing a good deal more about the background of her charges. And discussions in staff meetings were never purely theoretical or concerned with generalities but with the particular needs and reactions of individuals.

"This belief in her omniscience was shared by the Staff. Once a member of Staff went to tell her Headmistress that she had just become engaged to be married. Miss Wells greeted her, 'Ah, Miss So-and-so, I know what you've come to tell me.' And she did."

One of her pupils, Mary Simms (now Mrs. Longstreet) remembers that Miss Wells used to have, for morning break, egg and milk taken to her office in the new building. "It did her good. She was a good head mistress, really; rather Victorian, obviously, because things were then." A final picture in this kaleidoscope of impressions of the new Headmistress must be the photograph (see Chapter 11) of a senior girl playing leapfrog over a bent female figure, who, we are reliably assured, was Jane Wells herself.

Indeed the school had gained another remarkable Head.

* * *

And it was growing. Clearly a major new building would have to be undertaken before too long, but for the moment the old original building, which had been extended, improved and rearranged almost from the moment of its erection, would have to be extended and rearranged further. Miss Wells' second Prize Day had to be postponed, from October 1930 to July 1931, until new buildings were finished, and Sunny Hill had become "the proud possessors of two new form rooms, six music rooms, and four spacious cloakrooms, which accommodate over 60 people." In 1931 also a new library, known as the Gollege Library, was furnished with bookcases and fittings in light oak, the gift of Mrs Scott and Mr Gollege, and Henry Hobhouse, whose health was now giving cause for anxiety, was among those who gave new books. As pupil numbers continued to grow, the staff was increased by one, an Old Girl, Miss Mann.

1932 was "a red letter year for the School in that electric light has been substituted for gas. Gone are the dangers of dark corridors and the terror of fastening windows with only a waning torch! We are longing for the performance of 'Hamlet' to show off our fine stage lights to the public." Lessons, too, could now benefit from new technology. A new epidiascope proved of great value, as "several lecturers used it to show their slides, while the History and Geography Clubs also used it to illustrate talks." In the Christmas term, for example, Miss Cherry-Garrard gave a lecture on Morocco. "Her lantern slides were very unusual, being coloured."

In 1933 the science lab gained new fittings: benches with sinks, running water, and gas taps. The Cookery Room now had a Regulo gas stove and an oil stove. The hot water system was overhauled, and an electric pump installed in the yard. The girls found a constant and reliable supply of hot water comforting in cold weather. The arrival of the new benches prompted this piece of writing in ye olde style:

"And behold! in that seemingly great seminary for young ladies stood many stools and benches of great age, upon whose beautiful surfaces were many carvings of wonderful design… those of the wonderful carving were changed for new benches with neither decoration nor inscription … a decree was passed saying that no person should spend her valuable time working out wonders of decoration upon the new benches, however plain." (M. Westover.)

Individuals helped with gifts of furniture and decorative items. Easy chairs for the Blue Room came from Miss Cox and Mrs Golledge. Miss Bennett gave "a coloured print of Monet's 'Cap D'Antibes' as a leaving present; this also hangs in the dining hall." Josephine Holmes gave "a lovely vase for the Blue Room." Some Old Girls took up the Head's suggestion that they should present the School with light oak dining room chairs that had been designed specially for Sunny Hill. These cost "one guinea, carriage 1s. extra." Each had the donor's name and the dates of her period at Sunny Hill engraved on the back.

More, much more, was to come. The Old Girls affected to find all this most bewildering when they gathered at the school for their 1934 reunion: "We were all delighted to hear of plans for enlarging the School yet again. It is difficult to imagine Courts A and B covered by classrooms, and the old classrooms made into dormitories (or vice versa - I cannot quite remember which, for both are equally staggering!)." The centre of balance of Sunny Hill was going to change permanently with the moving, in 1937, of the day school down the hill to the new building and the giving over of Old House, as it was thereafter called, to boarding and dining.

In 1930 the Governors transferred £1,000 to a reserve fund; next year £1,529 went into the building fund; in 1932 a total of £1,416 was squirrelled away. The staff and pupils also did their bit. A sale of work was held to raise funds for furnishing the larger Library, which was to be in the new building, "in a manner worthy of the present Golledge Library." Such efforts by Governors and school did not at all meet the cost of the new building, but were an indication that the new building was no longer just a pious hope, but would materialise before the Thirties were over.

*   *   *

Meanwhile daily life was fuller than ever. At the end of her first year Miss Wells arranged a Hobbies Competition for the summer holidays, with a 16 shilling certificate as first prize. "There were many delightful entries of Art, Handicrafts and Literature." A History and Geography Club was started, with expeditions to Wookey, and Vallis Vale near Frome. After its first year this club divided into two, one for History and the other for Geography, each with appropriate expeditions to Wells Cathedral and Cheddar respectively. The Literary and Debating Society continued with play readings of, for example, 'The Rivals' and 'Pygmalion,' and debates such as "If by pressing a button you could kill a Chinaman in Pikin and inherit £10,000, would you do it?" (to the school's shame, a majority voted in favour); and "The craze for Yo-Yo is a sign of softening of the brain" (Lost). The Field Club remained active with competitions for fungi and moss, and other such delights.

In 1932 La Société française was added to the list of clubs. "It was decided that at meetings French games should be played, French songs sung and that everyone should speak French. This rather difficult rule is being strictly obeyed and all the members should pass French Oral with honours." In fact the amount of French decreased meeting by meeting. "At the first meeting we played 'Ou est ma place?' which is the French version of 'Come and sit in my chair,' while various people acted French jokes, and Joan Beechey and Jacqueline Lodwidge acted 'Le Renard et le Corbeau,' by La Fontaine. A French girl had been invited and she sang two songs for us. The meeting ended with the singing of 'Bon jour, Mlle Agathe,' and 'La Marseillaise.'" The next meeting featured a play acted by seniors and written by Miss Goldsmith-Browne. The third meeting had just one game, and then music! In subsequent years members compensated for the lack of French at the meetings by writing the magazine report in French.

In the Summer Term of 1933 a Sunny Hill branch of the League of Nations was formed, and membership soon rose to 85, a tribute to Miss Wells' success in getting girls to look beyond their own narrow interests.

Games were played with enjoyment and increasing success. In 1932 Sunny Hill won the inter-schools hockey tournament on goal average, against Frome, Ilminster, Minehead, Sherborne and Yeovil. There were house competitions in hockey, netball, tennis and rounders, and with the aid of the newly installed electricity, "on Feb. 11 the School and a number of other hockey enthusiasts from the neighbourhood assembled in the Blue Room to see the Hockey Film, produced by the Women's Hockey Association."

Amid all this happy and enthusiastic activity, it is hard to know how seriously to take the following view of boarding life by two day girls who were in Form IVa in 1932:

> Oh who would a boarder be,
> Having no freedom?
> Only on Sundays cake for tea
> If others leave some.
> Have to go to bed at eight,
> A disorder if you're late.
> Five of these is a terrible fate.
> Oh, would you be a boarder?
>
> Oh who would a boarder be?
> No time for quiet.
> The half-hour's leisure after tea
> Is but a riot.
> Six o'clock and prep. begins,
> Silence till the next bell rings,
> Then you hear the supper things.
> Now, who would be a boarder?

*   *   *

And always there was drama. One could fill a chapter with accounts of the plays continually being produced, but we may fill out one girl's recollections as an example. Suzanne Seward (née Giddings), who left in 1934, wrote to Miss Cumberlege, the headmistress at the time, a letter dated 7 Feb. 1967: "Another very pleasant memory is going carol singing all round the countryside, with Miss Goldsmith-Brown and her violin, calling on people like the Hobhouses. We also did a Nativity play most years. But the plays I remember best were the musical adaptation of Pilgrim's Progress, to the music of Brahms; the mime presentation of Spenser's Faerie Queen, with Shannah Melhuish, Muriel Lydford, Sylvia Green and I reciting in chorus before each scene; and of course, Hamlet. The hockey team used to give excellent concerts. In fact, we always were a theatrical school. Are you still?"

Suzanne's memory did not play her false, but during her time at the school there were more plays than she mentioned. In the 1930 Mid-Somerset Musical Festival, girls acted a scene from Henry IV part 1 and came third, with 85% and a first class certificate. The following year the Gleam reported: "We have kept up our acting reputation this year with three plays." They were 'The Faerie Queen,' a rhythmic mime, 'The School for Scandal' at the end of the Spring Term (proceeds from this production went towards a motor mower), and a Nativity Play "presented again in its simple form." In addition there were play readings of 'Quality Street', and 'The Barretts of Wimpole Street.' In 1932 a feature of Speech Day was the performance of Gilbert Murray's translation of the ancient Greek play 'Alcestis' by Euripides. This followed hot on the heels of Shakespeare's 'The Merchant of Venice,'acted by Forms Va and IVa. Miss Makins produced this, a set text for School Certificate.

Suzanne mentioned "and of course Hamlet." This 1933 production evidently made a great impression, helped by the new electric lighting, as we have seen. The Gleam review is as glowing as the new lights:

"It was Elizabethan. The small theatre in itself contributed to this; it gave the spectators a feeling of intimacy. The stage, too, with its depth, and facilities for expansion and contraction of scene, helped the effect of fluidity in performance and belongs by right to the Elizabethan drama. The most abiding impressions of the play were gained in the moments when acting, speech, costume and lighting magically coalesced with the whole spirit of the play: the silhouetted figure of the pacing sentinel against a dark blue sky, and the slow, silent passage of the Ghost in a faint beam of silver light; the rich massing of colours in the room of State, with one sombre figure sitting alone and aloof from the chatter of expectant excitement; the exquisitely mimed dumb show on the steps at the back of the stage, with the sinister poisoner slowly advancing; foils clashing in the midst of a crowded stage with a courtier's delicate flourishes in the background."

With all this theatrical experience to draw on, girls formed a critical audience for a visiting lecturer on Shakespeare. The Gleam contributor must have enjoyed holding tongue firmly in cheek while writing her last sentence: "Mr Edward Lugg, an elocutionist of considerable skill, rather exaggerated his subject. He spoilt his speeches and made his characters unreal. His lecture did not cover as much ground as we had expected, and did not touch upon the depth and meaning of Shakespeare, but his elocution was of the type that we do not often get the chance of hearing."

Above: The Day School, completed in 1938;
Below: The new School Hall was used for the 1938 Speech Day

Chapter 10

The New School

S uch varied activity could not disguise the fact that the school had outgrown its buildings yet again. Eyes were turning to the Governors, and hopes of a major new building were rising. It was time that piecemeal extensions and temporary huts gave way to a properly planned, permanent day school, that would free the original building for boarding and catering.

Let us look at the governing body at this period. Some of the 'founding fathers' were still serving in 1933, and we can read letters between three of these, Henry Hobhouse, Rowland Hughes and William Knight as they chose the most suitable person to fill a vacancy in their ranks. On 5th December 1933 Rowland Hughes wrote to Henry Hobhouse:

Dear Hobhouse,

Thank you for your letter. As I said at our interview I am inclined to the suggestion we then made that Miss Woodforde is the best person to recommend, but she should be sounded, I think, as to her willingness to accept the position. The only difficulty I anticipate on her part is that of locomotion in getting to our meetings, but as there are several people who come from Castle Cary this can be overcome.

I think it is desirable to have someone from Castle Cary rather than from any other direction.

With regard to the other persons mentioned I think the second on the list should be Miss Warren, she does a good deal of work in Castle Cary, has ideas and is not afraid to express them. I have some doubts as to the suitability of the other three ladies mentioned, and I doubt whether Mrs. P... would act. Her husband at any rate does not care to take any part in local work, at least, so he told me. With regard to Mrs Ph..., I have never heard of her as being a person who takes any interest in public work at all.

Yours very truly,
Rowland T.A. Hughes

Two facts stand out from this correspondence. One is the sort of person the school needed as a governor, hardworking, public spirited, full of ideas and outspoken. The other is that although this vacancy was one which the County Council had the right to fill, it was the recommendation of those most closely concerned with the school that would carry the day. On January 4th 1934 the governors' secretary wrote to the County Education Office in Weston-super-Mare, with a copy to William Knight:

> With reference to the appointment of a new Governor, consideration of which was adjourned from the previous meeting from the H. E. Sub-Committee, I have been asked by the Chairman and other Governors of the School to suggest for consideration of the Sub-Committee, the name of Miss H. M. M. Woodforde, St. Anselm's, Ansford, Castle Cary.
>
> Miss Woodforde is very well known in the district and has devoted many years to W. I. and other social work which has brought her into close contact with the parents of girls attending this School. She has had some teaching experience and is generally a person very well qualified to be on the Governing body.

Three weeks later the County Education Officer could write back:

Dear Mr. Hobhouse,
I beg to inform you that the County Education Committee at their recent meeting, decided to appoint Miss H. M. M. Woodforde as their representative on the Governing Body of Sunny Hill Girls' School, Bruton.

*   *   *

One 1935 new girl was William Knight's granddaughter Pamela (Mrs Richards). She remembers her school days vividly:

> "When I walked across to take the entrance exam, Brena Pangbourne showed me round and everyone was so friendly that I felt at home at once. Miss Wells, the Head, then took me to a music room - I think it is now part of a House mistress's flat - and sat me down with the papers. She forgot about me and I fell asleep but was eventually rescued and taken down to lunch. I am a slow eater and was so embarrassed when everyone got up to say grace while I was still struggling with the last bit of my jam tart! I was not put in Brena's class but the one below. I had never done French and found it an effort to pick it up (it was the middle of the Spring Term) for in those days

you were not coached to cover any gaps. The other subjects presented no difficulties and I liked them all. I was a day girl to start with and enjoyed taking home what I had achieved, hot from the oven, on cookery days. I was sorry when, later, the form divided and I was put in the language section, especially as, for once, we were to learn German instead of Latin.

"After my grandmother died, I became a boarder but was allowed to go home on Sundays to make tea for my grandfather and wheel in the trolley, already laid by our housekeeper before she went out. This was a great privilege. I loved boarding school life. In the evenings, each form had a territory called a 'cosy' where we met after prep and gossiped, played games, argued or knitted. Once, I remember, it was in the wings of the stage, round a Tortoise stove, in the old Blue Room, now no more, between the old and new buildings. In summer we appreciated the school gardens, especially Rosy Corner, and it was great to play tennis after supper. There was a patch of clover by the San where you could find four- and five-leaved leaves, which made us feel very lucky.

"On Saturday nights there was always dancing, and no lack of girls who could play the piano for this, or we got up some form of entertainment. Either a form or a dormitory would organise this and although it was largely impromptu, it was great fun. On Sundays we walked to church, in a crocodile of course, one week to Pitcombe and the next to Shepton Montague (this was before the fire there), clutching our penny for the collection. We were checked out by matron as we left, to make sure that our hats and stocking seams were straight, we were carrying our prayer books and wearing our gloves. Sometimes we went to Bruton church and were sternly admonished to keep our eyes straight ahead and not look at the King's or Sexey's boys. I didn't enjoy church then (we played the alphabet game, silently, during the sermon) but am glad we were made to go as I do now.

"We were never allowed any tuck (if any was sent, it was confiscated and returned at the end of term) except on Saturday afternoons when we could spend twopence from a supply kept in the gym cupboard and doled out by a member of staff or a prefect. Most of us wolfed down our one chocolate bar or tube of fruit gums at once. In those pre-fluoride days, we had rather good teeth."

*　　*　　*

In January 1936 Rowland Hughes died. He had been a governor for 24 years, and had taken over as chairman when Henry Hobhouse's health declined in 1931. On June 25th 1937 Henry Hobhouse himself died aged 83. The passing of the two chairmen of governors, both of them founding shareholders of the school, within eighteen months marked the end of the old era.

The building of the new day school marked the beginning of a new era. It is hard for someone looking at the school buildings today to imagine how the school could have managed in the original building and some temporary huts. The School Inspectors in 1935 were sure it ought not to have to manage for much longer:

"In view of the imminence of new quarters for the School there is no need here to enumerate the various defects of the present buildings.

"From time to time the original buildings have been extended in order to meet the needs of a growing school. Additions are varied in character; some the result of private enterprise, some of public funds, some temporary in structure, some permanent, some for boarding purposes, some for day school, some attached to the Main School, some detached. The Governors are right in deciding that such patchwork extensions, while they have in their day fulfilled their purpose, must now come to an end. The School deserves a building worthy of its established position."

The Inspection team could not, however, refrain from commenting on the gym:

"An exception is made in the case of the gymnasium, a temporary structure in many ways behind accepted standards. The floorboards are warped and there is no accommodation for changing. The Governors should bear in mind its limited life."

This was the building welcomed so enthusiastically in 1919 ("Jim who?") which was still in some kind of use in the 1980s.

The Inspectors' report noted the prudent financial preparation made by the Governors:

"In view of future extensions to the school buildings profits have recently been placed in the Buildings Account. This at the date of the Inspection had accumulated to over £8000. In addition there is a balance in the Bank of several hundred pounds, which may go to swell the above amount or may be used for sundry school purposes.

"For the last three years the annual profits on the administration have been about £2,000, £1,113 and £1,786 respectively, and this in spite of expenditure on electric light installation, water supply and the Science laboratory.

"The financial position is therefore sound, and in the opinion of the Inspectors the Governors can embark with confidence upon a building scheme which will meet adequately the needs of the School."

This did not mean that they had all the money they needed. The building cost £30,000. Somerset County Council gave a grant of £10,000 and a loan of a further £10,000, interest free, which the governors were still repaying after the war when Sunny Hill had become independent. Mr Pictor, who designed the original 1900 school, was still the school architect, and designed the new building, although he did not live to see it completed. Aims and priorities had changed, however, and the day school looks very different from what would now be known as Old House.

* * *

It was all very exciting for the girls, and a little frustrating for the staff, when building began in earnest in 1936. The Gleam for that year, published in April 1937, reported:

"The work of the new School buildings is progressing rapidly, and already the face of the land is changing. But although we feel a tinge of regret at the disappearance of so many familiar landmarks, we are all looking forward eagerly to the time when there will be a completely new day school, which is to contain a large hall, laboratory, geography room, domestic science room, classrooms, library and music cubicles, while in the present buildings the dining room and kitchen block are to be extended. It is hoped that the day school will be finished in September 1937, and that the rest of the building will be ready by January 1938."

The next Gleam, however, had to retract that hope:

"The whole School is looking forward to the time when the new buildings will be completed. We are already using one wing, and part of another, and although we are frequently distracted by the builders' noises, and amused by their songs, on the whole we find the new School easier to work in. The rooms are light and airy, and we are especially proud of our new Art room, with its large windows.

"At present, owing to the lack of a covered way between the new School and the old, galoshes have been very much in demand, and the lack of them has led to so many awkward situations that we are surprised they did not suggest themselves to the minds of our poets as a subject for verse - grave or gay.

"We hesitate to fix a date for the completion of all the new buildings, remembering our rash prophecy in the last number of the Magazine."

Those builder's noises and songs found their way into a sketch, The English

Lesson, written by Miss Allen for the 1950 historical pageant and encored in 1975. This is the opening:

Scene: A classroom 1937. Tramping outside, subdued at first. A form (UIV) preparing for English. Enter a girl in a rush: "She's coming!"

CAPTAIN   Stop talking, Betty. Go to your place, Ann. Be <u>quiet</u> all of you. That includes you, Pat.

(Silence. Enter Miss X)

MISS X   Good morning, Upper Four.

FORM   Good morning, Miss X.

MISS X   Sit down. (They sit) I am so glad that you were waiting quietly for me. It is just the right opening for our lesson, which is, if you remember, the reading of quotations from the quiet poems which you have prepared in prep. (Sound of a lorry backing) May we hear yours first, Ann?

ANN   Sleep, by Wordsworth.

A flock of sheep that leisurely pass by,

One after one ..

WORKMAN Tip 'em on the floor. (bricks tipped from lorry)

ANN   ... and the sound of rain, bees murmuring ... (fall of gravel off)

... the fall of rivers, winds and seas,

Smooth fields, white sheets of water

(bucket of water poured out, off, and cement mixed)

... and pure sky ...

WORKMAN (off, yawning) Sky looks black, don't it?

ANN   I have thought of all by turns ...

FOREMAN   (off) I'm thinking as you oughter be fired.

ANN   ... and yet do lie sleepless

WORKMAN (off) I didn't get ter bed till one. (They bumble on)

Young poets of 1937 and 1938 celebrated the new building, too. Diana Gibbs, Form Vb. had discovered enjambment:

OUR NEW SCHOOL

Our new school is very grand,

It's quite the best for miles around.

The rooms are very large and clean,

Whereas the old form-rooms had been

Draughty, dark and very cold,
With scarcely room enough to hold
Desks for thirty girls or more,
And countless cracks along the floor.

Our new rooms are not painted yet,
The walls aren't dry enough to let
The men begin to paint them o'er.
And there are "port-holes" in each door.

Alas! the builders, they will deign
To sing "The Poppies Bloom Again,"
While Miss Marin says, with a sigh,
"We cannot help their lullaby."

Another young poet spared a thought for what had disappeared:

...
The third form went, the bike shed too,
They passed like fleeting dreams,
I stood within the new school doors
Where the brass-work gleams.
...
I walked along the balcony
And never a word I'd say,
Shining steps and corridors
Took my speech away...

Miss Wells in 1960 looked back on the upheavals that the building works caused:

"The first gymnasium the school ever had was in the present Garrett Anderson sitting room and was also used as the cookery room. That room had many vicissitudes but its highlight was in 1937 when the kitchen block and the dining hall were in the hands of the builders, and it became the school kitchen with the now VIth form study next door as the larder, and the passage way from the kitchen to the big school room through which the meals were carried by the domestic staff. The big school room had become the dining hall for the whole school - then about 230, and the Flower Room dealt with all the washing up. It sounds impossible, but it *worked*, owing to the amazing goodwill of the domestic and teaching staff and the girls. Miss Allen had to teach Form II in the then new staff sitting room to the noise of a large concrete mixer just outside and a set of jolly workmen who broke into song at unexpected moments."

*   *   *

Alongside the excitement of the new building the school suffered several losses at this time. The late Chairman of the Governors, Mr. Rowland Hughes, whose death was recorded above, was commemorated by a black metal Rood Screen designed by Mr. W.H. Blacking, F.R.I.B.A., and erected in Bruton Church. A large number of the Seniors attended the dedication service on Thursday, 29th September, 1938, and also in the congregation was Anne Satow, who had come to the school in September, 1935, to take School Certificate in the following July, and died on the Sunday after the dedication of the rood screen. When she left school, Anne stayed at home and threw herself with interest into local and Church affairs where her friendliness and readiness to help endeared her to all.

Mr Pictor, the School architect, died on November 29th, 1938, and by his death the School lost one of its oldest and truest friends. Mr Pictor was not only the architect of the new buildings, but he also designed the original buildings in 1900, and was responsible for each additional portion when the increasing numbers made enlargement necessary.

In 1936 the school had joined the Ship Adoption Society. The girls were interested to receive logs from a ship at sea, and grew to feel that Captain Bullock, who wrote long letters about s.s. African Trader, was a friend. In 1937 a letter, full of British understatement, gave warning that the dangers were real:

> We went to Antwerp, where we loaded the rest of the cargo. All of it was foodstuffs for the Spanish (Basque) Government. We left there on May 25th for Santander, but on the way we had to call at Dover to pick up a Non-Intervention Observer. His job is to see that no munitions of war are carried in the ship. The particular man we had, and still have, is a young German merchant service officer, who speaks perfect English. We arrived [at Santander] on May 29th ... We got there early in the morning, and at 9 a.m. we were treated to our first air-raid warning. That was an easy one. The 'planes just circled over the town, but dropped no bombs. After a few days we got used to that sort of thing. There were very often three or four a day. There were two submarines in the port and they used to fire at the 'planes, but never did any damage. One day the 'planes came over (five of them), and dropped about 60 bombs about a mile from us. We could see all the bursts, but had to keep under cover as they had put an anti-

aircraft gun just alongside the ship and the shrapnel was dropping on the wharf alongside. Not too pleasant! ...

We entered Gijon quite quietly. There everything was calm and peaceful, though we were only 20 kilometres from Oviedo, the front. .... Really it is very quiet in Spain. I do not think it was in Bilbao. I met a Captain who had to leave there in a hurry the day before it was captured, and his description of it was something like a inferno.....

Sagunto. July 3rd, 1937

Well, we have got this far, and to be quite honest, I am not a bit pleased. Last night a warship arrived off the port and started shelling the place. This morning at four o'clock two or three 'planes came along and dropped a few bombs. It is really uncomfortable. The bombs were less than a hundred yards away. Two of the engineers were a little bit late [entering a bomb shelter] and got damaged a bit. ... Sunny Spain is very nice in normal times, but just at the moment it is rather unpleasant.

Now in 1938 The Gleam had to announce that the Ship Adoption Society link had come to an end "with the tragic death of Captain Bullock, who was killed when his ship was bombed off the coast of Spain in June of this year."

One obituary in the magazine, however, was not so serious:

"It is with regret that we record the death of an old friend - the Elm. For many generations the elm has served not only as a useful landmark, but as the goal of the boarders' short runs in cold weather, so that we had come to regard it as our own property.

"It is interesting to hear from local authority that the elm is supposed to have been planted by Sir Thomas Ludwell, who left this district in the middle of the 17th century to go to America. Later he became Secretary of State for Virginia, died in 1678, and was buried at Bruton Parish Church, Williamsburg, where the inscription on his tomb states that he was a native of Bruton 'in the County of Summerset in the Kingdom of England.'"

Finally we may turn to reports of a death which were, like Mark Twain's, greatly exaggerated:

ODE OF THE EXECUTION OF LATIN
Thus said Miss Makins in the Room that looks o'er Avalon,
Calling to the children of the newly made Five A:
  "Latin's passed away

On the smoke of Judgement Day.

That our work may now go forward please put your books away".

Clearly this rhymester was guilty of wishful thinking, since another, Sara Woodford, wrote:

EXAMS

… But the wretched clock ticks on

And my paper's a blank as yet.

O for a squint at my Latin book!

Whatever's the English for "iubet"?

..Break! Break! Break!

O break the news gently to me,

You say I have passed in Latin:

To all the gods - praise be!

*   *   *

We shall not end this chapter with deaths, real or imagined, but will join the rejoicing as the new building was finished and used for the host of customary Sunny Hill activities.

Preparations for the first Speech Day in the new School hall included a flurry of letters, including news of the Speaker, and an amusing response:

17th June, 1938

Dear Lady Langman,

We have secured Miss Theodora Clark an ex-Headmistress of a leading girls school [Croham Hurst School, Croydon] and resident in the county, to give away the prizes and address the School on Friday 22nd July at 3 p.m.

She is lunching here on that day and we should be very glad if you would come and meet her (1.15).

Yours sincerely,

North Cadbury Court

Yeovil

Somerset

Thurs. 18th

Much hope that Miss Theodora Clark will not be able to plumb the Governors' ignorance on educational matters in the course of luncheon but feel I find I must risk that and accept with pleasure for luncheon at 1.15 on 22nd.

Yours sincerely
Eleanor Langman

[Another man who was invited, Mr Howard Fox, refused; but said of the new school buildings: "I have often admired them from the train and can congratulate you at any rate upon the site and elevation."]

More seriously, it immediately became clear that the new building would not solve the problem of accommodating all who wished to come to the prizegiving.

28th June 1938

Dear Miss Wells,

With reference to the invitations for the Prize Giving, could you now let me see your list of persons, other than Governors and Parents, whom you propose to invite. Now that we shall have extended accommodation, I think it is worth while reviewing this matter.

Yours sincerely,
A Hobhouse

June 29th '38

Dear Mr Hobhouse,

We find that we can only seat 378 people in the body of the hall, and as there are 183 girls + 20 (about) Old Girls who have books or certificates to get, we shall barely be able to accommodate the parents.

We could probably seat an extra 16 or 18 people on the platform, but there will be little, if any, space to spare in the hall.

The only way we can invite extra people beyond those whom you may wish to seat on the platform, is to invite them to tea and the entertainment, and that will give them a chance of seeing the school and, if they are interested, some of the work.

Yours sincerely,
J.T. Wells

The great day arrived and The Gleam tells us that "Arthur Hobhouse as Chairman reported on the progress of the buildings during the previous two years. He mentioned the enormous difficulty in the planning and constructing of the new buildings, in so limited a space, and commented on the success in overcoming these difficulties under the guidance of our architect, Mr.Pictor, and builders, John Long and Co., of Bath."

Fortunately we have the script of the speech, which included: "Many of you who have attended previous Prize Givings in the old school may feel rather strange in these new and beautiful surroundings, but I am sure you will not be disappointed with the big changes which have taken place and I hope that you will entirely approve the results of the time, energy and cost which has been expended." In fact according to the Accounts for this year £19,750 was paid to the contractors on account; £6,000 War Stock was sold, Somerset County Council gave a loan of £9,000 and the Hut was sold for £23!

"When we met last in July 1936 I outlined the proposals of the Governors for the rebuilding scheme at Sunny Hill and now that the work is complete, I think it may be of interest to summarise what has been done.

"Our original building which contained both Day and Boarding accommodation, has been re-planned and extended for boarding accommodation only. The temporary wooden buildings which were added after the War through the energies of Miss Radford for extra classroom accommodation, have been removed after a long life of   years, [the gap is in the original typescript] and this new building has been provided for Day School purposes. The problems which confronted the Governors of the School in connection with this scheme which has been successfully accomplished, were very considerable. In the first place, it was essential that there should be no break or serious interference with the current work of the School, and you will appreciate that it is of course very much easier to build a new school than to convert it as a going concern. However, by a carefully planned programme and with the ready co-operation of the Contractors, it has been possible to avoid any disorganisation or interference with the teaching at Sunny Hill, and the Governors feel that the school owes an immense debt of gratitude to Miss Wells and the Staff in having made this possible.

"In the second place, owing to the circumstances of the site, great difficulty was experienced in deciding where to build this new Day School and in carrying it out. After much thought and planning, the Governors finally adopted this two-storey building on the slope of the hill, with, I hope, the best results. But the character of the ground not only gave the architects much greater difficulty in planning, but increased the labour and costs of the Contractor. On behalf of the Governors I should like to say how pleased and satisfied we are with the execution of the work.

"You will, I hope, all make a full inspection after the Prize Giving of this new building. It is a complete new Day School, equal in every respect to the most up to date standard laid down by the Board of Education. There are ample classrooms for about 200 children, with a finely equipped laboratory, Domestic Science room and Art room, and in addition, we have this fine Assembly Hall, especially valuable to this school in connection with its dramatic work. The only portion of the undertaking which is not yet complete is the lay out of the grounds, and completion of the drives. But we are proceeding with this as rapidly as possible, having regard to the need of economical work and making the surroundings permanently attractive.

"Of almost equal importance to the erection of this building are the big extensions and re-planning of the original building which has now become your boarding house. By adding to the building on the south side, the Headmistress now has, for the first time, suitable and sufficient accommodation in the form of a self-contained house, but connected with the remainder of the building. The old kitchens have been completely rebuilt and extended and proper domestic quarters are provided on the floor above. In addition to this, there is ample Sick Room accommodation built on the top floor of this wing.

"Various other improvements have resulted in the re-planning of the Boarding House. The Dining Room has been enlarged so as to accommodate not only the Boarders, but as many Day Girls as may choose to take the school dinners. The south-western dormitory has been enlarged and a new and very attractively situated Staff room has been provided on the ground floor below. Last but not least, sitting rooms have been provided for the girls in the boarding house by converting some of the old classrooms for this purpose.

"You will see from this short account that the school has been completely remodelled. Not only have we an up to date Day School second to none in the county and with ample accommodation for about 200 girls, but our Boarding House is immensely improved in every respect and will amply house about 80 boarders in addition to the teaching staff."

So much for the facts. It is fascinating to hear an Old Girl's impression. Sarah Woodford wrote:

"It was with grave misgivings that I approached Sunny Hill on the afternoon of July 22nd, to join in my first Speech Day as an onlooker and an Old Girl; I felt sure that new faces, new buildings and a "generation that knew not Moses" would contribute to the feeling that I no longer belonged to Sunny Hill. I went in School-end gate and that feeling was slightly alleviated when I saw two or three silk dresses approaching - girls playing that old trick of trying to catch a few words with their parents and friends before the ceremonies began; as we walked down the steps to the new building it was a great comfort to see the faces of Miss Clarke and Miss Rowell at the entrance to the hall.

And of the entertainment she wrote:

"It has always been amazing to me that Second Form have the courage to stand up before so many people, with a self-possession worthy of a Queen's Hall orchestra, and give such a very creditable performance with their percussion band. The French songs were an innovation for Speech Day, which I hope will continue; Forms III and IVb were very gay, catching the spirit of the songs and acting them so well that even the non-French part of the audience could understand and enjoy. Of the Senior Choir, trained by Miss Rowell, one cannot speak too highly. The play "Michael" was a performance I shall not easily forget.

"For all my misgivings on my arrival for Speech Day, I left Sunny Hill feeling that nothing had substantially altered, and that everyone was just as friendly as they ever had been."

Chapter 11

Rationing and Ragwort

The Biology teacher Miss M.N. Pruce was in Canada when the second world war began. She had sailed out in *The Empress of Britain*, with many Czech refugee children on August 5th, 1939. On the return journey on September 7th, after the outbreak of war, she saw the *Empress* being painted grey for war service, and had to transfer to the *Duchess of Richmond*. As she waited to sail, the *City of Flint* came in to Halifax with survivors from the *Athenia*. The passage home was in a convoy of eight ships, escorted by two destroyers and four flying boats. "And so began the long journey across the Atlantic," she wrote, "the monotony varied by 'Abandon Ship' drill, fitting gas masks, etc. We arrived back to find Britain at war - policemen with tin helmets - buildings sandbagged - trains in darkness, and other unfamiliar sights."

The war was not unexpected. In July the Chairman of Governors, presiding at the second Speech Day to be held in the new School Hall, had assured parents, after mentioning work which had been done during the year in connection with the drives and terraces, and after noting with pleasure that the numbers of the School were increasing, that the safety of the girls "would receive the utmost attention should there be an outbreak of war."

*   *   *

Indeed the school entered the war years in good shape. In September, 1938, the number of girls in the School had reached 195, 82 being boarders; the Sixth Form with 21 members was larger than ever before. The finals of the Senior Hockey League had been held at Sunny Hill on March 25th 1939, an unusually cold day, and Bruton won the cup for the first time since 1926. Snow was falling as Miss Radford presented the Cup. She said that she had had it a great many times in her hands, but this was the first time she had had the pleasure of presenting it to Sunny Hill.

At the beginning of the year '38-'39 there seemed to be a growing desire in the

Senior School for the abolition of Houses. The school magazine reported that they 'held a debate, "The House System is of no value to the School," which the whole school attended. The vote taken at the end proved that the majority was in favour of Houses, but it seemed that people disliked House Competitions. Therefore, instead of continuing the usual Music and Dramatic Competitions, it was decided to hold a "Parents' Afternoon," to which each House would contribute a half hour programme. It was hoped that the production and preparation of this event would unite the members of each House. The "Parents' Afternoon" was a great success.'

Gardening was an important occupation, and with war looming attention was paid to growing vegetables. "After a wet summer, most of the gardens had become overgrown with weeds, and have taken some time to clear up. Enthusiasm has been shown by several forms, and new ground has been broken up and manured, with the idea of growing vegetables as well as flowers next year. The toolshed has been restocked and the gardens numbered. More care could still be shown in clearing up rubbish and cleaning tools after use." Soon the school welcomed "our lady gardener, Miss Williams, who, in spite of the hard weather last winter, managed to carry on cheerfully to improve the appearance of our new grounds and produce a good crop of vegetables. She must also be congratulated on having inspired so many of the girls to 'dig for victory.'"

* * *

Pamela Knight has written of the autumn of 1939:

"The Sixth Form brought our first taste of freedom but it coincided with the beginning of war. I had spent part of the summer holidays, with Pam Lane, making blackout curtains for the old building. The new buildings were just finished and we were able to spread ourselves in what seemed vast and light rooms but we had to go back for prep in the dining room, squashed together, all the boarders, reading, writing, sniffing and coughing. When we complained that it was difficult to concentrate we were told, crisply, that there was a war on and if we learned to concentrate in these difficult conditions it would stand us in good stead for the rest of our lives. It certainly has. We were glad to work in our new form rooms, however, when the lighter evenings came. The new tennis courts were ploughed up for potatoes before a single set was played on them but at least we had the old ones. Numbers of girls arrived from parts of the country at risk from bombing and we had several refugees from Europe who opened our minds to what was going on across the channel. The food, which had always been excellent, became a little sparser as time went on."

Above: Joan of Arc production

Left: P Herrin leaping over Miss J Wells

Right: Pam Knight in her 'Gondoliers' costume

Below: Pam and friends enjoy a Sixth Form picnic

A recent clear-out in Old House turned up a picture postcard of a dog with the legend: 'Lying Doggo.' The other side was postmarked 12th November 1940 Gravesend, and bore the address,

Miss Joy Jessup
Sunny Hill Girls School
Bruton
nr Bath
Sommerset [sic]

Darling. hope you are well. I expect a letter tomorrow then I'll answer it. We had a very rough night last night. We are all safe and well. No need to worry. Nurse Dodd sends her love, and Mary.

Much love Mummy.

As the bombs fell, devastating London and areas of strategic importance like Gravesend, so even Bruton heard the sounds of war occasionally, and gave careful thought to blackout and camouflage. Mary Simms (Mrs Longstreet), a pupil of Sunny Hill 1937-1942, recalls "Whilst I was at school, Castle Cary Station, being a junction, was bombed and we all came down into the stairwell of the stone flight of stairs in the old school as an air raid shelter. A German plane came down at Lamyatt. That was an excitement because it caused a big bang. I don't think we had any other bombs. We had some kind of blackout in the old building".

Indeed, according to the Editor of The Gleam, "During the first year of the war, the black-out has proved to be one of our greatest difficulties. The usual clubs and societies were discontinued but in their place a system of after-school activities was introduced. These proved popular and, on the whole, well attended." They were held in the daylight from 3.30 to 4.30 p.m., and included a juniors' Handwork Class making felt toys, under the Art mistress, Miss Lee, attended by about 20 girls. Priscilla Lee, "an American who was a total breath of fresh air," according to Mary Simms, "was absolutely brilliant, very tall with shocking ginger hair. She was very artistic and great fun. She would take us off for a walk down by the river, down into Cole and up the other side."

There was also a pipe-making class, in charge of Miss Rowells, about whom Mary Simms comments: "We sang a lot, because Miss Rowell was an extremely enthusiastic and very good teacher. She got us all to be enthusiastic." Pamela Knight seconds this view: "Miss Rowell was a wonderful music teacher and producer, and her Gilbert and Sullivan operas were always a great success. She had the knack of combining discipline with inspiration and we always gave of our best. She also founded an orchestra, in which I played the violin (badly) and we sometimes went down to play with the King's School orchestra - an awesome experience."

There was a Dancing Class in charge of Miss Cuthbertson. For the seniors, there were Current Events Meetings, in which Miss Clarke, the Second Mistress, who taught History, answered girls' questions. Miss Brown conducted the Senior Play Reading Group, which was a great success. The First Aid Class, which was very popular, was taken by Miss Rain. The Greek Class, instructed by Miss Rabjohns, was attended by six girls, who were very keen to study the language. Miss Voelter joined with some of the seniors in a French Play Reading Group. All these activities were much appreciated in the dark days of winter.

Even the performances of Gilbert and Sullivan's operetta 'The Gondoliers' had to be held in the afternoon owing to black-out difficulties. Costumes for this "were contrived from the contents of our elastic acting cupboard, augmented by costumes kindly lent by Day Girls." It was a case of 'silk purses out of sows' ears.' Mr Barnes' gondola was pronounced a great success, and proceeds from 'The Gondoliers,' which amounted to £46 ten shillings, were divided between the Finnish Relief Fund and the British Red Cross.

Not only did windows have to be blacked out, but also made splinter resistant in case of bomb blast. Arthur Hobhouse wrote to consult the County Architect's Department on the matter:

"Miss Wells reports that Messrs. Hobbs have started hanging the cellophane but that their two men do not appear to be very rapid or expert. Possibly Hobbs is short of men used to this class of work. Miss Wells asks whether she should carry out the cellophaning of the boarding house windows by the School labour. Also whether such windows in both buildings as have been treated with textile material (I believe butter muslin) need to be cellophaned."

Expert advice soon came in reply:

"With regard to the application of the cellophane to the Boarding House windows, the success of this is materially affected by the method of application, and it is essential that it should be properly applied with the proper gum, and steps taken to ensure that all air bubbles are carefully removed with a squeegee. In these circumstances, therefore, if you do not mind, I would prefer Messrs.Hobbs to carry out the work, but as they do not appear to be very rapid, I will certainly instruct them to get a move on.

Those windows which had already been treated with textile material do not need to be cellophaned."

The question of whether and how best to camouflage the school buildings, particularly the new Day School, caused prolonged and serious debate. On 5th July 1940 the County Architect's Department set out the issues:

"Dear Mr. Hobhouse,

Bruton, Sunny-hill School

"In reply to your memo of the 3rd instant, you will no doubt appreciate that there is a marked difference between "camouflage" to a building and merely changing its appearance by painting it a different colour. Camouflage, if done properly, as at the Yeovil factories mentioned in your correspondence, is a very scientific process involving the obliteration of all ground shadows as well as the efficient screening of the building. It is also a very costly matter on account of the quantity of paint and "foliage" netting required.

"With regard to the suggestion that certain public buildings, such as school etc., should be camouflaged on account of their prominence from the air, if I may be permitted to give my own views, I do not consider this essential because there still remain many other conspicuous landmarks from which a pilot may obtain his bearings, such as rivers, reservoirs, main roads, etc., and in particular the monastic dovecote on the hill at Bruton which is so close to the Sunny-hill School.

"If the Governors consider something must be done, I would strongly advise that they should not embark on any make-shift proposals of patchwork painting on the wall surfaces because there is the danger of this conveying the impression to an enemy pilot that an obvious 'attempt' had been made to camouflage the building and therefore it must be of military importance.

"I would suggest that the wishes of the Governors would be well met by merely changing the present colour to a different shade of say a drab green or brown throughout. There are approximately 1650 sq. yds. of wall surface. This could be treated with two coats of ordinary external distemper, the cost of which would be approximately £100, plus of course the same cost for reinstatement after the War."

This sensible advice did not end the matter. The Air Raid Precaution Officer was making his own investigations, and this delightful bit of officialese resulted:

WESTLAND AIRCRAFT LIMITED

Yeovil

From Mr. J. Ramsden, Pilots Office.   to Mr. J. F. Milne, A. R. P. Officer.

15th June 1940

JR/IMC/500

re: W/JFM/DW/1101.

With reference to the above memorandum and the correspondence forwarded with it, I now append my report.

Sunny Hill School, Pitcombe.

This building stands out very distinctly.

(signed) J.Ramsden

Meanwhile the military authorities offered their own views in their own literary style:

S.C.5/60174/Q/(b).   H.Q. SOUTHERN COMMAND,

SALISBURY

5th. July 1940

Dear Sir,

I am to refer to your letter No. 1301/25 dated 29th. June, 1940, and to say that it is considered that the following building should be camouflaged: -

Sunny Hill School, Bruton.

(Signed) Golhill

Major for Colonel,

A.Q.M.G. (b) Southern Command

Wisely, the School took no notice, and discussed instead which dull colour the Day School should be painted, No. 5 Ivy Green or No. 51 Deep Cement. Fortunately the debate was still going on when this short note ended the affair:

20th August, 1940

Dear Sir,

Sunny Hill Girls' School

Reference your letter of the 7th instant and subsequent telephone conversation, I confirm that the proposed recolouring of this School has now been cancelled in view of the policy adopted by the Authorities not to attempt any camouflaging of civil buildings.

*   *   *

Such correspondence was not seen by pupils, but the girls were well aware of the threat of bombs and of the part that blackout played. Pamela Knight remembers: "We heard the German planes throbbing across the sky to bomb Bristol and later, as they limped back, hung out of the dorm window to see the red glow in the night sky as the city burned."

Patricia Ford, aged 13, wrote:

A.R.P.
After sunset every night
No one must show a speck of light,
For then King Black-out reigns, you see,
Oh, bother all this A.R.P.

You hear the tramp of warden's feet
Marching up and down the street.
You wonder if your light he'll see.
Oh, bother all this A.R.P.
....
A siren sound - a raid has come -
You listen to the engines' hum.
Your heart beats fast - alas! alack!
But all is dark, the whole place black.

And then - the gladdest sound you hear,
The signal saying "All is clear!"
No damage done, and so you see

Our thanks are due to A.R.P.

Girls also played their part in 'the war effort' in many different ways. The Gleam reported:

"In the summer term of 1942 Miss Wells suggested that the School ought to become more active in the war effort and, therefore, after form meetings to discuss the matter, we arranged a system whereby each girl agrees to do a minimum of four hours war work a week. This work is carried on enthusiastically from the Sixth to the Second Form, and includes such activities as knitting, gardening, herb collecting, salvage collecting and housework. For girls of sixteen and over, classes have been organised in First Aid and Despatch Carrying."

The gardener was not convinced that 'enthusiastically' was the right word. Writing about the School Land Army she admitted that "the day-girls have been very useful," but had to add: "The boarders have helped, especially the juniors, but most of them only under pressure." She explained that "Owing to the necessarily increased vegetable production, the gardening staff have not been able to give the children's gardens as much attention as they would have liked, but it is hoped that the whole of the San. grounds will be dug up soon."

Mary Simms has a rather different memory. "Lady Langman was a governor and had a lot of land, and was much involved in WarAg and all the wartime things; as our war effort, we went over on Cadbury Castle, Cadbury Ring, South Cadbury, and pulled ragwort by hand, until our hands were absolutely raw. That was our war effort."

✳　　✳　　✳

Pamela Knight mentioned that the food became a little sparser. Mary Simms was not aware of a noticeable change. "Life went on, because it was fairly basic even before the war. We were used to rather stringent meals. At one point we were let loose to cook on the old Esse stoves down in the kitchen, for some speech day or special occasion. We used to queue for lunch in the bottom corridor going up towards the headmistress' house, under the dispensary. We would turn right into the dining room. On special days like speech day when we had get to our food over quickly, we always had currant buns and bananas as a pudding. And ghastly, ghastly fish every Friday, with potatoes and boiled beetroot, on which they put a white sauce which went pink!"

To provide for the increased number of girls was not easy. Mr Hobhouse reported:

"Miss Wells finds the cooking facilities inadequate for vegetables and steamed puddings. A quotation was obtained by Miss Wells for a 30 gallon gas-heated vegetable boiling pot; after discussing the matter with Miss Wells and the Cook, they agreed that the lifting of such a large pot was rather beyond the capacity of the female staff. I left with Miss Wells a leaflet illustrating a modern gas-heated steaming oven for potatoes and puddings and I consider this preferable in the circumstances."

It was sweet rationing that hit hardest. Mary Simms again:

"I coped with the coupons for sweet rationing. We had to keep a book. Everyone was allowed so many coupons a month. It depended on your personality how you used them. You either had one glorious moment or you spread them out systematically through the month. We used to put a form out in the old asbestos Gym on a Saturday afternoon, and you were allowed in to take your ration. I indulged once a month in one large peppermint cream, which was absolutely delicious. Other people would have three sweets a week.

"We also had bags of fruit sent up on Saturdays from a little shop called Fish in Bruton (Peggy Fish was at the school). They contained apples and pears. I think there were oranges, but they would have been very few - or possibly bananas. This fruit was kept in a little room across the corridor from the Old House sitting rooms."

Wartime conditions affected practical school subjects. Mary Simms reports:

"For my School Certificate in Domestic Science we had to do patches. Miss Mostyn, the Irish Domestic Science teacher, made sure that the pattern all joined up. You had to learn to darn, and to sew a piece of tape on. No one would do such things in this day and age, ever again. 'Prepare a meal for a miner and his family using one gas ring only' was one School Certificate cookery assignment. We were prepared for this ordeal by cooking supper for the staff on various occasions. I remember having to sieve lumpy custard. We did sewing in the same Domestic Science room. Because it was war time, for School certificate we had to have made a renovated garment - make do and mend."

Mary still has a photo of the dress she made.

On academic work in general, Pamela Knight says: "The teaching in those days was relaxed and School Cert. came on one without undue fuss. Exams were taken in one's stride." Mary Simms agrees: "You were not made to work in those days. There was no encouragement to work hard. Of course you were told that you should get good results, but nothing like the pressure put on the young today. We had prep supervised by prefects, with a member of staff walking round the various rooms making sure there was not chaos. As for external exams, they said 'Your exam is next Tuesday and you go and do it.' There was none of the present pushing or great swotting or urgency about it."

* * *

The war took its toll in unexpected ways. Men of military age disappeared into the forces. Mr H. T. Crapp, Clerk to the Governors, could not get the Accounts ready in time for the June meeting. In a hand-written letter dated 18th May he says:

> I may say, and I am sure you will understand that I am working under great difficulty at the present time owing to depletion in office staff and Special Police Duties. I get little or no clerical assistance apart from the typing of minutes and all the routine work normally done by Clerks in the Office under my supervision is now done by me. My wife has helped me with the applications for fees but she is now in a Bren Gun Factory.
>
> I hope therefore you will forgive me if the accounts are a little late this year.

Lorna Windmill, of Windmills, the Bruton ironmongers, mourned a brother killed in the war - an event which affected all the pupils. They were allowed to choose hymns on Friday morning, and "we were always choosing 'Eternal Father, strong to save.'"

Yet when Old Girls met in the summer of 1942, and everyone was anxious to hear from Mrs Newark stories of Singapore and her experiences whilst escaping, the school seemed a haven. It is surely a credit to the Governors, Headmistress and Staff that this could be so. "On account of rationing we all brought our own food and Miss Wells provided tea for us," wrote one Old Girl. Mrs Newark herself wrote: "It was a great joy to come back to the Summer Reunion. Sunny Hill looks so safe, so happy and so secure; after all these years I felt at once as though I still belonged. There wasn't a trace of strangeness even in the new school. I hope that no S. H. S. girl will feel too 'old' to go back, for she will get the warmest welcome."

* * *

Dining Hall

Chapter 12

Nettles and Green Knickers

The school went on growing. Numbers increased from about 195 girls before the war to about 260 in 1943. As a consequence, Sunny Hill developed into a two-stream school with parallel classes for all age groups except in the bottom and VIth Forms. This made it "possible to grade pupils in the same age groups. We have been very fortunate in obtaining sufficient additional staff to meet the increased numbers." So the Chairman.

With no further building possible until after the war, the system was under strain. The school sewage system could scarcely cope, and after a visit by an engineer the Chairman promised to 'go into' the matter; one hopes for his sake that he spoke metaphorically. It took over a year for men to be spared from Government demand work to cut a trial hole under the allotments below the school gardens.

*   *   *

For the girls, a topic of major interest was the renaming of the Houses.

"For some time there had been a feeling that names with more significance than Blue, Brown, Red and Yellow, would be desirable and would probably help to stimulate a greater spirit of unity within the Houses. The most difficult question was the actual choice of the new names. Many suggestions were put forward, including famous Admirals, Prime Ministers, famous women, the School Governors, and the names of the Royal Residences.

"We chose famous women and drew up a list of the thirteen we considered most suitable - among them were Joan of Arc, Grace Darling, Millicent Fawcett, Jane Austen, Marie Curie, Florence Nightingale, Edith Cavell, Elizabeth Garrett Anderson and Madame Chang-Kai-Shek. In order that our choice might be more discriminating, accounts of the lives of each of these women were written by different girls and read to the School.

"Finally, Red House chose Marie Curie, the discoverer of radium; Yellow House chose Elizabeth Garrett Anderson, who opened the medical profession to women; Brown House chose Millicent Fawcett, the leader of the Women's Suffrage Movement; and Blue House chose Florence Nightingale, whose work during the Crimean War was of such lasting value in improving military hospitals and medical conditions for the services, and laid the foundation of civil nursing as a career for women. By choosing the names of these four great pioneers we have not only honoured them for their work, but have set ourselves a standard of life."

These names continued in use, along with the colours, until the abandonment of the house system in 1998 in favour of 'halls' named after stately homes, reminiscent of the 'royal residences' rejected in 1943.

Each house adopted one of the Services to support during the war years. In 1943, for example, Blue House reported its main activity had been knitting comforts for the Army: 100 garments were sent to the depot; Brown House was able to send up six parcels of knitting to the Royal Navy knitting depot; Red House members were enthusiastically knitting for the Royal Air Force and several parcels of garments were despatched, while Yellow House, who knitted for the Merchant Navy, produced 100 garments; they did complain, however, that their "work was held up by frequent shortages of wool and it is still evident that the bulk of it is done by a few industrious members of the House."

*   *   *

Early in the war the Current Events Group debated the motion, "The House approves the evacuation of schoolchildren," and it was carried, after lively discussion, by a small majority. M. Young, aged 11, may have received one such child. At any rate she wrote this verse:

A PUZZLED EVACUEE

From London town has Tommy come,
To stay down on the farm,
That while the war is going on
He will not come to harm.

He finds the things so very strange,
It puzzles him full sore,
To think that milk should come from cows,
Not bottles at your door.

One day he ran away a mile,
Because he saw a cow,
"I thought it was a bull," he said;
He knows it isn't now.

He came in all excited once,
All hopping on one leg,
"Do you know what your hen has done,
She's laid a boiled egg!"

He thought the pigs were raving wolves,
- He'd never seen a sheep,
Excepting in a butcher's shop,
All cut up in a heap.

Now Tommy's having lots of fun
And lots of things to do;
But sometimes thinks of Mum and Dad,
And wants them with him too.

The Current Events Group, however, "was decidedly opposed to the idea that the bombing of our civilian population calls for retaliation." After the bombing of Bristol, as Pamela Knight recalls, "That August we opened the school to give a holiday to a party of bombed mothers and children. A group of us came back and were allocated jobs. Mine was to prepare salads and vegetables, all freshly picked from the school gardens. In the evenings we put on concerts and entertainments. One mother lost her wedding ring and couldn't remember which washbasin it had fallen down. Groups of frantic girls unscrewed U - bends and peered down plug holes and drains in a vain hunt for it. 'Never mind,' said the woman when she came on this strenuous activity. 'I'm always losing them. I'll get another from Woolworth's next week.'"

* * *

The School became more and more self-supporting owing to the difficulty in obtaining gardening and domestic help and "essential work" - washing up, preparing vegetables, gardening etc. - became as much a part of the daily routine as Arithmetic and French. "Essential Work", though much reduced, was still a feature of boarding life in the 1990s.

Owing to the shortage of gardening staff the school was asked to give more help with the upkeep of the grounds. It was eventually decided that each form was to be responsible for some definite part of the garden. Names given to these areas may not mean much to present pupils, but will bring back memories to some Old Girls:

VI, middle terrace; Upper V, banks below the new buildings; L. Vl, border along the road hedge; LVm, grass slopes near the covered way; U.IVm, the top terrace; U. IVl, Rosy corner; L. IVa, bottom terrace; L. IVb, the sides of the drive to the new building; IIIa, the path to the San; IIIb, the gym lawn; II, the path round the San.

Girls also worked every day when possible on a large vegetable patch near the grass netball court; this produced satisfactory quantities of cabbage, lettuce, beetroot, carrots, parsnips, leeks, and broad beans, all of which disappeared with great rapidity into the school kitchen. Another large piece of work which fell to the girls was the cutting and care of the tennis courts and the cutting of the grass netball court. Irene Trim admitted: "To be quite truthful, I used to detest gardening but it had to be done." She evidently warmed to the work, and reported: "Soon I had finished weeding and digging and I planted some seeds, carrots and turnips, onions and swedes, all in many even rows. My carrots, onions and swedes are now in store, but my turnips are still in the ground. I know they taste quite nice, though, as I've cooked some."

Indeed, in other areas of school life, so girls complained, "activities have been increasingly handicapped by the lack of materials and perhaps more seriously by the curtailment of our free time owing to the steadily increasing demand made upon it by the needs of our own community as domestic and gardening staff grew fewer."

Despite this, much good work was done. A special appeal was made to the School at Christmas 1942 for 1000 books for the Merchant Navy, in answer to which 1052 books and 42 monthly magazines were despatched; later in the Spring two further sackfuls were sent. In May Wincanton Hospital sent out an S.O.S. for eggs for putting down for the winter, and, thanks to the kindness of local parents, were sent a contribution of over 10 dozen. In spite of the shortage of wool Forms II and IIIa knitted squares and two blankets were sent to Dr. Barnardo's and the U.G.S. Owing to the restriction on the despatch of flowers by rail and post in the Spring the school was only able to send a few boxes to the London Settlements. Tinfoil for Dr. Barnardo's was collected as usual, though it took longer to fill the sack.

Having voted for the motion that " All schoolchildren over the age of twelve should be released in the summer to help on farms," it is not surprising that girls were busy in the countryside. It is not surprising, either, that Katherine Blair, a childhood friend of the future headmistress Jean Thomson, should have written so well about one countryside activity, being the daughter of a Professor:

"Picking nettles was a familiar duty for all during the summer months. Armed with a stout pair of gloves and perhaps some covering for the arms we could approach the most hostile clumps of nettles and pick them stem by stem. Bunches, each containing twelve heads of nettles, were tightly tied up with whiskery string and carried by hand or barrow to the "Chamber of Horrors". A network of strings, each suspending a number of bunches, clothes peg fashion, filled most of the hanging space of the shed.

"The smell of drying herbs filled the air as the bunches of dried nettles were removed from the lines and the shrivelled leaves stripped off into large tea-chests. The contents of these were finally stuffed into sacks and weighed, prior to being sent to the warehouse for medicinal and other purposes. The bare stalks were stacked in readiness for paper making, whereas the string was salvaged for future use."

Jean Martin wrote on collecting rose hips: "The beautiful posters hung on various notice boards in the school could not but rouse our energies to the collection of hips. These posters showed alternatively rosy and robust babies (thriving upon Vitamin C) or bottles of a sickly pink fluid -Vitamin C. During our walks we scanned the hedgerows for the divine fruit. Returning home we sorted our victims. We hope the Nation's babies will become fat and rosy."

June Johnson's job was less romantic, but no doubt just as useful: "Every week Miss Graham used to take some of us down to Pitcombe to collect and sort salvage. We went round to the cottages in twos and collected small bundles of cardboard and paper. While doing this, we were often forced to listen to local gossip. The sorting centre was a cellar under the village hall and it opened on to the lane. There was a damp earth floor, and the whole place always smelt strongly of mildew. We had to jump the puddle in the doorway and sort the salvage in the semi-darkness of the cellar. While sorting we bumped against one another, got in the light or repeatedly knocked our heads on the low beams. On fine days we sorted outside in the lane, watched by an inquisitive audience of children."

There was recycling nearer home, too. Just as today canny parents use the second hand uniform shop, so they did during the war, with even more urgency. Old Girls were begged: "Look out as soon as possible all your old school uniform and unused games equipment and return it to us for resale. Green silks, panamas (these can be re-blocked), velours, scarves and berets can not be bought and are therefore specially welcome, but school coats, tunics, blouses, pullovers, belts - all are much appreciated by parents and save coupons. Even if well worn they can still be of use."

*　　*　　*

In spite of the war, Pamela Knight found being in the Sixth Form was an exhilarating time. "The work was stimulating (we had to write a sonnet once for prep). Besides English I did French (I had more or less caught up) and Geography. I also had to do Latin, as it was a necessary qualification to do an Arts degree at university then. We had extra Current Events lessons and knitted for 'our boys at the front.'

"Never having been much good at games coming up the school, I suddenly gained confidence and found myself in the first hockey eleven and the proud possessor of the green stockings we wore for matches. How we relished our contests with other schools, and how often it seemed to rain on match days! I was lucky enough to be in the first tennis team in my last year. On Friday nights we whitened our tennis shoes and set them on the dorm windowsill to dry."

Mary Simms has this to add: "We used to play hockey quite a bit, but it was difficult during the war because there was not much transport. The Royal School, Bath, were evacuated to Longleat, and we played on the front of Longleat."

Pamela continues: "Pam Lane was Head Girl for my first year in the Sixth, and set us a good example, so the next year, with Zoe Veale as Head Girl, we prefects took our responsibilities very seriously, tolerating no nonsense from our juniors! My sole act of rebellion was noticing a copy of 'Gone with the Wind' in the bookshop window in Frome, while I was in the dentist's waiting room opposite, and darting across to buy the hardback for five shillings (25p.). I smuggled it back to school and we read it avidly, the more so as it had been banned as unsuitable for our tender years. Others were more adventurous and, as the years go by, I have heard tales of going out at night and even planning to meet Sexey's boys. On this occasion the girls were caught on their way out, so the boys took the school gates off their hinges and put them in the field. This must be an old tradition as my aunt Teddy told me that my father did this when he was at Sexey's."

Mary Simms remembers that the vicarage [now Old Vicarage] was occupied by the Reverend Alan Leslie, who had a little Austin Seven, with a Wiltshire number plate beginning AMW. "We used to go down to his house for Confirmation preparation in the evenings. That was something, to be allowed out to go down there. We used to be the choir at Pitcombe Church and Mr Jennings, the local farmer, used to play the organ." In 1943 Mr Leslie left Pitcombe for Langport. He had served the school both as Vicar and Governor. A number of the boarders responded to the new Vicar, the Revd. Kenneth Ashcroft's appeal for volunteers to spring-clean the church and spent a very busy Saturday afternoon cleaning and polishing. Eight girls were confirmed at a special Confirmation Service for the School at Pitcombe towards the end of the Summer Term. As a change from Pitcombe and Shepton Montague, Mary Simms says, "We probably went to church in Bruton two or three times, no more. The boys used to wear boaters in those days, and piled them at the end of the pew. Someone would put a foot out; if you flicked it properly you could get them all rolling down."

To meet boys was, as Mary explains, a rare event. "The only time girls were allowed into Bruton was on a Saturday, if we were on the Bruton List, when prefects were allowed to go with girls' shopping lists, to get toothpaste and what have you. Other than that, in all the time I was there we had, I think, two or three concerts in the new King's Memorial Hall. We did not meet boys. We never had any other chance of going down to King's. Even if we went to a concert, we were escorted into our seats and out again."

*   *   *

Instead of the company of the opposite sex, there were walks, although occasionally one could lead to the other.

"We always went for a walk on Saturday. We used to walk miles in crocodile. On Saturdays and Sundays we might go right round Redlynch, which was quite a long way. We must have had a very hard glazed frost once, for the trees at Redlynch were absolutely fantastic. I had an old family friend, Mrs Eddles, living there, a lady in waiting to Lady Suffolk. The Guards were stationed in Redlynch House for a time, including quite a lot of very well known names. I can't think how I managed to visit our friend there from school, but we did.

"We used to have a vote to decide where we would go on a walk, and the poor member of staff on duty had to endure this. Occasionally we would go up the Pigeon Tower. Up Cannons and down Green Lane was a great favourite: down past Cole Station, through the village, to a lane on the left, only a cart track. We went up there, just round the back of Pitcombe Church, and on until we came out on the Shepton Montague road. That was a fairly mild walk. Redlynch was a really long way, but being girls we used to like to go up there to see who was about. The Hall School was at Bratton in those days, and another walk was down to Bratton. Because we always went to Shepton Montague for church, we did not do that on weekdays.

If we were being punished, or were slovenly, we were sent on an enormous run up Creech Hill, towards Evercreech. That was awful." (Mary Simms)

*　*　*

As an ignorant male, I leave discussion of school uniform entirely to Mary Simms:

"The uniform was tremendous. We had so much. All the gym slips and pullovers, and for weekends we had navy blue serge dresses with beige collars for Sundays in winter, and green dresses of dreadful tussore silk for high days and holidays and summer dresses. We wore green leather belts with our summer uniform and all those cotton tunics. I have one still. When I wore it later with a cotton frock, someone recognised it at once. There were awful lisle stockings, and you had to have so many pairs of shoes.

"We had panama hats for the summer with the Sunny Hill badge, and awful black velour hats in the winter. We had summer and winter badges for our hats. The summer ones round our panamas, and the others for the velour. They had vicious little spikes to fit them to the hats, because you had the same band for all your hats, and the bands were all the same size, and the spike fitted behind the badge. We had green Harris tweed coats and green berets which we were allowed to wear on everyday walks. It was on Sundays we had to wear the black velour. The velour hats were so ugly.

"In the summer we wore summer tunics, but the gym slips with velvet facings we wore in the winter. They were quite pretty. Tebralco blouses with short sleeves. All uniform came from Marsh's.

"We did eurhythmics, this awful Greek dancing, and we had to have special things for that - a Greek blue tunic. We ran around barefoot and pranced about the new Hall like very lumpish oafs, I think, when someone played the piano. Eurhythmics was compulsory for part of the time, perhaps the first year.

"But what everybody mentions are the green knickers. They were for every day. We were sitting in a hotel lounge after dinner three years ago and talking to a stranger about friends we both knew in Somerset. My husband said to her 'Did you go to Sunny Hill by any chance?' She obviously sounded like that. She said 'Yes, I did.' And she looked at me and said 'You'll remember those awful green knickers as well.' This is the thing that old girls of our vintage all talk about."

*　*　*

To finish the chapter on a more exalted note, here are three revealing glimpses.

Evidently the war called forth serious thought. Fay Yells reported that "A group of senior girls studied C. Lloyd's book 'Democracy and its Rivals.' A summary of each chapter was followed each week by lively discussion. It was interesting to learn what drastic changes in the existing social order some of our girls would like to make after the war."

Despite a more relaxed approach to teaching, academic results were good. Here is the 1943 French Oral examiner's report.

"The standard of spoken French at this School is remarkably high and reflects great credit on the teaching staff. I was agreeably surprised to find that the girls conversed with facility, employing a wide range of words and choosing the one with the correct shade of meaning. Pronunciation and accent were both excellent. I was told that it was the practice for the pupils who sat at 'High' to speak French with the members of the staff, and I consider that this is an excellent plan that might well be introduced into other boarding schools."

Among motions carried by the Current Events Group was this: "The Arts should be continued in war time." Accordingly, on November 14th 1942, the School gave "a concert to help the Bruton Tank Drive, the proceeds being invested in National Savings for the Radford Scholarship Fund." The school hall was nearly full. Performers included the Junior Choir, a Staff Choir and soloists from both girls and staff. Miss Allen produced two plays. The concert raised £30 and a White Elephant stall at the event brought in £10.

Meanwhile Sir Arthur looked to the future. He said: "We have recently heard of the new post war changes in education which if carried through will have big results and may even affect this school." The topic deserves a new chapter.

Hockey Team

Chapter 13

The Butler Act and
the Bruton choice

The post-war changes to which Sir Arthur referred soon became law. The 1944 Education Act, seen through Parliament by R. A. Butler, introduced a national system under a newly created Ministry of Education. Secondary education for the first time was compulsory and free. The Somerset Local Education Authority was now a committee of Somerset County Council. Schools were divided into primary and secondary. Secondary schools were for children aged between 11 and 15, the new minimum school leaving age. Pupils could stay on to 18 to take the School Certificate for entrance to university or other higher education institutions.

Thus Somerset County Council, through its LEA, was responsible for setting up and administering complete facilities for primary, secondary, and further education. Children were allocated to secondary schools on the basis of the 11-plus, a selective test taken in the final year of primary education. The big question for Sunny Hill was what place the school would and should have in the new co-ordinated educational scheme of things.

The Governors applied for Direct Grant status. This would retain something very like the existing position, with the direction of the school largely independent of the County Council, but with a considerable amount of the funding paid by the Council. The County refused the application. The school appealed to Board of Education. Professor James, one of the governors, wrote frankly to Sir Arthur Hobhouse on 10th June 1945:

"It is very unlikely that we shall get what we want. I think that unless the County is prepared positively to support us, our application is not likely to get serious consideration in Whitehall; but I came away feeling that the mind of the County (so far as it is represented by the Chairman on Monday and the two officials) is set and set hard against us; it was not a really open mind. Not one of the three, I thought, advanced a really considerable argument; in the last resort, the school, they said, must be worked into the scheme for the County which they are required to set up under the act. This is mere officialism; and I am afraid that this mere and frightful officialism will choke us. It would be a splendid thing if the County would come over to our side and vote away its (strong) chance of controlling us and 'working us (God help us!) into the County scheme under the act.'"

By 1946 the possibility of Sunny Hill becoming independent was aired in The Gleam: "Miss Wells and the Governors felt that by coming under the County the activities of the School would be too restricted. Accordingly a Direct Grant was applied for. This, unfortunately, was refused and so if possible it is hoped that the school may become Independent, but its future status is still rather uncertain."

Margaret Carter, who was School Secretary between 1952 and 1965, and Senior House Mistress from 1965 to 1971, put the matter as she saw it thus: "Sunny Hill applied for Direct Grant status under the '44 Act and was refused, because the County thought 'Aha! We'll have that!' and the School absolutely shattered them by going independent; it had been Grant Aided before that. Then the County looked round and found they had no grammar school in the area for girls, so they came cap in hand and said 'Please will you take our 11+ girls?'"

In fact in 1947 the Governors had to decide just how co-operative to be. Sunny Hill, like other schools, was facing a period of great pressure for school places, and was indeed feeling the need to extend its buildings. After enduring what Professor James had called 'the mind of the County .. set hard against' them, the Governors' attitude was understandably a trifle cool. "In reply to the County's request for 2/3 rds of annual vacancies and a certain proportion of boarding places it was agreed to offer the County up to 20 free places for the year 1947-48 subject to the acceptance of each pupil by the Governors but that no boarding places could be guaranteed owing to uncertainty as to number of vacancies."

In fact Governors and County reached a *modus vivendi* that was good for both. Many Somerset girls received a good Sunny Hill education, at a very reasonable cost to the County, and Margaret Carter as Secretary "merely sent the bill to the County, and the money came in. We were one of only two such schools in the country, I believe."

Some figures given by the Chairman at the 1947 Speech Day may be useful to record. "Out of 285 girls at present at the School, 118 are boarders, of whom 44 are from outside the County or abroad;167 are day girls of whom 164 have been admitted on the County list or admitted from primary or private schools in the neighbourhood and for whose fees the Local Education Authority are entirely responsible, and 9 who are receiving bursaries." Sir Arthur also jotted down in his notes: "School Fees. Termly Boarders £90 p.a. Weekly Boarders £78 p.a. (21 termly and 2 weekly boarders at reduced fees) Tuition fees £35 p.a. (21 day girls have remained at the old fee of £12 p.a.)"

* * *

The saga of relations with the County has taken us from war to peacetime. The transition was marked in true Sunny Hill fashion. L. Jarvis and K. Wells reported:

"On V E Day 1 at 3 p.m. we assembled in the hall and heard Mr Churchill's speech. We began our V E celebrations with a rounders match: VI Form v Staff. VI Form won 1-0. After that we had an open knockout tennis tournament. In the evening the boarders went to church at Pitcombe to the Thanksgiving service, and then listened to the King's speech.

"The next day we were granted a whole holiday, the day girls either sharing the celebrations at home, or coming to join in the revels with the boarders. These festivities were our own choice. Our first thought was for our early morning rising and, on appeal to authority, we were allowed an extra hour in bed. After a hurried breakfast, many of us being too excited to eat much, we went for form picnics. Most of the forms chose places where paddling was possible: for once it was theVIth which went to the pool instead of the IInd form, and the other forms camped along the length of the river. Although the day was hot and sunny, VIth form camped on the island and lit a large bonfire.

"At 3 p.m. the sports, arranged by Vth form in the morning, took place on the hockey pitch. The people of Pitcombe had been invited, and many of the children and grown-ups entered into the fun with great zest, giving us a feeling that we were celebrating a national victory in a united way. Much fun was derived from the side shows, especially the beauty competition which was won by the Vicar. The dressing up race, during which we watched Mr Ashcroft, Mr Golledge, Mr Salisbury and Mr Hunter struggling into bonnets, skirts and pyjamas, was great fun for the audience.

"In the evening the Sixth Form arranged a programme of party games, dancing and singing. By 10 p.m. everything had been restored to order and the school was silent; not so the village of Pitcombe, which carried its festivities far into the night in the form of bonfires and fireworks, shouting and singing. Many of us were kept awake by Roll out the barrel, Abide with me, God save the King and Auld lang syne in just such an amazing order."

The Gleam Editor had to admit that "The declaration of Victory in Europe has made very little difference to our school life. We still have two days of essential work to be fitted in by each form." Brenda Marsden (Hurst) noted one example of essential work in her diary: "Terrible job, swishing round in a mixture of gravy, cabbage, jam and mock-rice!" That was what passed for washing up. On the other afternoons, however, girls could enjoy a variety of new activities, no longer hampered by the blackout. "We have made a good beginning with the art, dramatic, music, architecture, handwork and stamp collecting clubs. At the moment the Current Events clubs are compulsory, and as such they are not a great success."

*　　*　　*

There were signs that not all was well with the school spirit during the first post-war years. The Gleam in 1945 confessed that "the year has not been at all peaceful or placid, and many of us have been aware of restless undercurrents both in the boarding house and day school." It was no better in 1947. "Things seem to be getting more unsettled than ever, and even in our school we experienced great sorrow at the departure of so many staff, especially that of Miss Rowell, who has been with the school so long." Turnover of staff was indeed a problem. Five left in 1945, seven in 1946.

The Gleam complained in 1946 that the School Council for the past 3 years had not been such a useful instrument of a self-governing school as it could have been. "Ridiculous agenda is [sic] brought up and when points of interest are discussed, no sensible arguments are expressed, but direct negatives and affirmatives are given without any reasons."

The House system came into question at the same period. Miss Wells felt in 1945 that the Houses were growing too large, and suggested that Millicent Fawcett and Garrett-Anderson should produce daughter Houses. The plan was presented to the staff, who vetoed it. The next idea came from the school, suggesting that two new houses should be formed from the new girls and volunteers from the existing houses. Miss Wells felt that this division would leave out certain age-groups in the new houses, which therefore would be without seniors to lead them in the future. Then the Senior School, by a unanimous vote, decided that Houses should be abolished until the school felt the need of them again; but the majority of the School did not wish Houses to be abolished and the Old Girls looked on them as an integral part of the School. It appeared that only drastic measures could revive the traditional "House spirit."

Eventually, in 1946, four new day girl houses were instituted, each affiliated to one of the boarder houses, which remained as Marie Curie, Millicent Fawcett, Garrett-Anderson, and Florence Nightingale, each with a separate block of the boarding house for dormitories, and its own sitting room. This arrangement caused dissatisfaction amongst some of the girls, "but" hoped the Gleam, "this may decrease when the system is past the experimental stage."

* * *

Such unsettling changes were by no means the whole story. In 1945 one girl entered the Medical School of St Andrew's University, and another gained a place at Lady Margaret Hall. There were performances of the opera 'Iolanthe' in May 1945, and a public gym display with folk dancing and a ballet version of Alice in Wonderland that same term.

The production of 'Iolanthe' was a triumph of determination over austerity. The Gleam reported: "The fairies danced and sang very delicately. The speaking parts were clear and nearly word perfect. Thanks to the ingenuity and unremitting labour of Miss Woodroffe, Miss Esam, Miss Burrow and Miss Wilson, the clothes were as good as Sunny Hill usually produces (the peers' cloaks were all made of cubicle curtains from Dorm 2) and the makeup was very good. Juniors and seniors alike have got tunes from Iolanthe on the brain." The producer of this, as of so many plays over the years, was Miss Allen. The 'orchestra' consisted of Miss Speight on piano and Mr. Fiori on violin. £101. 15s. 0d was raised for the International Schools Fund, for rebuilding education in countries devastated by war - and this at a time when Sunny Hill itself was gratefully receiving food parcels from schools in Australia and New Zealand, and, as The Gleam reported in 1946, "from Dr and Mrs Goethe, of Sacramento, California, we are being sent the American Natural History Magazine for a second year. This beautiful non-austerity magazine is enjoyed by everyone and usually looks well-worn by the end of the month!"

In the autumn term of 1945 a public Speech Day could once again be held, and at the end of term the Nativity Play cast its accustomed spell: "It portrayed a little refugee girl falling asleep to the sound of children singing carols in the village school. In her dream she saw the angels in heaven and Gabriel, who brought the news to Mary; she heard the heavenly music telling the shepherds of the Saviour's birth, and finally she saw the scene in the stable. The play was watched by a spellbound audience at both performances. The most beautiful and striking things were the wonderful colour of the angels and the grace of their patterned movement."

* * *

One item from the minutes of a meeting of the Governors well illustrates the shortages and regulations that were taken for granted: "Electric Plug Points. Licence to install these in Music Room of Day School had been applied for. If cuts in electricity prevented this the heating boilers to be stoked a little harder on very cold days."

Into this austere school in 1946 came the first "County Girls," including Sheila Watts, whose husband Colin Watkins headed the school's Science in later years. She remembers that

"The school was very stark then. The windows were still covered with blast paper, semi transparent paper stuck on the windows to stop them shattering if bombed; that was peeling off, so it really looked pretty horrible. There were no curtains in the dormitories. There were curtains on the rails between the beds, and you could pull them round and make a cubicle, but none on the windows. and I remember it as bitterly cold, but of course it was the winter of 1947. It wasn't the school's fault, because coal was rationed and the heating system wasn't very efficient. It was a gravity feed, with great big pipes and old-fashioned big radiators. It used to be so cold that in the Cosies we used to make tents of blankets round the radiators and get inside to keep warm.

"I was sleeping in the dormitory on pillars, at the top of the covered way. I don't think it's used as a dormitory now, as it's considered too cold. It was a store room. You can imagine that in 1947, with three walls, the floor and the roof exposed to the outside. It was grim.

"We had to wash with washstands and jugs; every morning when the rising bell went, two people went with these big white aluminium jugs, down to a bathroom where there was hot water. They came back with this supposedly hot water, and poured it in your icy cold bowl, and you washed quickly before it froze. I can remember standing at the top of the covered way and feeling so cold, and thinking I should never be warm again. But that first winter was so cold. They ran out of coal, because coal was rationed, and we all sat around in our overcoats for about 24 hours, and then they sent us home because they couldn't heat the school. I still have the scars from the chilblains on my feet from that winter. We had fun. MrsDonaldson let us use the meat trays from the kitchen to slide down the hill. Of course they would never allow that now.

"We had iron bedsteads and flock mattresses. We had to provide some of our own bedding ... not blankets, but we brought an eiderdown and sheets. Every morning you had to strip your bed off, put everything on the chair at the bottom of the bed, and then lift the mattress and turn it over.

"We had a matron called Miss Hill, who was universally known as Deadly. So much so that one of the new girls didn't realise that it was not her name and addressed her as Miss Deadly. She used to come round and inspect to see that you had properly stripped your bed. This became so ingrained that when I went to Bristol and was sharing a room, the first morning I stripped everything off the bed. My room mate said 'What are you doing?' Seven years of indoctrination lasted all of a week!"

Sheila's memories were of a life that would now be considered very hard. "The other thing which would be different from nowadays was that we all had to do essential work. Essential work was vegetables, laying the tables, clearing the tables, and helping with the washing up. Each person did it about 3 times a week. It took about half an hour, evenings and mornings. Cutting up swedes, preparing vegetables. Swedes were a real problem. When you are 12 you are not terribly strong. With great big swedes and knives, it was as much as we could do to get the swede into half, without cutting up the rest of it. It was quite nice in the summer when you were shelling peas."

It is not altogether surprising that Sheila remembers one or two girls running away. "I can remember thinking I would run away, but then thought Mum and Dad would just send me back."

✳   ✳   ✳

Two views of the academic work at this period come from an outside examiner and from Sheila Watts. In 1945 35 girls took School Certificate and 30 passed. 17 took Latin. All but 4 took Art. (There were only three entries for Higher School Certificate, including one in Physics.) Two years later there were 50 entrants including the July and December exams. Only 6 failed to get the Certificate.

In 1945 a French Oral report by E.J. Arnoud was most encouraging. "A good performance both in reading and conversation. In reading, the intonation was very good indeed, often better than the pronunciation, where a few difficult sounds, such as nasal vowels, seemed to elude a number of candidates. The conversation was also very satisfactory. Most candidates understood the examiner very readily and acquitted themselves very well in their answers. A few proved to have reached a really high standard, and none were far below the pass mark. Such an even performance, with a large number of entrants, is in itself a most creditable tribute to the teacher."

Sheila's view was this: "After the war everything was a bit unstable. The teaching at school was good on the whole. We had a big turnover of teachers. In my year we had 5 Latin teachers in the first 2 years we did Latin, a new one practically every term. Each new teacher began with the First Declension again. We knew the First Declension very well, but otherwise we were very bad at the subject. When we came to the Upper 5th Miss Wilson took out 7 of us and put us through the entire Latin course in one year."

She goes on to claim: "I only just got through Latin, by a happy accident. Miss Wilson chose for our Mock unseen the same passage that we happened to get in the summer. She had been through it afterwards with a fine tooth comb and told us what we should have done. It was all still there in my mind. In fact the examiners must have been puzzled because all the rest of the paper would have been pretty poor."

Brenda Marsden (Hurst) thought well of the French dining room, an institution which probably helped win the examiner's admiration for the girls' oral French. "To eat in the French room was pleasant - a small, quiet room, which developed a family feeling. We were supposed to speak only in French - I think at least we tried hard and Miss Wilson and Mrs Monks were very patient with our efforts!"

A pupil's eye view of the staff can give a strange impression, but may be of interest: "The staff room was a tiny room behind the school office, on one side. On the other side was the little Head's office. They were fairly well crushed up in the staff room! Every time the door of the staff room opened, there was a tremendous overpowering whiff of cigarette smoke. Miss Allen used to smoke a tremendous amount. When we were in the 6th form doing Geography at A level, and had double periods, we used to take bets on how long she would last out before she would say 'I must just go down to the staff room and collect ....' and then come back reeking of smoke. The only male teacher was Mr Fiori who taught the violin, and he was another one who went round in a haze of tobacco smoke. In fact when we wanted to smoke we used to go into the music rooms, because they all smelled of tobacco."

*   *   *

Despite the post-war instability, Sunny Hill was growing and thriving. In 1947 the Chairman of Governors reported: "As the numbers show, this, like other schools, is facing a period of great pressure for school places, and the Governors and the Headmistress are doing their utmost to provide the maximum accommodation so that the greatest possible use can be made of education at Sunny Hill."

He pointed out how fortunate the school was to have built its new building prior to the war, but added: "At the time, it was thought to be a very generous provision, but at the moment we could well do with still greater accommodation, especially for some of the outdoor pursuits of the School, such as further playing fields. The Governors thought of the possibility of levelling the front field for this latter purpose, but abandoned the scheme in favour of extended vegetable garden, which should amply provide for the difficult catering requirements of today."

This public statement came out of many detailed discussions in Governors' meetings. At one meeting "The question of the field in front of the School was again considered. Mr Hamilton stated that it would make a full size Hockey Field but his further estimate of the cost was £1,250. He also reported a difficulty in disposing of the sewage from the new Cottage without causing a nuisance to those playing if it was used as a playing field. Agreed that the Front Field should be cropped as garden land and that about $\frac{3}{4}$ an acre of the allotments would be of use to the School in connection with boarding house sewage disposal." At another meeting "The use of Mr Spratling's Field adjoining the School for hockey was considered and after an inspection by Mr Hamilton and Mrs Makins, who reported that it would be suitable, it was agreed that further action should be left to the Chairman." The Governors were also collecting estimates for making two hard tennis courts.

Financially the school was in a healthy state. Out of total receipts of £15,129 in 1945, the Head's salary accounted for £675, the teachers' salaries £5,331, wages of servants £1,346, and after all other expenses including the year's repayment of Somerset County Council's 30 year loan for the new building, it was possible to transfer £2,500 to the Reserve Fund.

Soon the Governors were faced with a major decision, when they received the following letter:

Oct. 21st '48

Dear Sir Arthur,

I wish to tender my resignation to the Governors to take effect at the end of the Summer Term 1949. I do this with regret, but feel that it is time the school should have some one younger at its head. I think that it will be best from the School's point of view to stay till July......

Yours sincerely
Jane T. Wells

❋   ❋   ❋

Miss Chappell

Chapter 14

Jubilee and Miss Chappell

The year 1950 was marked by a great Jubilee celebration, and a pageant telling the school's history in dramatic form. It also saw the retirement of Jane Wells, only the second headmistress in the 50 years of the school's existence, and the coming of the small but formidable Enid Chappell.

Less noticed was the retirement of Miss P. M. Hayward (born Sept. 2nd 1894) who had been School Secretary from 1917. Miss P. M. Clarke, History teacher and later senior mistress, called her "a sure stay and support, whether it were in the recurring minor crises of examinations and speech days or the major upheavals of building operations and European conflicts. Always busy yet always cool, quiet and orderly as her own handwriting, I never asked her help in vain, even when, long after normal secretarial hours, I rang her up at Wayside and she might reasonably have replied that she was off duty. But her standard of service knew nothing of official hours or off duty." When the Governors were settling her pension, the Clerk, Mr Taylor, wrote from Church Street, Wincanton:

> Miss Hayward's Salary. I am afraid that I can only trace records from 1941; apparently the earlier ones must have been destroyed by the bomb.

The retirement of Jane Wells was the occasion for many tributes, some of which appeared in a previous chapter to help sketch her character when she arrived. The Chairman of Governors Sir Arthur Hobhouse said at her final Speech Day: "The Governors, the Staff, and the School have, through all these difficult years, admired the wonderful way in which she has maintained the high standards of school life with wisdom, foresight, and inspiration. She has devoted her energies, without any selfish consideration, to the well-being, present and future, of the School. As Chairman of the Governors at the time of two critical decisions - to build the new Day School, and to become an Independent School - I can testify to the large part which Miss Wells took, and how she fought fearlessly for what she thought was in the future interests of the School." In fairness, the apparent reservation in the phrase "what she thought ..." does not mask any great disagreements between her and the Governors, as far as the surviving correspondence shows.

Miss Wells took over a school of about 130 girls, and in her 1950 annual report she could announce that "the total number of pupils has reached the record of 302 and it may remain a record as the day school has already outgrown its buildings. I feel that the School may lose something in quality if it increases much in size."

Miss Allen commented: "Miss Wells was Headmistress of Sunny Hill for 21 years. Her own characteristic comment was, 'and what is 21 years? It isn't really very long' - for she would always belittle her own effort and achievement. This modesty and her steady refusal to claim or to accept credit where it was certainly due perhaps really did hide from us the full extent of our indebtedness."

And Miss Allen as Senior Mistress added ruefully: "Finally we remember her reaction to difficulties. Sometimes she would tell you, with an air of positive radiance, just exactly how complicated a situation was. I remember coming back to school early when the term-not-yet-begun was already bristling with difficulties. Someone told me how short we were of staff; of many domestic crises; of the fact that two dormitories were out of action and we had not yet found anywhere for the girls to sleep. And the recital ended, 'But of course Miss Wells is in great form.' What she would say and how she would act were unpredictable to the end. And each year, if not each term, she found new ways of approach. Thus, though no member of her school could be unaware of the standard held before her, yet Sunny Hill could never settle down into a monotonous routine. There was always a certain apprehension in the air - sometimes puzzled, sometimes resentful, sometimes amused. But in general the bracing element was healthy. It certainly added a zest to life."

A final comment from one of Miss Wells' last Head Girls: "I was one of the Big Four in 1950. We left with Miss Wells, a lovely lady who made a great impression on my life. I was a little country girl who came here on a scholarship and because it was war time I had led a very sheltered life. I learned a lot about how the rest of the world lived. Miss Wells always took a class in her own subject, French. We used to call it 'Jane's French.' She made us value Sunny Hill."

*   *   *

A service of dedication and thanksgiving was held on Saturday July 22nd 1950 in Bruton Parish Church. The Order of Service shows a formal and reverent occasion: "We are gathered here in the sight of God and in the presence of one another to give our humble and hearty thanks to God for all the many blessings He has vouchsafed to Sunny Hill School since its foundation, and to dedicate ourselves afresh to His service." The hymns, psalm, readings and prayers led up to a sermon by the Bishop of Bath and Wells on Psalm 144 verse 12: "that our daughters may be as corner stones, polished after the similitude of a palace."

The Chairman of Governors looked back to "that wonderful service in Bruton Church ... Gratitude that in the changing world Sunny Hill had clung successfully to the splendid ideals of service and complete womanhood inculcated by our Headmistresses."

What one pupil remembers, however, is what happened to the hats: "We had to look our very best, and to accomplish this the matron of the day decided to steam many of our battered Panama hats to improve their shape. The steam was too hot, or perhaps the time was too long, and I remember walking down to Bruton looking more suited to a Wild West Show than a church service, and I was not the only one."

*   *   *

The Pageant was an experience long treasured by all who were there, despite the continuous rain. The script was printed and offered for sale later: '1000 copies at 2/3, post free.' The Gleam asked: "How did Miss Allen and Miss Wilson, but especially the Producer, just how did they manage to fit the extraordinary amount of work they did for the Pageant into their already crowded timetables? I am still wondering, still abominably curious, when I say how grateful we all are to those two versatile staff. We also owe our thanks to MissVinall for the English Lesson, and to Miss Coles, who made those hideous early school uniforms." J. Browne of UV L remembered particularly "that hilarious Bristol scene" and the early uniforms: "those straight-on-the-head boaters, black stockings, and pinafores over those hideous straight tunics." A pupil recalls that "Almost every girl played some part or other in the Jubilee Pageant that year."

So successful was the pageant that in 1975 the same script was updated and used for the Third Jubilee.

*   *   *

After the nostalgia of the summer term came the new broom that was Enid Chappell. She aroused strong feelings, whether of admiration or dislike. Sheila Watts was not impressed. She compared her two headmistresses like this: "Miss Wells and Miss Chappell were very different. Miss Wells was very strict but fair. You really minded your p's and q's with her. For example, when she taught us French, we sat bolt upright with our arms folded behind our backs. 'Good for your deportment, girls!' She used to have us in to her room on a Sunday evening and read to us. That was great, because there was a real fire! She used to read very nice books and that was a really enjoyable time."

Another pupil has similar memories: "In the First Year we all looked forward to 'Jane's Reading'. This was on Sunday evening when Miss Wells had all the First Year boarders in her sitting room and read to them. She had a wonderful reading voice, and these evenings made us realise that our very stern headmistress was really very kind and understanding. Miss Chappell continued the tradition, but we heard that she read from the Bible, so we were very glad to have had 'Jane'." (The rumour about reading from the Bible was untrue!)

Sheila continues: "Miss Chappell - I didn't get on with her at all. I always felt that her smile never got up to her eyes. I can't put my finger on it. We just didn't jell. She was very much an English lit person and I think she felt all the 6th form ought to do English. I started off doing English and didn't like it and wanted to change. Since I wanted to change to Art, which I am sure she thought an absolute cop-out, it didn't go down very well. I think she had a very hard life, because she had to look after her mother, a rather difficult old lady who lived in school and had to have all her food specially prepared and minced, so as not to have any lumps. She cared for her loyally for years, which couldn't have been easy."

Sheila may not be completely fair to Miss Chappell, who later had cause to announce: "Those who soar to State Scholarships are in a happier position. Both Gillian Thomas and Sheila Watts obtained them with distinctions in Advanced English, Advanced History and Advanced Art. … Sheila entered Bristol University where she has become an intrepid cave-explorer, with dire results but she will be back 'caving' again when her leg has knit."

Anthea Cox has different memories: "Miss Chappell was really like the Queen Mother, with her fur stoles, lacy hats and handbags. She spoke like her, dressed like her, had a stately air of royalty about her. We could scarcely believe she was human, but she was very sweet and kind. If we were at the bottom of the covered way and she was at the top, we would not dare go through the door but would stand holding it open while she did her stately walk all the way down. When it came to Honourables or detentions we would queue outside her office to have our book signed, and I still relive the sensation when waiting to see the Head of the school where I teach. She used to read us stories in her sitting room on Sundays. Miss Chappell seemed to us quite old, and her mother seemed ancient. She had a cat called Ginger, and a pale blue Morris Minor."

Margaret Carter, school secretary and later house mistress, saw a side of Miss Chappell that the girls did not. "I have always worked very hard, have as it were been married to my job; but I had never before worked as hard. Miss Chappell and I used sometimes to pass each other at 5 a.m., she going back to her house after working through the night, and I starting the next day's work, since I work best in the morning. Miss Chappell would have a couple of hours' sleep before starting again. She was an incredibly hard worker.

"She was a wonderful person who made the School what it is now. She sowed all the seeds. It used to be a very poor school financially; we were very careful with the money, but gradually we built up. First two huts adjoining the Netball courts and then the extension containing the Gymnasium were built in Miss Chappell's or Miss Cumberlege's time.

"She also moderated in the holidays for one examination board. She did a tremendous amount in the Headmistresses' Association, and made the School known. She worked all the hours there were. She had a passion for gardening, and used to garden by electric light! She was tiny, and was known locally as 'Queen Victoria'. She always looked through the steering wheel when she drove her car."

We gather something of Miss Chappell's grasp of practicalities from these extracts from a letter to Sir Arthur Hobhouse dated 24th October 1950, half way through her first term.

Last Monday and this Monday the water supply to the School entirely failed. I cannot get to the bottom of this failure. Our supply failed at 12 o'clock, just as we were facing lunch for 350. I am more than a little anxious about this, for first, we have to wash up in dirty water which is serious with infection about, and secondly I cannot keep an even temperature in the school. We have shut off the boilers as a safeguard. I believe there is nothing else I can do, besides complaining to the Wincanton R.D.C. I am enclosing the correspondence now.

The Southern Electricity Company has been over to look at some Macrocarpa trees which are interfering with the electricity cable. They will send our men to top them. They are the trees flanking the hard tennis court but they have all grown too tall and thinned out underneath.

I saw Vickery again about the Kitchen Garden elms and discovered what he would really like best would be for the gardeners, when Barker arrives, to top them.

I wanted to inform you that I have found a Mrs Down living in one of Miss Brook's cottages, at the Hall School, who will, this term, when Miss Brooks does not want her, come in to help us out. She is unqualified but very capable, and can do a little cookery with the girls and help with a few games periods. She would not by any means be full time, and as we are working two Academic Staff short this term and the Staff have been carrying this extra burden, I might use her at an hourly rate until Miss Masters arrives.

I did not tell you at the Governors' meeting that Miss Masters will be non resident. I have no more accommodation for the staff, and Mrs Vickery has told me she would prefer not to have a member of staff after this term. Unfortunately there is no legal agreement about our using a room in the Lodge.

Elliott has today asked me for a rise. I discovered they are living in a two roomed cottage, and the wife is eking out their income by two hours daily in the Ansford canteen. I felt I ought to inform you, as this has been in our minds.

Yours sincerely
Enid Chappell

* * *

Those who were interviewed for jobs by Miss Chappell retain abiding memories of the experience. Charlie Biesheuvel says: "I came for interview on a Friday and Miss Chappell at 5 p.m. told me I could have the job. I said 'I want to talk it over with my wife.' She had to be employed as well; she was a trained secretary and a trained nurse, and she had to do cleaning. You would never believe it, at nine o'clock the next morning, Saturday, Miss Carter, Miss Chappell's secretary, came down the Rocks to Pitcombe where we lived in a cottage called Twilbee, asking why I had not answered! I know now that there was a Governors' meeting on the Monday afternoon; so she had to have an answer, I can see that now. But she didn't give me much time. I only had one evening to talk it over with my wife. [The card reads: "I have had no acknowledgement of my letter..."] That was typical."

Another applicant, in 1960, was Sandra Hollister (Mrs Howe). "When I applied for a post at Sunny Hill I received a summons to interview which involved my arriving, by the train from Exeter, at Bruton Station dressed in suit, hat and matching gloves and handbag, and wearing stiletto heels after the current style. No one met me, and I had to find my own way to the School. This, I later found, was par for the course. There was never anyone to meet a person if Miss Chappell was involved. I finally arrived at the School and was interviewed by Miss Chappell in her dining room. She sat behind a big desk with her back to the bay window, so that I could not see her face against the light. During the interview she looked up and said, 'Miss Hollister, I see that you are still wearing your gloves.' 'Yes, Miss Chappell.' 'Are your gloves hiding something? Is that a ring I see on your finger?' I took my gloves off and confessed that it was, and that I was engaged to be married. 'Ah!

How long, then, can we expect you to be with us?' These were questions that today one would not be allowed to ask.

"I had to walk back to the station because nobody offered to give me a lift. I spent several weeks waiting for a letter from Miss Chappell, but heard nothing, until in May I received a telegram to this effect: 'Do you want this job or not? Phone immediately.' When I phoned, she said 'Why have you not replied to my letter?' I said 'I haven't had your letter.' 'Oh you must have,' she said. I repeated that I had not had a letter. 'Oh, I wonder if it was ever posted. I am offering you the job. Would you like it?' When I said 'Yes,' she promised 'I will write to you.' I have the letter still."

John Howe's appointment was equally idiosyncratic. Sandra tells the story: "Miss Chappell once invited John and me to dinner, and towards the end of the meal she asked, out of the blue, 'Would you miss your cricket terribly?' 'Sorry, Miss Chappell?' 'If you came here to teach Geography...' That was John's interview! She tended to assume that when she had thought something, she had said it, and the other person knew it!"

* * *

One former pupil, who unfortunately did not give her name, has written this detailed account of boarding life in the early 1950s:

"The dorms had bare boards, no curtains except for half length nets, and there were marble washstands. Every morning and night, water (hopefully hot, but often barely lukewarm) had to be collected in tall enamel jugs from the nearest bathroom, and then poured into china washbowls. After we had washed and cleaned our teeth, the dirty water was tipped into a communal slop-pail which was always filled till it overflowed, since we all hated the job of lugging it to the bathroom to empty it, and so insisted there was room for just one more bowl-full! Any water left in the bowls or jugs overnight would often be frozen solid by morning. The central heating in the entire school was not very adequate, and whether it was that, or whether winters were much colder in those days I do not know, but chilblains were a regular problem.

"The uniform at the start of my career was not designed for warmth, and consisted of gym slips, worn with short-sleeved blouses with square necks and V-necked pullovers. It was no good growing one's hair to keep the neck warm, because any hair long enough had to be tied back, and plaits had to be tied together.

"Most of the dorms did not have radiators. When we reached the Sixth Form, a kindly matron decided to allow the boarders hot water bottles, which she would fill with hot water, but since there was one radiator at the very end of the Sixth Form dorm, we were excluded from this privilege, and bottles surreptitiously filled with lukewarm tap water were not the same! We were allowed only 5 ornaments or other articles on our chest of drawers; everything else had to be put away out of sight, and nothing could be stuck up on the walls. Our beds had to be made with immaculate hospital corners, but we were permitted a soft toy, which gave the otherwise bleak dorm a more homely feeling.

"We were allowed 2 baths a week, on a very strict rota basis, and unbelievably hair washing was only once every 3 weeks! Quite incredible in the light of present day safety awareness, we had to dry our hair in front of gas fires, usually as many as 4 to a fire, all pushing and shoving to be in the front. (I had very long hair and it was frequently singed on hair washing day.) As we moved up the school and became more aware of our appearance, to avoid greasy locks we developed the habit, while bathing, of 'slipping down by accident, Matron'.

"The laundry system contributed very little to personal hygiene. Washing one's own clothing was strictly forbidden. Each weekend the laundry was collected, in piles of like garments, in the middle of the dorm floor, and carefully counted. Each girl was allowed to send one and only one of each article. Wearing the same white shirt for a week was bad enough, but looking back I cannot imagine how I could have borne to wear the same pair of thick green knickers and pair of lisle stockings for 7 days! As for our school tunics or skirts, no provision for washing these was made unless one spilled all one's dinner over them; and so at half term our mothers were simply amazed at the colour of the water they were washed in. It resembled the muddy cocoa we drank at morning break together with half a slice of bread and margarine.

"One lot of washing was done by a lady in Pitcombe village, and two members of the Fifth Form were allowed to take the huge laundry basket on a kind of trolley to her house on a Saturday morning. This was enormous fun, if somewhat dangerous, for we would both sit on top of the basket and let the trolley roll freely down Rock, praying not to meet anything at the bottom.

"Every morning after breakfast we had to run 'round the elms' - the triangle made by going along the main road towards Bruton, back down the hill and then up the lane. This, in the middle of January, at 8.15 a.m. high on the hills was guaranteed to cool even the hottest blooded girl. We also had to have a run after school, this time the longer one, round Pitcombe, which many of us so hated that we would take turns to hide in the very large cupboard in the cosy, so that the prefects would not find us and send us out. When we in our turn became prefects, we stopped anyone doing this by taking a register half way round the run! Poachers make the best gamekeepers.

"Since the war was not long over, rationing was still in force. This must have made feeding hungry girls no easy task. Inevitably bread played a vital part in our diet, and particularly at tea we would consume vast quantities, ordering extra by holding up fingers to show the number of rounds we wanted. It was considered very clever if one could manage all ten; this must have led to weight problems for some in later life. Most of the bread was eaten dry; we each were served with one small cube of butter, and one small dish of jam did not go far among the 14 girls on each table. Wednesday teatime was special because we had currant buns, and on Saturday and Sunday we had a cake each for tea.

"Having just been shown round the new Sixth Form accommodation at Highcroft we all feel we had a rather more deprived existence, although we did not realise it at the time. The Upper Sixth Common Room was the little room just inside the main door of Old House, and is now a cloakroom. In here we spent all our spare time and even had our prefects' tea there. We never considered that we might be allowed to wear other than school uniform except in the evenings, and that concession did not include Sundays, when we stayed in our navy blue / green school dresses all day. The only thing I remember resenting was that the house mistress thought it necessary, if it was pouring with rain on Sunday, to come and tell us that we were to wear our mackintoshes to church. I thought that at the age of 17 I could have worked that out for myself.

"Bedtime for the Sixth was 9.20 p.m. with lights out at 9.45. The pattern throughout the boarding house was for each year to go to bed 20 minutes later than the younger one, starting at 7.40 for the 11 year olds. We considered ourselves very lucky when, in the Lower Sixth, we could go shopping in Bruton on Saturday morning, and in the Upper Sixth after school as well, provided we were back in time to change into mufti for prep at 5 p.m.

"On both Saturday and Sunday afternoons walks were the order of the day, unless it rained in torrents. Initially one went in the junior crocodile, under the charge of a member of staff, but 2 seniors could choose two juniors to take on a group walk instead. Juniors who were not chosen became discontented, and the system changed: everyone walked in the croc until the fourth year, when girls could sign out to go in groups of four. Any contravention of walk rules (Wear your beret at all times; no going anywhere near Bruton; no going into fields, hedges or barns with King's boys) meant being sent back to the junior croc.

"The 'cosies' were anything but!: bare floorboards, a minimum of furniture, very few comfortable chairs. Each Colour House had a cosy. Much of one's life centred on the House system: each house produced a play for the other houses, sat in house tables at teatime, and to a certain extent slept in dorms organised by houses. We were barred from the cosies, and of course the dorms, of other houses. Nor were we allowed into dorms during the day, except to change into mufti before evening prep. One favourite way of reaching our dorm at this time was to climb up into the roof space and come down through the appropriate hatch into the dorm. It was easy to lose one's way with only a much-used torch as guide; once, to our horror, it was the hatch above a staff bedroom that we opened.

"On the last night of term it was traditional to sleep in odd places. This might simply be under the bed, but the more adventurous would attempt a good night's rest on top of the Judy box (the open-fronted cupboard where we hung our clothes) or even curled up in a drawer. This, after a midnight feast, meant a crowd of very bleary eyed girls greeting their parents next day.

"After lunch at weekends we had silent reading in house cosies. This lasted far too long; even if one had a good book to read, the lack of chairs meant sitting on the floor or on window sills; this, together with a ban on even the quietest whisper, was guaranteed to make the most avid reader fidgety by the end of the session.

"Saturday night was dancing. All the boarders donned their party frocks and spent the evening ballroom dancing with each other in the hall, supervised by the Housemistress. The Sixth Form planned the programme to include valetas, Gay Gordons, barn dances etc., and for putting the records on the wind-up gramophone with its steel needles. Soon after my arrival one house raised money to buy an electric turntable; the end of blunt needles did much to improve sound quality. All the records belonged to girls. Once the Housemistress decided that the music played was most unsuitable, and censored our records. Those she disapproved of she confiscated, including Doris Day's 'Secret Love' and Frankie Lane's 'Answer me, my love.' In fact she seemed to consider love a four-letter word. We were so cross that the next week we played 'The Little Shoemaker' continuously all evening until she was driven to distraction. When she complained we said it was the only record we liked out of those she passed. Our tactic worked. She reviewed her decision and returned a fair number of confiscated records., though we were not surprised that Johnny Ray's 'Such a Night' never met with her approval."

Chapter 15

Faith, Scholarship, Building, Polio (and poems)

Miss Chappell set herself to raise academic standards by every means, including regular exhortations to parents on Speech Days. This is from 1951:

"The world cannot afford the luxury of silly women, especially when it has not a monopoly of sensible men. There are plenty of Mr. Collinses who need sensible wives. I should like to see more real struggle for sound scholarship, producing a slightly larger proportion of entrants to the University. This year there has been some giving up and entry into lower planes of employment. Unused talent is bound finally to lead to a sense of frustration and disappointment. Three girls only have tried to enter the University field this year."

Miss Chappell had spent five years investigating Grammar School Curriculum, and had been "struck by the liveliness of planning of many girls' schools up and down the country." She was grateful for the lack of rigidity in Sunny Hill, and felt that they had possibilities of experiment that older, more traditional schools would not accept. This meant that the coming of the General Certificate of Education held few terrors for Sunny Hill, but results in the last year of School Certificate and Higher Certificate showed that while the lower exam was passed by 29 out of 33 entrants, only 2 out of 6 passed Higher Certificate. Sixth Form teaching needed attention.

By 1952 a Sunny Hill Internal Diploma had been devised and awarded for the first time at Speech Day. A Stage 1 Diploma was awarded to all who had satisfactorily covered the minimum course to the Upper Fifth year, and a full Diploma to those who went on to a Sixth Form course. These diplomas also recorded service to the School and outstanding characteristics. That year a Sunny Hill Scholarship was awarded for the first time.

Miss Chappell found the sexism of some parents distressing: "To me personally, it is more serious to find parents still arguing that a girl does not need as good an education as a boy, especially when it may be her privilege one day to bring up her own boys. We talk glibly about equality of opportunity and when educational opportunity is available by State decree for both boy and girl alike, it seems folly for parents to oppose it. One of the most heartening remarks this year came from one of my fathers: 'Even though my elder child is a girl, she is my first born and her education will never be sacrificed to her brothers.'" The challenge that followed was interesting: "Wouldn't every father feel the same?"

Miss Chappell's drive towards academic excellence met considerable difficulties. She reported: "The staffing problem becomes daily more acute. There is a shortage of women teachers, particularly specialists, and a rural school has the last priority. Yet only with a full complement of staff can a school thrive. The fear that dogs the steps of a Head is a time table blank. Already we have faced it in Domestic Science and Classics."

Glenys Perry remembers some of the staff at this time: "First there is Miss Vinall. She taught English and no-one ever misbehaved in her classes, I do not know why because she was a gentle lady and a wonderful teacher. She certainly had presence and commanded great respect. She was in charge of the library. When we left school many of us kept in touch with her until she died. She was very interested in her old girls. She had a book and if one had produced an outstanding piece of work one was honoured with the invitation to write it in her book.

"Next is Miss Allen, apparently known as Sally to the staff but Little Char among the girls. She taught Geography, was deputy head and produced the school play. She was also the Sixth Form mistress and her spiel on first meeting us as Sixth Formers included something like 'You left the fifth year as school girls and it is obvious that you have come back as ladies!' I must confess that I never got to know Miss Allen well for I did not pursue geography to O Level even.

"Miss Haskell taught Maths and we were all terrified of her. She was however the most brilliant teacher that you could wish for, though I remain bemused by some aspects of Maths to this day. She taught us to understand what we were doing and my bemusement is my failure not hers. I must admit that I enjoyed helping with Maths while doing supply teaching and found that I was good at teaching the subject. She is a lady with a tremendous sense of humour and even though we were so terrified we could still recognise the great kindness and concern for us that went with Miss Haskell who never seems to age."

Margaret Carter recalls: "Miss Wilson, who taught French, was a character, an eccentric who kept the staff entertained over supper with tales of her great-uncle who always took a hip-bath with him, just in case he needed it.

"The staff when I came used to change for supper. Miss Allen would sit at the head of one table and Miss Dare at the head of the other, while a third table was for staff liable to be called away on duty. Miss Dare, the House Mistress, was a battleship, very strict. She had been a house mistress all her working life. She was large and imposing, and no girl argued with Miss Dare. Nobody on the staff argued with Miss Dare!"

A school inspectors' report in Miss Chappell's early days concluded by endorsing her ambition: 'If, without losing the care for the slower individual which distinguishes Sunny Hill, and without any undue forcing, the school can introduce its abler girls to the discipline and inspiration of Scholarship, it will have set the crown on a very fine achievement.'

Was it a reaction against Miss Chappell's emphasis on academic achievement that called forth this poem?

ROADWAYS (With apologies to John Masefield)

One road leads to Cambridge,
One road runs to gowns.
My road leads to freedom,
To the green rolling downs.

One road leads to Oxford,
Where the great brains laze.
My road leads me homewards,
Where the white sheep graze. ....

My road leads me, lures me,
Away from schoolgirl strife.
Most roads lead degree - wards,
My road leads to Life.

To add more truths to the knowledge
Of all truths of the mind,
In quest of that one beauty
God put me here to find.

Mary M. Coney (16 years) VI. H. B

*   *   *

Pupils notched up achievements in several fields. In 1951 Mary Pearse had a life drawing hung at the Exhibition at Selfridge's. Gillian Thomas won a prize in the Poetry Society's annual competition and her poem 'Hero Worship' was published in the Poetry Review. She also won the 1st Prize in the National Book League's competition for an essay on Modern Poetic Drama which was included in a touring exhibition. Lilah Perry broadcast in Children's Hour and at the Taunton Festival won 3rd prize in the piano class, 1st prize in the open cello class, 1st prize in the singing class, and the Westlake Cup for the competitor with the highest individual marks - 93% for cello playing.

Cultural life was encouraged by visits to Bath for a concert of Bach's music, one by the Halle Orchestra, and a performance by the Ballet Rambert. Girls visited Bristol University to hear German Lieder, and Bath to see 'The Merchant of Venice' performed by the Young Vic. There was a cinema trip for 'Scott of the Antarctic,' and films were shown in school on Indian life, Penicillin, and 'Our Heritage'. Joint ventures with King's School included play reading, a film, a concert and Marlowe's Doctor Faustus.

House plays continued to flourish, one of the most restrained and delightful being 'Alice Through the Looking Glass' and an operetta. The Compass Players visited the school and gave a superb performance of Milton's Comus.

International links were made by visits from Fraulein Schwartz, a German headmistress, and Siv Rosberg, a Swedish student. That year's Confirmation was held jointly with King's, with a combined tea to follow, and there were two informal dances, one at King's, one at Sunny Hill. In 1952 Fraulein Dieckmann, an English teacher from the Teletta Margaretha Schule in Leer went away with admiration for Sunny Hill School Assembly and green uniform, for "the humour and gaiety of heart which inevitably tempers the seriousness in England, for our village community life, stone cottages, and the Service in our village churches." She declared that her stay at Sunny Hill had made her love England whereas six weeks in London had nearly driven her back to Germany. Miss Wells' International School Fund had by now furnished two classrooms in Leer and Sunny Hill sent off a consignment of English books as a 75th Jubilee gift for the nucleus of their English library. Miss Chappell was invited to take out 17 girls for their Jubilee celebrations.

*   *   *

Above: Caesar and Cleopatra

Below: Kenneth Ashcroft, Vicar of Pitcombe and VE Day beauty competition winner

Enid Chappell came with another fervent wish, also: to strengthen the spiritual life of the school. Girls were encouraged to attend a Missionary Day at King's with the Bishop of Barbados and C.M.S. missionary Harvey Cantrell as speakers. They also attended a series of Lenten addresses by the Franciscans of Cerne Abbas in Bruton Parish Church. Miss Chappell herself helped to prepare girls for Confirmation, after her idea that her brother, Rector of Buckerell, Honiton, should do it proved impractical. Local clergy were ruled out, because, as Miss Wells had written in 1950, "Parents in this neighbourhood know that the views of the clergy are not always those they themselves approve of."

One long lasting innovation was a voluntary Boarders' Sunday evening service. Sheila Watts was not impressed. "Miss Chappell started a Sunday evening service which she said was voluntary. She pointed out to me that I hadn't been for a few weeks. I didn't think much of that. If a thing is voluntary it should be voluntary. That was how voluntary things tended to be." A year later Miss Chappell had to admit "It is still a little difficult to persuade the majority of the Boarders of the value of this quiet half-hour to herald another busy week."It was not for want of a varied programme of speakers, including the Heads of King's, Sexey's, and Frome Grammar; Miss Ferguson on her work in India, Mrs Tuanama on work in Peru. Miss Sayle of the Sunday Schools Caravan Mission showed slides of Canada, and there was an epidiascope evening with Oberammergau Passion Play pictures.

A choir joined each year in a Festival of Church Music at Wells Cathedral. In 1951 a Carol service was held in school, evidently the first. "The weather proved very suitable for a Christmas service - large snow flakes falling continuously throughout the afternoon. We sang many festive songs, both in parts and in unison, and several members of the School read extracts from the Bible on the birth of Christ. We all sincerely enjoyed this service, and hope that it will become an annual occurrence." There were plans to add to this a Nativity Play.

In 1952 the Sixth Form, at request of the School Council, began to read the lesson regularly at School Assembly on Fridays, using a new lectern given by the Parent Staff Association. Lent lectures were again given by Franciscans from Cerne Abbas. The Vicar of Pitcombe, Rev Kenneth Ashcroft, visited each term to speak at Prayers or take the Boarders' Service, and prepared 14 confirmation candidates. One hopes that he was one local clergyman that parents approved of. Girls heard a missionary lecture about Burma.

In 1954 the school held a Bible Week to celebrate the third centenary of the British and Foreign Bible Society. Some of the Lower Fifths were taken to Bible House in London and set out an exhibition in school. Local vicars and others gave talks after prayers each day. Mr Ashcroft of Pitcombe brilliantly compressed the vast theme,

'The Origin, History and Authority of the Bible', into 20 minutes. Other topics were, 'The Bible as a means of Salvation,' 'The Bible as a Way of Life', and 'The Personal Use of the Bible.' During the week, £18 worth of books and Bibles were sold in school and there were 17 new members of the Bible reading societies. About 100 girls belonged at that time to the Bible Reading Fellowship and Scripture Union.

The Head may well have approved a prize-winning poem in traditional style by Jennifer Dunn, VI H, called 'Cathedral'.

> Dim holy palace, house of God on earth,
> Off'ring to Him of that which was his gift,
> (Most precious gift to those of lowly birth):
> Power to create a bridge to span the rift
> That lies 'twixt immortality and Man
> Who has a mortal form but soul divine -
> Its perfect beauty and majestic span
> Mirror the grace of God in every line.
> Delicate trac'ry, virgin-pure and white,
> In arch and column soars to vaulted dome;
> And lofty windows stain the sun's bright rays;
> And many a gilded angel hovers bright
> Among the shadow'd heights of God's own home.
> In silence here I kneel to offer praise.

*   *   *

Once again the school was outgrowing its buildings. Extra staff accommodation was needed, and was provided by building on to the Gardener's Cottage at the bottom of the drive. This meant that five more mistresses could be housed within the school grounds, although the architect had planned for four bed-sits and a box room! In the difficult post-war era with its infinity of bureaucratic delays such building was an achievement. In December 1950 there were complaints that the Ministry of Education were taking 'some considerable length of time' over their decision. When Mr Vallis, the architect, made enquiries he was told that the school's application, which had been sent to the Ministry of Works in April 1950, and had reached the Ministry of Education that August, had been put back for review in March 1951. The school had sent constant reminders, but it was only a personal visit by an H.M.I. in January 1951 that got things moving.

There was friction over the architects. Mr Hamilton, an associate of the original architect Mr Pictor, had sent a sketch plan for the Cottage extension, but had been passed over in favour of Vallis. He was, however, given the work of designing new classrooms, and various ambitious plans exist for a two storey building at the end of the day school. Soaring prices forced the Governors to settle for the present more modest four classrooms which were opened in 1953 (and therefore known as the Coronation Wing), now housing the Art Department.

A third pressing need was for a gymnasium. It was planned to build one on the site of the old wooden hut (where the Hobhouse building stands), and in view of government curbs on such building a prefabricated structure was proposed, but even this was not allowed. The Chairman gave parents what consolation he could: at least Sexey's was even worse off.

*   *   *

On September 3rd 1953 three polio cases in Bruton during the summer holidays were reported to parents. The County Medical Officer was consulted, and parents were given the option of not sending their daughters back, and term was to begin on September 16th. This was put back to 24th, but on 31st October a girl was admitted to hospital, and the school closed until 9th November. Then came this letter to parents:

> *25th November*
>
> I must inform you that there have been a few additional cases of this very mild polio (which are without paralysis). The school is under constant medical supervision and the MOHs wish it to continue at work. As a precaution, outside school engagements are being cancelled and parents are therefore asked to use discretion in home activities.

The County M.O.H. told Sir Arthur Hobhouse: "I have asked Miss Chappell to check the hygiene of the kitchen and the health of the kitchen staff and I have also asked her to look at the bed spacing in the dormitories seeing that they have at least 6 feet clearance between the beds and I have advised 'topping and tailing' the beds in these dormitories."

On November 27th the school was closed for the rest of the term, but on December 18th there was good news from the M.O.H.: "I had a telephone message from Dr Thompson yesterday evening saying that he had considered every aspect of your outbreak and had come to the definite opinion that the cases were not poliomyelitis but probably one of the 16 forms of Coxsackie Virus Disease (probably the Bornholm variety)." Coxsackie viruses cause sore throat or fever with chest or abdominal pains.

The school could return to normal.

Margaret Carter remembers, "That was in the days of the great Mrs Stell, a sea captain's widow in her late sixties, who had trained at Glasgow Royal in the days of real nursing training. She was diagnostically superb, and although we had nine cases of polio, no girls suffered permanent paralysis. She would see a child in the passage and would take it up to sick bay, put it to bed, and not allow it even to feed itself, even to move. Three days later it would develop symptoms of polio. When we asked her how she knew, she replied 'You can see it in the eyes.'"

And for another view of Matron Stell:

A SAD STORY?
(Song of Matron)

If you're feeling ill,
I can give you a pill,
From the little green box on my shelf.
Though others have died
From what is inside,
I don't think it will injure your health.

If you come back at Break,
I'll your temperature take,
For it's only one hundred and three.
Though that may seem quite high
I don't think you will die,
You don't even seem poorly to me.

Now then don't stay in bed
'Cause your body's all red,
And you're feverish, hot and then cold.
Scarlet fever I know,
Gives the symptoms you show,
But it's not so infectious, I'm told.

Now don't worry I know
You've not got polio
Though your body is paralysed through.
You can still move your eyes?

And let out painful sighs?
Well, we won't call the doctor for you!

If you've got a bad cough,
Or you've cut your thumbs off,
Or you're ill from the fish cakes at tea,
If you've measles or mumps,
Or feel down in the dumps,
Remember, dear, just come to me.

Kathleen Clothier (14 years) L.V.L.

✳   ✳   ✳

The beech tree opposite the main entrance to the new building (among those planted to celebrate the Coronation) nearly died. Miss Vinall led the following delicious parody as an incantation round it. According to one source it recovered. Others say it died, and the present glorious tree is its replacement.

VI GENERAL'S COPPER BEECH CHORUS
(after reading "Murder in the Cathedral")

We are the members of VI General,
Idle, ignorant schoolgirls, noisy and shallow,
Living and partly living, irritated by regulations
Harried by our form mistress, misunderstood, frustrated,
Preferring chatter and laughter to mental exercise,
Yet of some use to the School, immersed in petty duties:
Cocoa at break; cocoa at snack;
Thank you letters; votes of thanks;
Notices at prayers; notices at tea;
Break charge; library charge; leading in to meals;
Archives; turning out; distributing tuck;
Essential work; bell ringing; stamps and serviettes;
Care of junior dormitories; care of junior forms;
Maintaining silence in the school; confiscation; locking up.
The cares of the school weigh heavily on our shoulders.

Our beech tree was to have been our memorial,
A symbol of our golden-hearted happiness.
Its roots travelling to depths unknown: its slender trunk reaching skyward.
Glossy of leaf; smooth of bark,
Silhouetted against the dull black of the coal shed,
Glorifying the magnificence of the Somerset countryside:
But all is gone.
Now our beech tree withers from its topmost branches,
With caterpillars on the leaves, fungus on the stem.
The worm at the root and drought in the soil;
A blight on our beech, a blight on VI G,
A blight on Sunny Hill, a blight on the world.

Yet Miss Chappell promises us another copper beech:
The birth of new life, as we ourselves
Travel our different roads - to colleges, hospitals and universities.
As the tree prospers and flourishes
establishing itself in this seat of learning,
So we, the members of VI G, transplant ourselves
From Sunny Hill, to the world beyond.

So this, our naming ceremony, is three ceremonies,
At the same time a christening, a funeral and a rebirth.
We make merry for the christening,
We mourn for the death, we rejoice for the rebirth.
(All life is both a mourning and a rejoicing,
A birth and a death). Margaret labels our dying tree,
And this same label shall name our living tree,
VI G's copper beech, copper, copper, dying beech,
VI G's glorious shady, living beech.

K. L. V[inall] and some of VI G.

*   *   *

The path leading from Cole Station to the Day School, before the building of classroom huts, later replaced by the Thomson building, beside it.

Chapter 16

The "Seamy" Side

Turn your Armani suit inside out and you see "the seamy side," the side where the seams show, and learn a little of how it was tailored. It is good to be aware how much work goes into the smooth running of the school, and the time around the year 1955 is as suitable as any to illustrate this. What gets only a passing mention in a public speech may have taken months, even years, of careful thought and planning; what is never mentioned in public at all may have required the wisdom of serpents to negotiate.

When parents and friends gathered for Speech Day on 16 July 1955, there was a relay to the Gymnasium for 1st year pupils and their parents. Miss Chappell mused in her speech about her own position.

"In an exploratory conversation with some junior members of the school who collected round me gardening one evening there was some attempt to define a Headmistress's job. It was, they said, not to garden in the school garden - though she might garden in her own - but to look after the girls, and finally: 'A Headmistress may do exactly as she likes.'

"It is pleasant to contemplate a freedom as untrammelled as this and interesting to define the limits that make it less of a reality. An ever growing community and the limitations of low fees prevent my doing exactly as I like with my time and with the ambitions which we all have for the school. Here I am poised between bureaucracy on the one hand and benevolent despotism on the other - and my emphasis is upon benevolent for I am always grateful to Sir Arthur and our Governing Body, who with their vision and kindly wisdom can bring some life into the valley of dry bones of rules and regulations."

She went on to list the year's many achievements, and to show the life of the school such that a visitor remarked: "The more I get to know the school, the more I am impressed and I feel very glad indeed to be connected with it." Sheaves of correspondence, agenda, minutes and hand-written notes, however, reveal some of the anxieties, crises and hard decisions that Head and Governors, particularly Sir Arthur their Chairman, faced to keep the life of the school so impressive.

* * *

Among the improvements happily announced was mains drainage. It is strange to think that Sunny Hill had survived without this for over half a century. A dip into the thick pile of paper on the topic brings out some interesting letters, starting with one with a whiff of cloak and dagger from Edward Hamilton, the School's engineer, to Sir Arthur Hobhouse, March 5th 1951.

> Dear Sir Arthur,
> As you know, for some considerable time it has been a problem to disperse the effluent from the Boarding House sewage system, and I have for some years, without any really considerable expense, managed to cope with the situation. However, the exceptionally wet summer and winter have now made the position critical. ... I have not approached the Local Authority directly ... as I did not wish to draw too much attention to our predicament.
>
> Since the last Governors' meeting I formulated a plan ... If this matter is freely discussed at a general meeting, the information may be too widely circulated, with possible prejudicial effects. ...
>
> *Yours truly,*
> *Edward Hamilton*

It eventually became clear that the local authority, Wincanton District Council, had plans to bring mains drainage to the area, but was taking its time about it. As an incentive, in 1954 the School offered £700 towards putting in mains sewage for Pitcombe. Sir Arthur backed up the offer with some cogent arguments contained in a letter to Lady Langman, one of the Governors, but given wider circulation:

From letter from Sir Arthur to Lady Langman, 16th July 1954:

... It seems to me that the Authority should accept our figure of £700 for the following reasons:

1. There is a general obligation to provide sewage disposal at a reasonable cost and this matter has been outstanding for a long period of years.

2. There is considerable urgency on public health grounds to carry out a sewage disposal system ...

3. Sunny Hill School is a non profit making institution serving some 150 or more residents, apart from approximately 200 day school dinners, and as a large ratepayer it has a special claim.

4. If a public sewer is not provided now, by reason of the School having to provide its own disposal works, there will be no sewer constructed for other properties requiring connection in the future in the Sunny Hill area.

Sir Arthur ended with a plea to Lady Langman, but it appears that this was not all he was doing:

I hope that if you are present at the Wincanton R. D. C. meeting on the 21st you will put forward these points so that the Council decides on the above arrangements at once.

Before long came this hand written note from Lady Langman dated July 23rd:

My dear Arthur,
Thank you for the useful "priming" but you had lobbied Bully so successfully that he sprang into action and there was no opposition (except a bleat from Wyatt about the rest of Pitcombe being left out) so it slipped through easily and I never had to say a word. I am sure it is much the best solution for the school. .... Now I hope they will hurry up.

That same day Sir Arthur received the official letter from Wincanton Rural District Council accepting the School's offer of £700. The mains sewer was coming none too soon. Vallis and Bird, the school's architects, wrote to Sir Arthur on October 5th.

The effluent ... is leaking out of the bottom of the cesspool and percolating through the earth and discharging at a point in close proximity to the south east corner of the Coronation block. This liquid is obnoxious and is polluting the area around.

* * *

One can imagine the satisfaction with which the Governors heard the news that the problem was finally solved. On the catering side, too, there was much work and worry behind the no doubt traditionally excellent Speech Day tea. Later that year the Housekeeper Mrs. Gaskell-Williams, who began work only in September, within a month seemed unlikely to settle. In December she gave in her notice. She was leaving at Easter. Miss Chappell had no choice but to accept her notice, because there was so much disturbance among the domestic staff. The Cooks evidently thought that they could manage the catering without any direction, and their obstructive behaviour made the Housekeeper's post almost impossible. The truth was that the Cooks did not have the training to cope with catering and costing, but would not face the fact.

The grounds were probably looking their best on Speech Day, but the Caretaker Mr Stone was not contented. During 1955 he kept asking for more perks, more money (an increase to £6.10.0 was authorised on July 6th), and less work. He became slack over the incinerator, and Miss Chappell pulled him up about it. His reaction was to give in his notice. The fact that he had nowhere for his wife and himself to move to must have helped Miss Chappell to persuade him to relent. She was quite sure that he would not stay long, however.

Simmerings among the men began again soon; they came first from Charlie Biesheuvel the Head Gardener who said the post was too big for him and he would want to move. (Fortunately he is still working in the gardens today!) The Kitchen Porter - "an honourable, pleasant man" as Miss Chappell described him - made enquiries about his wage from his Union and was told he should be paid above Agricultural Wage. Miss Chappell pointed out to him that the School had no scales except Agricultural for the men and Burnham for academic staff. However she felt she ought to write to the Union Secretary in Oldham. She thought that by subsidising a cottage and providing meals the Porter's package was in fact above the Agricultural Wage level. What with this and that, as Sir Arthur confided to his Vice-chairman, Miss A. K. Daniel in October, "The problem of ordinary staff (domestic and outdoor) is a continual worry."

* * *

In her speech Miss Chappell was able to say, with pride: "Among Old Girls' successes this year special note must be made of the School's first LL. B. obtained by Sylvia Barwick and a number of prizes won by nurses in training at Bath and Weymouth Hospitals - Ann Buffett, Phyllis Catley, Megan Sharp and Christine Chatfield. At Barts., Lorna Gilson came 1st of her group and 2nd of her year in the first examination. Gilliam Hobbs obtained her Horticultural Diploma at the end of the year as Head Student of Studley. Isobel Mildon has been elected Senior Student of St. Mary's, Cheltenham." Academic successes, though, were not achieved without more anxiety behind the scenes, over providing staff to teach and classrooms to teach in.

That year some long serving staff left. First, Miss Wilson, who had arrived to teach French in 1942, and had become 'an institution'; Wendy Edwards, the Gleam editor, asked the girls: "Stop and imagine, if you can, Sunny Hill without Miss Wilson. In almost every sphere she could advise. Her versatile personality will be sadly missed." And then Miss Vinall, Senior English Mistress and Librarian since 1941. Her health had been failing and her nerves overstrained. She took a month of complete rest, and this restored her temporarily. When she came back she was given a lighter load, but a spinal operation some years before had weakened her and she took the decision to resign, long before retirement age, and to teach near her home in Lewes. Her name lives on at the School in the Vinall Library Award. Miss Chappell knew her value and told the Governors, "This will be a difficult post to fill."

In a year when Sunny Hill joined with King's to sing Bach's St. Matthew Passion, perhaps the greatest work ever written, the musical life of the school seemed to flourish. Then Mrs. Davies the Head of Music found the post too strenuous and the school too large. She began to ask for concessions - seven fewer periods of teaching and exam work each week. This would either have been detrimental to the music of the school or penalised her colleagues. Before the October half term Miss Chappell offered her some minor adjustments, but it came down to a demand for 7 more free periods or resignation. She resigned at half term. Her post was advertised at once, but only one woman appeared worth an interview, and she turned out unsuitable. The Head was forced to appoint a man. Lewis Leslie was excellently qualified with suitable experience, and in fact turned out to be a gentle and excellent Head of Music, and a composer who dared to make his own setting of The Gleam; but as a man he could not do boarding duties, and so was not seen as the ideal staff member at that time.

This may be the point to reveal the sacking of a Classics teacher a few years earlier. A selection of letters, with the teacher's name changed, tell the story:

Somerset
4. xii. 49

Dear Arthur,
Lady Langman and I saw Miss Eastman at Sunnyhill yesterday as requested by the Governors. You may remember that she is the non-resident Classics mistress who

had not fallen in with the arrangements for non-resident staff sharing some of the resident staff's duties for prep, walks etc. and had appealed to the Governors ... She has a home to keep for her mother but I don't think the work is beyond her. We did not like her attitude which is definitely non-cooperative and we feel she should be got rid of as her influence cannot be good for School or Staff. She will not resign ...

A. K. Daniel

North Cadbury Court
Yeovil
Somerset
Dec. 7

Dear Arthur,

I quite agree with everything Katherine Daniel has said about our interview with Miss Eastman. Her attitude reminded me more of a shop steward than a teacher of the young idea. It all boiled down to her choosing to say that Miss Wells in her description of the one term weekend gave the hours as $1\frac{1}{2}$ - 2 and Miss E insists that that is the total hours, to include 1 prep and 2 walks! I pointed out that anyone intelligent could see that $\frac{1}{2}$ hour prep, $\frac{1}{2}$ hour walk on Sat and again Sunday would have been an absurdity, but she said that was what Miss Wells had said and that was all she had agreed to do! an impossible woman and I thought not quite sane on the point. I think she is a dangerous woman and we ought to be careful how she is dismissed but she must go.

Eliann Langman

The Glen
Bruton 18.3.50

Ladies and Gentlemen,

I have received, in your name, a notice of dismissal from the Staff of Sunny Hill School at the end of this term, March 31st. No reason has been given.

As no assistant mistress can be dismissed without a stated cause, I wish to know the reason for your action, and to claim my right to a hearing before the whole body of Governors in order to answer any charges you may have to make against me.

Yours faithfully,
Daisy M. Eastman.

She was interviewed 11 a.m. May 12th, but, according to The Gleam, had left at the end of the Spring Term.

*   *   *

Getting the right teachers, and enough of them, was a continual headache. Finding teaching rooms was difficult, too. Ideally, girls should have been in sets for French in more junior forms, but there were no teaching rooms. Cookery and needlework classes had to be taught together. In fact the Headmistress reckoned that a point of saturation had been reached, because there were no extra rooms for sets and insufficient large rooms to carry more large forms. Numbers of pupils were increasing - there would be over 50 in the Sixth Form the next year - and the need for extra rooms, and if possible extra staff, was urgent.

To add to the worries, that summer there was a heat wave, during which the school's water supply failed five times. A call to the authorities found that the reservoir was at full level and the pressure up. This meant that the school storage tanks were not filling. The worst failure occurred on the Friday before Speech Day when there was no bath water available even for the youngest girls who went first to bed at 7.40 p.m. There had been no undue drawing off of water that day. It could only mean that the supply pipe to the school was furred up and inadequate.

*   *   *

Of such anxieties, apart from the water failures, the girls were almost completely unaware; which is as it should be. A Fifth Former, Angela Kemp, could experience the surroundings of the school as if all worked without effort, and could write vividly of a moment to remember:

> A red glow seemed to fill the sky, as I came up Sunfield Lane, touching the edges of the small clouds with gold, and turning the sky pale mauve. The Tor stood out, dark against the sky, and far away. Then a sharp wind blew up and hurried the pink tinged clouds away, replacing them with angry black ones, while the sun sank, and all its glory with it.

*   *   *

Above: New House, built in 1957 as an extension to the Sanatorium
Below: The hut built beside the path from Cole. It housed two classes,
and the space under its lower end was used by girls for smoking.

Chapter 17

"Uncommonly Together"

The years 1956 to 1960 were full of changes for the school as for the country. Among the topics for debate by the Inter-Schools Discussion Group, a forum for seniors of the three Bruton schools at one time chaired by Ned Sherrin, was this, in November 1957: "That town councils are justified in banning the film 'Rock around the Clock'". It was defeated, and the rock 'n' roll era came to Sunny Hill, welcomed, quizzically, by Josephine Willy of 6H A as follows:

> A flurry of legs
> and flying skirts,
> a breathless mob
> of teenage
> humanity, moving
> in an agony of
> motion;
> frenzied jerking to
> the strident
> chords of jiving jazzmen;
> minds immobile, tense,
> bodies whirling to the
> rhythm of
> discordant sounds,
> jarring notes
> crashing through space
> into oblivion.
> Sudden silence.
> A void
> to be filled -
> - by what?
> Is there an answer?

Classical music was also very much alive. 1957 saw the first Bruton Subscription Concerts with distinguished musicians such as Gervase de Peyer (clarinet), Gerald Moore, the famous accompanist, the London Singers, a string Quartet and Frederick Grinke playing a Stradivarius violin. "These concerts," it was reported, "were so successful that they are to be continued next season." They were in fact still going strong in the 1990s.

More controversially, Mr Leslie, the Music Director and one of three male members of staff, showed his intrepidity in writing a new setting for 'The Gleam', a strange and difficult composition "which brings out the meaning" a kind critic wrote, "of Tennyson's legendary poem in a fuller sense." The Old Girls found it interesting to hear both versions at their 1957 Summer Reunion. The ensuing discussion was lively. By the following year The Gleam reported: "M. Leslie's sensitive resetting and Composition of the School Song, which is more in keeping with the feeling of the age, is valuable to us, not only in itself but also because it has stirred up a slight controversy, as a break from custom usually does. The world may abound in Angry Young Men but there seems to be a singular lack of Angry Young Women, at Sunny Hill, at any rate on paper." The 1958 'Gleam' was sung at Speech Day for the first time, to varying reactions.

To complete this particular story we may mention two further settings, one by Christopher Welling in 1975 written for the Third Jubilee, a businesslike and easily singable version, perhaps more suitable for the full roar of a boys' school, and the latest by Jonathan Palmer, eminently fitted to girls' voices and very popular with those who have grown up with it. The author has heard girls sing it spontaneously on an ancient Roman stage in Pompeii and in the great Greek theatre of Epidaurus, despite protests by an officious custodian.

✳   ✳   ✳

Once again the school was outgrowing its buildings - there were 400 pupils by 1959 - and the Head and Governors kept their eyes open for local buildings which could be acquired and adapted. Pitcombe School had closed, and the building was considered in 1956, first as dormitory accommodation and then as a preparatory department. On 28th March 1957, however, Sir Arthur wrote to Miss Chappell: "Concerning the old Pitcombe School, I think that now it is unlikely that we can regard it as a possible preparatory department, as the Pitcombe Trustees have arranged to sell the Old School for conversion to a dwelling house."

In 1956 Sir Arthur and Miss Chappell, with the Vicar, Mr. Ashcroft's consent, had inspected the Pitcombe Vicarage to see if, should that building come on the market, there was a possibility that it could be used as a subsidiary Boarding House. They reported that " it appeared, that with some extension, it could be converted to accommodate 30 to 35 Boarders."

Meanwhile the Sanatorium was to be extended to make what was to be called New House. In 1956 schemes costing £4,500 and then £3,500 were considered, and the 1957 Gleam welcomed the first signs of action: "It was an exciting moment to see the site of New House pegged out and the huts appear, with a view to occupation in September. This provides 34 extra beds and 3 staff rooms and will enable boarding to continue to develop a little further."

When the building was completed on time, the first residents were overjoyed. Two Sixth Formers, Jennifer Shearn and Susan Orledge, wrote:

"Of course we had seen the foundations of the new boarding house before we left the familiar dark-brown-corridored old building for the Summer holidays, but little did we dream to what sumptuous splendour we were chosen to return. We had hardly arrived before an excited babble of voices informed us that we were 'over at New House'; little did we imagine how new it was!

"We stood bewildered in the spacious pillared hall, with its neon lighting and its ticking clock. Bewildered and awed we climbed the steep stairs and opened our door; gay red contemporary curtains, light oak furniture, built-in wardrobe and sink, soft bedside mats, thick beige counterpanes -'Oh it must be a staff room'; but no, it was ours for the whole year. We heard shrieks and exclamations of delight from the other new rooms, each with its own colour-scheme and design. The glory in which we sleep is rivalled by the glory in which we wash. Downstairs, white basins and baths gleamed in separate cubicles, blue-towelling curtains hung at the window and shelves of mugs stood erect in regimental order. Not only are the house and furniture new, but also, in a sense, the scenery, for the wide windows are a vantage point from which the familiar countryside takes on an unfamiliar appearance."

Contrast the report presented to the Quantity Surveyor:

SUNNY HILL SCHOOL NEW DORMITORIES
General Conclusions

It has not been a comfortable job for either the Chairman or Headmistress or Architect, but it has been completed just in time for school term without any major mistake and with, it is hoped, not a large extra expense.

1.   The major reasons for our difficulties in carrying out this building were, it seems to me,

(a) Insufficient time for overall planning in advance of letting contract.

(b) The large number of p.c. items in contract (40%) which required more time for planning before subcontracts.

(c) Amount and variety of built-in furniture which required still more time to design before ordering.

2.   Variations in overall plan did not delay the Contractor as they were limited substantially to early alterations in structure (e.g. adding to depth of entrance hall and insertion of 4 windows in frontage to School) which were decided well ahead of actual work.

3.   Completion time has been over run by 7 to 8 weeks, and neither the weather nor building variations nor overall instructions can really be pleaded by Contractor. There was a period, roughly mid-May and June, when with extremely good building weather progress was slow (whether due to insufficient labour allowed on site or insufficient supervision or both).

New House was dedicated by Bishop Fabian Jackson, accompanied by the Vicar and the Rev. Owen Williams, of Brewham, on 9th December 1957, a cold but fine day.

The rising of New House demanded new resident house and domestic staff. Miss Butters became Assistant House mistress and Mrs. Barker was welcomed back to Sunny Hill "to turn her capable and willing hands to anything needed. Her brother, Mr Farrow, and his wife are our joint caretakers."

✳   ✳   ✳

Meanwhile the school was weathering something of a financial crisis. Two letters from Enid Chappell to Sir Arthur Hobhouse throw light both on the problems and on the Head's hard work and grasp of facts. The second shows also her selfless commitment to the school's well-being. The author's comments are in square brackets.

~ "Uncommonly Together" ~

Dear Sir Arthur,

Last night [she probably means literally all night!] I spent with the accounts and have some observations which I will enclose though you asked me not to go into detail. [There follows a long detailed letter] In principle I feel we have not taken fully into account 1. The real implications of Burnham [4 subsections follow]; 2. the new tariffs in gas and electricity; 3. the general rise in living costs which were not covered in our last boarding rise; 4. the effects of new rates in postage, wires and phones. I will add some notes.

At present showing I am about seven Boarders up for September but I am still waiting for final County decisions.

Yours sincerely,
Enid L. Chappell

NOTES ON ESTIMATES

Boarding

a.   I cannot keep up the figure of 130 without some risk in overcrowding and in taking toll of present House and Domestic staffing.

b.   In expanding boarding, a 4th Matron becomes immediately necessary and later an assistant House Mistress. The present boarding arrangements must improve to attract i.e. more must now be spent upon dormitory furniture - rugs, curtains etc. It is light and airy but very shabby. Washing and cloakroom accommodation must be considered also sitting room space.

c.   It is doubtful whether the boarding figure now leaves much margin. School dinners at 1/6 (except on the cheese day) probably now need a further review.

[Then many detailed comments about work needed about the school, including:]
Staffing ratio is still low for

1.   size of forms which demand more divisioning

2.   boarding expansion

Domestic Science: either some cookery must be cut out or divisioning begin owing to limits of cooking space.

Science: Chemistry with some Biology needed in 1957

Music: Healthy but consequent expansion of work through created interest, therefore more than time of our music staff must be included for general staffing costs. 3 full time salaries… 1 full time visiting covered by fees; 2 part time covered by fees.

[Then repairs, grounds, games, printing, advertising, postage, laundry, fuel, light and cleaning, with detailed quarterly bills.]

Miss Chappell to Sir Arthur November 1st 1956

It will be a difficult financial year for me as I feel that we are not meeting the rising cost of living on the Boarding side - school dinners and laundry probably show a deficit, the school is considerably understaffed, the salaries of House Staff must be considered in April, there is considerable internal capital expenditure to face. I think possibly this term may be the most difficult for making both ends meet.

In these circumstances, though I am enclosing the salary figure for the day school head of a comparable school which you kindly asked me to assess, it would help the School not to consider any salary increase for me at this point. It would be my contribution to a difficult situation.

*   *   *

Among the able and perceptive Governors during this period was Brigadier Cazenove, who had asked to be shown the school in action when first appointed, and who in February 1958 felt ready to share his concerns about school academic policy with the Chairman. An edited version follows:

My dear Hobhouse,

For a long time now, I have felt concern about the academic side of Sunny Hill. Basically the trouble is classes which are far too big. This is accentuated by the teaching staff not being very hot stuff. People pay for their children's education in order that they should be taught something and unless the teaching is good, fee-paying pupils will inevitably dry up and Sunny Hill will be left high and dry. I defy anyone to teach properly classes of 30 pupils. The bright ones will get along all right, but the slower ones are bound to get left and it is often the slower ones who, in the end, prove of greatest worth to the community.

For good teaching one must, of course, have adequate class rooms. One must also have adequate staff, both in quantity and quality; and if one is to have adequate staff in a rural area like Bruton, one has to look after them especially well. I rather suspect that we all ought to have a good think about the general policy before going much further.

Yours sincerely,
Arnold Cazenove

Sir Arthur passed this letter to another Governor, Ian Michael, for his comments, and received the following (also edited):

Dear Sir Arthur,

I see the force of Cazenove's objections: there is truth in what he says, but it is not, I think, seen in the right proportions. My agreement with him does not go far enough to make me doubt that our present policy is substantially correct.

Cazenove is taking as his standard, I assume, the middle range of girls' public schools - places such as Clifton, the Godolphin, the Royal School, to name only those I know. By their standard he is failing to do justice to our very low fees. My daughter at Clifton is in a class of 29 or 30, and is paying day fees of £35 a term - a difference of 40% above Sunny Hill day fee. Much of the teaching she gets is, from the little I have seen, no better than that at Sunny Hill.

I would say that Cazenove is right in saying that the quality of the Sunnyhill staff should be better, but unrealistic in expecting it for the fees he is paying. I think, too, of course, that he is wrong in taking the standard he seems to. As I understand the development of Sunny Hill, with its tradition of service to a locality and its emphasis on keeping its fees low, the standard to take is that of a local authority grammar school. In fact we can only keep Sunny Hill what it is by running the school on a comparable budget with a maintained school and giving as good, and better, value. If we raise the fees out of all comparison with the costs of a maintained school we shall merely be one more 'private' girls' school, too expensive for all but a few, and not expensive enough to provide an academic and cultural education of the very highest quality. Sunny Hill's strength lies in its being, in a small way, a pattern of what may happen in the future; it is forward looking. The 'private' school is entirely backward looking, and has, I think, no future.

I think Miss Chappell has raised, and is continuing to raise, the academic standard of the school. She might be helped to enliven the staff in only two ways that I can see: by any of us who can keeping an eye on possible recruits of good quality, and attracting them to Sunny Hill when a suitable vacancy occurs. The other possible way (and it would be very difficult to suggest in a way acceptable to an already hardworking staff) is some kind of staff forum, discussion group, reading party or suchlike, which would enable intellectual interests to be shared and maintained. But the further education of her staff is a formidable task for any headmistress, and even more so for the governors!

Sincerely,
Ian Michael

There follows a comparison with other girls' schools, including:

1. Compares favourably with other fee paying Girls' Schools, certainly after the relative fees are taken into account.
2. Is at least equal to the average maintained grammar school in the County.
3. Has a definite value in combining the girls from the neighbourhood with daughters of parents who have not wished (or have not been able, e.g. abroad) to use the local authority primary and secondary schooling.
4. By reason of the latter intake it is valuable in combining the children from a diversity of homes which many people believe is a great advantage under modern conditions.
5. By combining boarders (150) with day girls (250) it has sufficient numbers for an up to date efficient secondary day school situate in the heart of the country.

Two Sixth Formers, Diana Finlayson and Angela Kemp, saw the academic process is their own way, and in the metre of 'Hiawatha.'

> Thus the old decrepit sages
> Nursed the tender seeds of learning,
> Taught them to the little pupils,
> Sitting, deep in concentration,
> Safely bound with regulations.

*   *   *

Miss Chappell's 1959 Speech Day report goes some way to show how she was indeed raising the academic standard:

"On the academic side, 14 Advanced Level Courses are now launched. The Science of the School develops on sound lines and it was interesting to see at the front laboratory bench one day, future doctor, dentist, and pharmacist, and behind them a potential psychologist and physiologist. [They had all won university places in these subjects.] 25 girls took our Advanced Courses and 18 reached Scholarship Level in 12. On the Arts side, History, English and Divinity are the favourites. Susan Wright did outstandingly well in English: she was high on the waiting list for Somerville, Oxford, but has accepted a definite place in English at Bedford College, London. To show how exhausting these blue ribbon examinations are, Susan spent $74\frac{1}{2}$ hours upon them. 6 County Major Scholarships have been taken up this year."

Extramural cultural activities included an Italian trip, to Rome, Naples, Milan, Pompeii and Capri.

That same year a poem underlined the strain which some students could feel under the pressure for academic excellence. This was one entry in a poetry competition instigated by Principal Murray, speaker for Speech Day 1959. This proved to be a 'Psychological Stunt' according to one person, a 'penetrating study' according to another. The scripts were confined to his dustbin after the results were announced. Not all the girl competitors could remember their poems, but fortunately Pauline Atkins did:

THE SCHOOL DAY

Creep from the bed
To the grey tepid water
Crawl into cold hostile garments
And dazedly, hazily register
Consciousness -
Being.
I think we had breakfast -
The eight o'clock pips I remember.
Then creep to the cubicle
Crawling in sleep-twisted blankets
While clambering from pillows
Counterpane covering all
Faintly and drowsily
Wakening.

The calling, compelling, summoning bell
Sings hurry to lessons and learning.
Each bell means less time
And more things to learn,
So let's hurry
Let's read
Let us write, don't lose time.
There is thinking to do,
Reasoning, arguing, defining, suggesting,
Supposing and questioning
Hurry, do!

Lessons have ended
Now study must start
A slow silent plodding through work,
Chalk-coated throat, gym-wearied feet
All must be borne, fought against,
Suffered,
While learning.
At the end I may
Creep into bed,
Still learning.

Murray's comments on this: Very sensitive: nerves perhaps overstrained: vividly original: needs great care.

* * *

The Asian 'flu epidemic in 1957 was memorable, according to Margaret Carter. "The whole of Old House was the sick bay. Teaching staff were recruited to come up and serve meals. I was not allowed into any of the dormitories, but was allowed to stand and serve on the landing, because they were so afraid I would catch it. Matron, Mrs Stell, did not go to bed for about 10 days during the epidemic, except for lying down for a couple of hours when there were others to take over temporarily. She herself went down with the 'flu after the last girl had been discharged. Her generation was tough!"

Miss Chappell reported at the next Speech Day that "school shrank to the dimensions of 1912, and perceptibly as I looked at it each morning at Assembly. It was a nightmare period, I thought one evening when I was dishing out apricot jam in the dim light of the dormitories which had become a vast sickbay, with a sputnik whizzing through space at a furious rate. It is a tribute to Matron's skilled and watchful nursing that we had no complications beyond one pneumonia case, and a sign of her exhaustion that she succumbed herself very reluctantly when the worst was over. Our three nurses planned their mutual [sic] attacks in obliging succession but Miss Dare resisted all the proffered infection and was, as usual, a tower of strength. But the school was not closed for one day. To this major catastrophe we added a bad epidemic of German measles and seven operations and accidents to the staff. There was hardly a day of the Spring term without someone missing." To the governors on 3rd February 1958 Miss Chappell admitted: "The staff are still not completely fit and sick relatives also have sapped their energy and time. When extra invigilation has been needed, there have sometimes been no staff to cope with it."

One girl's jeu d'esprit on this and other school matters is recorded: "And it came to pass, in the reign of Victoria, that, near a town on the river Brue in the west of the island of England, there was built a House of Learning, where maidens could be instructed after the manner of their fathers. And authority sent forth a decree that the maidens should be gathered together in Houses, that every maiden might contribute to the honour of the House, that the best House might gain a trophy and much glory. Miss Coles, the Head of the House, was taken ill and transported to the House of Healing, whence she returned to initiate maidens into the mysteries of Biology and to watch the House play, 'The Tenth Plague of Egypt,' written by the Scribe of the House, a senior maiden of studious disposition and serious mien, who portrayed the sad state of affairs which would ensue if all the teachers were to succumb to the same Mysterious Malady, known as 'X', as the maidens had done that term."

*　　*　　*

To put the crises and worries in perspective, the chapter ends with two assessments of Sunny Hill. The first is a general comment on the school by a long-serving teacher, Miss Allen, writing to Sir Arthur December 9th 1956:

"It is surely significant that in 25 years here I have never had a chance to be bored, because Sunny Hill has always been changing and developing and yet without losing its intrinsic character. From what I know of other schools I realise that we have been particularly fortunate in our Governors and our Headmistresses who have been so sensitive to changing needs and so wise in their adjustments to meet them."

The speaker at the 1959 Speech Day, Dr. John Murray, "who did so much to found Exeter University" wrote to Miss Chappell of his visit to the school:

I got the pleasantest impressions at the prize giving. The children seemed to me uncommonly "together" and happy, and uncommonly intelligent! But the "constituency", all those parents and friends, seemed full of trustful cheerfulness about the School, as well they might be, and the harmony included them. I congratulate you on the happy "burden" of guiding the School.

Ever yours, John Murray

*　　*　　*

Above: School coat of arms, granted in 1960

Right: Wayside, formerly the home of Miss Hayward, was bought as a boarding house in 1961

Below: 1961 building, built as classrooms, laboratories and the gymnasium on the right

Chapter 18

"Another Motto or none at all?"

Miss Chappell was disappointed. The Staff/Parents Association had offered a present to celebrate the Diamond Jubilee of the school in 1960, and she had suggested a Coat of Arms, an idea which the Association at first rejected. Miss Chappell pointed out that the next suitable occasion would be the Centenary, "and few of us will be there to witness that!" In a private letter to Sir Arthur she marshalled her arguments: "I do not look upon the Coat of Arms as something extravagant. All self-respecting schools and institutions have one eventually and I look upon it as a crystallisation of history in a decorative form. I think it is a luxury that may be afforded without our feeling, at this point in the School's history, that we have lost a tape-recorder, stage curtains, or the hundred and one other things that we can gradually acquire but which would not be as lasting a gift as the Coat of Arms."

When the Association was convinced in October 1959, the design was eagerly discussed. Should the motto be in Latin ('sequere scintillam', perhaps)? A note in Sir Arthur's hand dated 27. Jan. 1960: "Miss C. rang. They want a "Coat," e.g. 4 quarters, consisting of (say) Glastonbury Tor, a white pea, Hobhouse crest, and something else." About the motto Miss Chappell wrote "I am not personally fond of "Follow the Gleam" merely because so few people nowadays know Tennyson's poem and understand the full significance of it." Sir Arthur annotated this letter: "30.1.60 Telephoned H. M. quite agree but try for another motto or none at all." Shortly after this, however, Miss Chappell wrote again: "5th February 1960: I find there is very strong School support for 'Follow the Gleam'." So it stayed.

It was Sir Arthur who in May 1960 found a place for the Tor: "a stylised emblem of Glastonbury Tor, either on a panel, as the cross is now, or better still just on the shield below the rising sun." With this and other suggestions, the project was handed over to the experts, and on 14th June Anthony R. Wagner, Esq., C. V. O. D. Litt, Richmond Herald, could write to Sir Arthur: "I am glad to have your approval of the design and will now put it forward for the preparation of the Patent of Arms." It was just in time for Speech Day, when the chairman of the Parent Staff Association, Mr. Matthews, presented the new Coat of Arms for the School to the Chairman of the Governors.

Brigadier Cazenove remarked in February 1959 to Sir Arthur, "I suppose we cannot find a new name for the School? Its present name militates against it!" The new name was not long in coming. A new Scheme (under section 18 of the Charities Act 1960) was sealed on 16th January 1961, which introduced the official name Bruton School for Girls. It set down the composition of the Governing Body as consisting of four appointed by the Visitors of the Hospital of Hugh Sexey, Esquire, four by Somerset County Council, two by the Senate of the University of Bristol, and one by the Bruton Parish Council. In addition there were to be four co-optative governors, to be appointed by resolution of the governors. No member of the teaching staff of the School was to be a Governor.

The new Scheme also provided that 'There shall be a Head Mistress' (not a head master, be it noted) and assistant mistresses or masters. This was to recognise the foothold that men were gaining on the staff. In 1960 not only was Lewis Leslie Head of Music, but Mr Fiori was a popular violin teacher. The following year the 28 full-time assistants, though still called Assistant Mistresses, included two men, Mr Leslie, and Mr W Trewartha to teach Chemistry and Physics.

Variations in fees would not in future need the Minister of Education's approval, and Elmfield, the field used by Sexey's for Cricket and Sunny Hill for Hockey, was now held by trustees jointly.

*　*　*

Buildings great and small were planned and erected, and existing buildings improved. School numbers totalled 400, including 175 full boarders, 9 weekly boarders and 216 day girls. By 1962 they included girls from Nigeria, Pakistan, India, Malaya and China. The boarding accommodation was extremely crowded, but at least it was becoming less dull. In 1960 a House reported "The Old House 'brighter dormitory movement' continues and Dormitory Ix has scarlet linoleum, pale yellow rugs and bedspreads, grey beds and Heal's yellow and grey stalactite wardrobe curtains. There is a glow of bright colour emerging and we hope that it may continue into Dormitory I."

Two timber classrooms - popularly known as "the huts" - were put up in 1958 and proved "an invaluable acquisition to the Day School." They stood near the present Science Building, and in their later years at least provided pupils with the choice of listening to their own teacher or the lesson going on next door, beyond the thin partition. They provided a grandstand view of work on the new and long awaited gym building. The Governors decided to put up not only a gym and changing rooms but also four new classrooms, two Sixth Form studies, general laboratory, Advanced Physics laboratory, workshop and darkroom in what may be called the 1961 Building. Neither this nor the pre-war Day School can be called beautiful, but they served, and continue to serve, a most useful purpose. A later Headmistress commented: "My general overall feeling of Sunny Hill is that it is like a Hardy novel: it just grows out of its environment. Although in physical terms its buildings are an absolute blot on the landscape, yet in spite of that the landscape accepts it."

In 1961 Wayside, a bungalow across the road from Old House, was bought, with the fringe land, after the departure for Bruton of Miss Hayward, who had given long service as secretary of the School. Conversion into a small boarding house began immediately under the guidance of the recently appointed Bursar, Major Hugh Fraser. It was ready, beautifully converted for 14 boarders, when the autumn term began.

At the same time the school began to furnish a Needlework Room and to plan a Junior Department in the Old Gym, with a playroom for the Juniors and space to house uniform stocks to relieve the Third Year Sixth Form study.

In 1962 pressure of boarding numbers led the Governors to take over a wing of Hadspen House, the Chairman's residence. Buses ferried girls to and fro. Governors' minutes reveal the thinking behind the move: "In reaching this decision they had considered the necessity to relieve the pressure in the main boarding house and also that the use of the extra accommodation would enable the Governors to test whether the present increased demand for boarding places would continue before spending a large amount of capital in building a fresh boarding house." Lady Langman was frank about their dilemma: "About the Sunny Hill plan I'm so frightened of more <u>capital</u> expense till we have paid off the huge debt on new buildings, and I feel more boarders would make huge expense in kitchen and dining room at Sunny Hill imperative! I do think the boarders at present at Sunny Hill are very overcrowded but if they were scattered about and not extra ones, there would be no extra income!"

Hard upon buildings came the rounding off of the frontage land of the school and the clearing away of the old vegetable acreage and its levelling for a second hockey pitch.

* * *

School television, introduced in time for the wedding of Princess Margaret in May 1960 proved a boon. Girls watched 'An Age of Kings' and Science broadcasts. By

1961 the prospectus could boast that "The School has its own wireless installations and television set, cine projector, film strip projector, epidiascope, and electric kiln." A tape recorder was next on the list of technical wants and was bought through the efforts of the Third Year Sixth in 1962. Further off was the hope for a swimming pool. Swimming had become possible for boarders at the Frome Swimming Baths, but the School longed for a swimming bath of its own. A site was chosen in 1961 and subscriptions began coming in. A pupil at the time felt that "We were for ever saving up for the swimming pool and the new gym. The proceeds from all our activities went to that fund. It would have been lovely if the swimming pool had been there in our time."

Proper equipment was essential for the enlarged pupil body. The proportion staying on in the Sixth Form was 72 per cent, far higher than the average for other schools. In 1960 a Sixth Form of 92 was launched. By 1962 there was a Third Year Sixth of seven girls, who were allowed to abandon school uniform. Science teachers were waiting for labs, and meanwhile Sexey's, in the person of Mr. Everett, helped with the teaching of science.

The moral and spiritual life of the school was not neglected. In 1960, for instance, a new cup for public spirit, determined by a vote of the Staff, was presented by Mrs. Alexander. 16 girls were confirmed in 1960, 20 in 1961; the Student Christian Movement and Bible Study Group met in the dinner hour on Thursdays; a conference of Sixth Forms was held in July; two groups of girls attended Quiet Weekends at Warminster Theological College; the School Captains attended the Diocesan Weekend at the Glastonbury Retreat House; there were Boarders' Services, Lent addresses in Bruton Church, and flourishing Scripture Union and Bible Reading Fellowship membership. The Gideons gave testaments for first time. The school had collected £1,500 for charities in the last ten years. They had also purchased a guide dog for the blind.

The link with Leer continued with exchange visits. On her return one girl wrote: "We became acquainted with many fresh things, including black bread, various types of sausage and bicycles which one cannot pedal backwards. I also tasted for the first time 'flaumen kuchen,' otherwise known as plum cake; it really is unique and absolutely delicious. On my first evening I was taken to hear the local band play in honour of the 'Schutzenfest.' This is an annual shooting festival. The entire town had turned out to see the spectacle, which also included some fireworks.

"Discipline here is considerably slacker than at Sunny Hill, and there seemed to be few, if any rules, yet the atmosphere was very friendly and happy."

Margaret Whitmore the following year agreed: "No uniforms are worn in German schools, and there are no lessons after one o'clock. Discipline is less stringent there;

in fact one German girl said that she hated to see our little ones standing so quiet and good! Another noticeable point was our relationship with the members of staff. In Germany it seems the teachers are treated more as sources of information than as friends, and have consequently less influence on character formation than in our own country."

*   *   *

The school's academic life was full and lively. The English Department, for instance, had seven staff, two full time, Mrs Hudson and Miss Pickering teaching 32 periods, and the Head and 4 others part time. Miss Chappell herself taught twelve periods. Her 6th form Scholarship Class studied an outline of critical theory. The syllabus read: "Plato's Republic, Aristotle's Poetics, The Renaissance critics. Elizabethan critics, with special reading of Sydney's 'Apologia for Poetry'; Milton, Preface to Samson Agonistes; Dryden's criticism; Pope's Essay on 'Criticism'; Dr. Johnson's Shakespeare criticism; Wordsworth and Coleridge, Preface to Lyrical Ballads; Shelley's Defence. Some modern critics." This was heady stuff.

Even the less academic 'Sixth Form General Course' had a two year syllabus which included: Art - Twentieth Century - the Modern House including Good and Bad design; History of the English House from Norman times; Contemporary room design, furniture, textiles, sculpture, pottery; Appreciation of sculpture and painting including Klee, Mondrian; Comparison between modern and mediaeval Church architecture. Music - Twentieth Century: Sibelius, Bartok, Stravinsky, Schoenberg, Neilsen, Honneger, Prokofiev, Elgar, Vaughan Williams, Delius, Walton, Britten; Broadcasting - studio technique, stereo, VHF. Mathematics had a practical edge: Maths in the home, commerce, industry, science; Statistics, machines; History of maths, great mathematicians. Geography included: New Zealand, South Africa; Colour bar; The changing pattern of settlement (with a hint of dealing with immigration), Middle East, South America; Nationalism; population problems; Eastern Europe, Communism, Religions. A Sixth Former who had been through this non-examination course would have been well informed and prepared to hold her own in debate on many of the major contemporary issues.

1960 university entrants were Sidonie Bailey (Theology at Nottingham), Pauline Atkins (English at UCL), Christine Hudson (Dentistry at Guy's), Anne McCarthy (German at Bedford College), Celia Warren (English at St. Andrew's) and Linda Parker (History at Exeter). In 1961 the school had its first qualified Aeronautical Engineer (Pat Taylor). In 1962 Miss Chappell could mention "Barbara Woodyatt's 1st Class at University College, and at the universities at present girls are studying pharmacy, dentistry, medicine, botany, theology, philosophy, physiology and psychology, geography, social science, mathematics, physics, English, French, German and Dutch, Music and Architecture."

The Governors were keenly aware of the hardship felt by some families with the increase in fees, and drew up guidelines for allocating bursaries.

(1) Decline applications from parents already receiving assistance from an L. E. A. as it is obviously the latter's responsibility to meet rising fees.

(2) Look after pupils already in the school who are in danger of withdrawal owing to the January 1961 increase in fees. (These were: Day £111 p.a.; Full boarder £297; Weekly boarder £276.)

(3) Look after exceptional cases of key pupils who by reason of their exceptional merits (character, leadership, academic brilliance etc.) should be retained at all costs for the benefit of the School.

(4) Look after local or overseas pupils who have for some reason missed County examination, but who in the view of the H. M. are especially suited for education at S. H. S.

(5) It seems inevitable that with our limited bursary fund, distribution to any one pupil must be moderate so as to spread financial assistance as widely as possible. For example, we cannot afford to give a bursary of £200. [This at a time when one father who applied declared an annual income of £473. 10s. 5d.]

* * *

A letter from Ian Michael, a Governor appointed by Bristol University, to Sir Arthur Hobhouse and dated 27.6.1962, sparked an interesting debate among the Governors. It read:

"I am increasingly disturbed by the rapid turnover of young staff, which must be making some of the teaching in the younger forms very unsatisfactory.

"I am aware of the natural difficulties which apply to girls' boarding schools in the country, but I do think also that there is a further difficulty in the Headmistress's attitude to young teachers: she expects them to be 'dedicated' in the same way which she magnificently exemplifies herself. But this is rather a different situation for a young girl nowadays."

Ian Michael asked for statistics about mistresses, under 30 years of age, appointed in each of the last seven years, and the number of terms each stayed. He continued:

"It is very difficult to get any information about how the staff feels at Sunny Hill. I hardly ever meet them except in the company of the Headmistress, and when I do any kind of direct questioning is obviously improper. My doubts come largely from the Headmistress's own remarks about young mistresses, from students who have spent a term in the school, and from friends who have had a close connection with some one on the staff."

Sir Arthur replied a week later, agreeing that the constant changes of staff were disturbing. The figures requested were hard to obtain. He enclosed a typical letter of resignation which gave no reason but wished much goodwill to the School: I would like to express my warmest thanks to Miss Chappell, through this letter, for her support, kindness and consideration. May I extend this feeling of gratitude to Miss Allen and Miss Haskell who have unstintingly given of their time and patience to help me in all circumstances…. Margaret W Green (Old Girl)

The debate spread, as witness a letter from Katharine Daniel to Sir Arthur dated 8.6.1961:

I am rather concerned about Mr Michael's views as I have a great respect for his judgement as a general rule. About a year ago he mentioned misgivings to me about the relationship between HM and younger members of the staff. I think that as a strong Quaker he feared that she was apt to drive C of E on her staff. I was so disturbed by his criticism that I went to Bristol to discuss the matter with Mr Michael. He appeared to think that students from Bristol found HM very demanding over attendance at Morning Assembly and School Services. I know two members of the regular staff very well, one quite young and the other has been on the staff for several years. The young mistress volunteered her great respect and admiration for Miss C as HM and compared her very favourably with the Head she had previously served under. The other mistress is an RC and definitely resented being asked to attend Morning Assembly. This I consider unreasonable as she agreed to attend Assembly when she accepted the post. I think her attitude has been influenced by the Bishop of Clifton's recent instructions to all RCs. Neither of these members of staff were questioned by me but I led them on to discuss staff relations in general terms. I have made enquiries from two other girls' schools, one town and one country, and gather that the younger members of staff tend to move on after about two years' service. One difficulty that I know Miss Chappell has faced has been the undignified behaviour of some of the students in public places.

Four days later Katharine Daniel wrote again:

I had a chance yesterday to talk to a member of the Gillingham Comprehensive School. She is about 26 or 27 and has been at the school for about two years. She told me that few of the younger members of staff stayed longer than 2 - 3 years. In fact she herself is considering "getting further experience." This interested me, as a mixed school with a number of masters on the staff might seem an attraction to young mistresses.

Naturally none of this became public, but Miss Chappell said in her 1962 Speech Day report:

"Staff changes and shortages take all vision out of planning and the fear of timetable blanks is a real one. Birds of passage bring some enrichment but even swallows stay long enough to launch one brood and prepare a second for flight. If only young teachers would appreciate this parable from Nature."

*　*　*

Any school needs what Miss Chappell called a "nucleus of stability", and in 1960 she could say: "This we have and are very thankful for it in Miss Allen, Miss Haskell, Mrs. Monks and Miss Coles, who between them have given years of service to Sunny Hill." Two years later she had to say farewell to Miss Allen.

"An epoch of the School closes as Miss Allen departs. 32 years of unlimited ungrudging service deserve retirement well earned. As Second Form Mistress, then Sixth Form Mistress, Head of Geography, play producer, Senior Mistress, Deputy Headmistress, she has enriched the school to an incalculable degree. The generosity with which she welcomed me and helped me to settle in 12 years ago I shall always remember with gratitude. Her loyalty as my Deputy, utter dependability, sense of humour and courage, her faith in us all in moments of crisis and difficulty, intractability and awkwardness, her tolerance and unfailing humility, have made a lasting impression. There are some like Miss Allen content to be anchored, creating the stability without which an institution could not afford change."

An unofficial view of Miss Allen comes from Sandra Howe, who came in 1960 as her assistant in the Geography department:

"Miss Allen, Deputy Head, was also Head of Geography, although her degree was not in Geography but from the London School of Economics. She was a real character, a chain-smoking little live wire of a woman, a Quaker and therefore 'beyond the pale' inasmuch as she did not conform. She was quite happy not to conform, and in fact made it her business, almost an act of faith, not to conform!

"She was near retirement when we knew her. The day after my arrival in Woodleaze began with a staff meeting, which, because Miss Chappell was late, took all morning. After a rushed lunch we had to be up in the girls' dormitories from 1.30 p.m. until 7 p.m., without a break for supper, ticking off their items of uniform on a list, and confiscating anything they should not have. At the end of this Miss Allen said to me, 'I expect you'll want to know what you are teaching tomorrow! Knock on my door at 9 p.m.' This was my first job; I had no experience; and I had been up till then told nothing at all. At nine o'clock, having been on the go all day and very tired, knowing that I still had to walk back to Woodleaze, I knocked on Miss Allen's door. 'Come in and sit down,' she said. 'Now, what do you want to know?' 'I should like to know what I am to teach.' 'That's easy. General Geography to the Thirds; Africa, Australia and South America to the Lower Fourths; Upper Fourths, North America and Asia; Lower and Upper Fifth, the O level syllabus. What do you want to do with the Sixth Form? Done monsoon Asia, have you? No? Right, you can do that! Take it in turns,' she said. 'You do the Physical with Lower Sixth,' she said, 'and Regional with Upper Sixth. And then you've got two periods a week doing what you like. That's enough about work, isn't it?' she said. 'Have a cup of coffee!' That was all she told me. I spent the whole of the first week of term dictating notes on the correct use of Best Books, while I prepared the topics!"

Above: The whole school visited Coventry Cathedral;
Below: Prizegiving with Miss Chappell

Chapter 19

Farewell to Miss Chappell

Enid Chappell was feeling her age. In March 1962 she wrote to the Governors: "I do hope that in these last years I shall be able to serve the School adequately. There are things to consolidate but I am sure that great benefit will be derived from a younger Head with energy and vision." It might be interesting to give a few examples of her workload at this time.

The domestic side was a recurring worry. Her report to the Governors on 8th February 1962 looked on the bright side: "Term began easily in spite of the defection of the appointed Housekeeper and her assistant ... I must warn the Governors that our cooking situation is constantly a precarious one and I have patiently to endure a good deal in order to avoid a major crisis." On October 18th that year she reported: "Term began well until tensions appeared which caused us to sacrifice our Cook-Caterer for the new Chef and his wife, even if they themselves may not be long-lived at Sunny Hill in spite of the importation of cat and bagpipes." The help of German girls, who left various careers for the experience of working in England, was much appreciated.

Miss Allen's departure brought new work. In April 1962 Miss Chappell wrote to Sir Arthur: "I think that she is really at the end of her tether and would like to go this year. I am not going to press her to stay." This meant the appointment of a new Deputy, and the choice lay between another teacher (still happily alive and active) and Miss Coles. The other teacher refused, and Miss Chappell wrote: "I am afraid we must respect and accept her decision. I am seeing Miss Coles tonight. She is younger and with greater energy and already runs the external exams and helps me over the timetable, but has the organisation of Science to cope with. She is a rapid worker but would not suffer fools as gladly as Miss Allen." Soon after her appointment, the Head told the Governors: "Miss Coles has entered wholeheartedly into her job and, as I forecast, combines conscientiousness, promptitude, good organising ability and kindliness in her post." In fact Wendy Coles proved an excellent Deputy for many years, continuing to serve under Miss Cumberlege and Miss Thomson.

Two other appointments that Miss Chappell made at this time proved long-lasting. Mrs Diana Biddick came in 1961 as Head of History and stayed until 1983. As for John Howe, it was Miss Allen who suggested that Miss Chappell should see "the young Schoolmaster who has married my Second Geographer!" Enid acknowledged (with a sigh, one imagines): "It will be inevitable to introduce more male teachers. They might make a good pair." On May 9th 1962 the Finance Committee noted: "This might be a happy temporary arrangement." The "temporary arrangement" lasted, happily, until 1998!

The school's Science came of age with Enid's appointment of Mrs Winifred Besly. No longer did girls have to rely on Mr. Everett of Sexey's for their advanced Chemistry teaching, although the Head was glad to acknowledge his great contribution, and to note that "both his last pupils are doing well and going to Queen Mary for Botany and Nottingham for Pharmacy respectively."

Miss Chappell was confident in 1962 that the English department was in safe joint hands: "Mrs Olive and Mrs Waller are good teachers, one untrained, one trained, but with Cambridge and Manchester degrees respectively." They were a learned and well-balanced team. Joan Waller, whose husband became Deputy Head of Sexey's School, encouraged the appreciation and writing of poetry, and Eileen Olive, related by their children's marriage to Winifred Besly, enthusiastically produced drama and left A level English students in no doubt of the correct opinions to have on English literature.

There were more down-to-earth concerns as well. On April 6th 1962 Miss Chappell wrote to Sir Arthur: "Conversion of Lower Garden. The main soil moving task is completed. Final measurement of the playing area will be almost exactly 100 yards by 60 yards. Cost of the project £1,000."

The following month she told the Governors of her phasing out of one of Sunny Hill's most characteristic activities, the weekend crocodile walk, and gave her reasons: "Expeditions this term on Saturdays have been to places of interest like Claverton American Museum and Wookey Hole, and on Sundays the Upper and Lower Fifths have been to the Poldens and Stourton. This means that I have substituted for group walks (which almost invariably included King's boys) organised activity, but we have left the Sixth Form boys and girls to meet unsupervised. I hope that this will be a better way of dealing with the younger adolescents' problems." Surely the times they were a-changin'. The great walkers of the school's early years would have shuddered to read that "The Guides have been on a 12 mile hike which exempted them from their normal Sunday walking owing to sore feet, an indication of a disappearing faculty!"

*   *   *

The demand of other nationalities for English education was increasing. In 1961 Miss Chappell was "very proud to have two Chinese girls from Malaya in the School and a Pakistani girl from East Africa, and would be glad to have three more Malayans and a Nigerian girl in the autumn." In September 1962 new girls included two Persian Muslim sisters, aged 8 and 11, a Punjabi Hindu to study Law in the Sixth Form, the daughter of a Malayan Ambassador, a Muslim, and a Nigerian Roman Catholic, both entering Upper V. Privately Miss Chappell described the Sixth Former as "a very able and delightful girl who obtained Latin in Cambridge Overseas Certificate at Ordinary Level in four months," and commented "We all value this interracial education, though the differing religions and outlooks break the unity of school worship."

Soon, ten girls from Africa and Asia were able to give a concert. Before performing dances and songs from their home lands they gave a parade of their native costumes, "all charming in line and colour, graceful, and much more flattering to dark eyes and complexions than European dress." There were Chinese shepherd songs, an Indian temple dance, a modern Indian dance, and an Indian song, 'In the Universe let there be stars.' Two Nigerian girls sang and mimed *'Iwe Kzko'* — 'Learning' — from which it was evident that learning is as hard a task for Nigerian as for English children. Another African contribution was a song from a pupil recently arrived from Basutoland. Three girls performed a Malayan dance, and one also performed a solo candle dance.

Boarders were concentrated at this time as follows: Old House: 114 + 8 staff plus secretary, housekeeper, caterer, two cooks, student. New House: 51 + 5 staff. Wayside: 14 + 1 Staff. Sunfield: 11 + 2 staff. Mr Salisbury's: 5 weekly boarders.

✳   ✳   ✳

Advanced Level in 1962 showed a pass rate of 86%, with 19 different subjects spread among 37 candidates. The Sunny Hill spirit shines through the comment: "As many were not outstandingly 'academic', this is an interesting revelation of what can be done in continued education." Scholarship Level papers were taken by 16 candidates in 12 subjects with 56% passes. Present day pupils will scarcely believe the Head's remark that "Ordinary Level was taken more light-heartedly, as usual by our girls."

Staff and girls alike bore witness to what the school meant to them. Ann S. Davies wrote a letter of resignation on 17th April 1962 speaking of the "privilege of being on the staff of Sunny Hill. I shall remember with gratitude my three years on the staff, especially Miss Chappell's helpfulness and understanding, and the friendliness of my colleagues. The School has a happy atmosphere which pervades every aspect of its life." Miss Allen the retiring Deputy wrote: "I have been fortunate to have worked in such a pleasant place and with such kind and sympathetic Governors to guide and help me at every turn. It has been very stimulating to be allowed the buildings and staffing to secure our academic progress."

The girls' perspective may have been different, but the message was similar: "I have been at Sunny Hill for seven years and leave next week with great regret. I will always appreciate my years at school. My two years in the 6th form have been a most rewarding experience, never to be forgotten." And from another leaver: "I have spent 7 happy years at Sunny Hill. If I am fortunate enough to obtain a place at St. Andrew's University for Mathematics in October, this will be my last year. If however I am unlucky, I will be joining the band of the Third Year Sixth. I feel that Sunny Hill has done much for me and I know that no door has remained closed to me while I have been there."

Lest we become too solemn, however, here are other recollections from around this time, from Anthea Cox (later Mrs Yelling, now Mrs Bell):

"When I was in the 4th form three friends and I decided that we could stand school no longer, and that we would head for Glastonbury, where I was sure my father would pick us up. We had walked nearly as far as Castle Cary Railway Station when we realised that it was a foolish enterprise, and tore back to school. I cannot remember what happened to us when we got back.

"We used to play April Fool jokes on the staff, for instance sticking their breakfast plates to the tablecloth with glue, and tying their chair leg to the table. We were always having midnight feasts, getting the day girls to supply some of the food. I seem from my reports to have been polite, quietly helpful and cheerful, but after lights out things were different: 'Anthea must learn that when the lights out bell goes she must be silent and remain in her bed.' The lights out bell seemed to be a signal: 'Come on girls, out you get!' We were the naughtiest dormitory. There were bars for curtains round our beds, but no curtains. We used to perform gymnastics on the bars. My friend used often to break the springs of her bed, and her parents would receive bills for their replacement. I once fell and cracked my head on the corner of my chest of drawers, for which I was marched down to Miss Chappell. We went scrumping apples at Pitcombe or Wyke Champflower.

"My friend Chris wore a plate with false teeth. She had forgotten to take them out one night, and was sick, and lost the plate down the loo. Mr Biesheuval lifted up some manhole covers to catch the false teeth, and they were found! She was ever indebted to him for her false teeth."

*   *   *

As Miss Chappell neared retirement, Sir Arthur Hobhouse was compelled to offer his resignation from the Chairmanship of the Governing body on account of ill-health. We have already noted his great energy and abilities. He had directed the affairs of the School since March 1936 and had been a member of the Governing Body since 1930. Tributes paid at the time claim what a study of his correspondence bears out, that he combined a large vision with close attention to detail. Lady Hobhouse "gave the impression of Eleanor Roosevelt, tall and spare and windswept," according to Sandra Howe. We may allow Anthea Cox to add: "Lady Hobhouse's petticoats were always showing. Instead of saying to each other 'Your petticoat is showing' we would say 'You're Hobhousing!'" When Sandra attended her first Speech Day in the hall, "There was a strong draught across the stage, and I wondered where I had come to. Half way through the proceedings Lady Hobhouse got up from her chair, announced 'I can't stand this any longer,' and wrapped herself in one of the velvet curtains before taking her seat again." Both Sir Arthur and Lady Hobhouse died in 1966.

Miss Katherine Daniel, who had recently been awarded an MBE, took over the Chairmanship, and served from 1963 to 1971. On her retirement Desirée Cumberlege traced her interesting life:

"She was one of the VADs of the First World War who used to work long hours and, when not actually nursing, would read to the soldier patients, help them to write their letters, teach them or play with them the games which helped to relieve their minds a little of the pain and anxiety of their situation.

"After the war she became one of the first woman farmers who worked their way into that position by sheer effort. She used to drive a milk float and with it supply all the milk for the schools within about a ten mile radius of here - including Sunny Hill.

"She was a member of the resettlement board that helped establish returning soldiers who wished to farm with a smallholding and very small government grant, and she has the phenomenal memory for names and faces that often seems to go with a life of cheerful and devoted service.

"She used to own one of the earliest bull-nosed Morris cars which she worked as hard as she worked herself, and I have heard tales from Castle Cary residents of summer holiday children's outings to the sea on a borrowed wagon being passed by Miss Daniel's Morris, straining every metallic muscle to get up speed to pass, but doing so with a courteous regard for the horse drawing the wagon."

The school was still in good hands.

* * *

So Enid Chappell came to retirement in the summer of 1964. She had seen the swimming pool finally opened in June 1963, and summed up some recent achievements and her hopes like this:

"The second Guide Dog for the Blind is nearing its realisation, the Lilian Ruth Willis Memorial Fund for Multiple Sclerosis relief and research is well established and an additional £50 for the Peckham United Girls' Schools' Settlement guaranteed. For ourselves the physical education facilities have reached fruition this year. The Swimming Pool declared officially open on Speech Day, and the Badminton Court marked out on the superb Gym Floor give further opportunities for physical activity. Now we must aim at the establishment of a Chapel Fund so that there may be in the heart of the school a place of withdrawal for quiet thought and prayer without which no human service or activity can thrive or find true and full expression"

It must have grieved her that about this time the revived Debating Society voted in favour of the motion "That the Ten Commandments are outdated," even though another, "That all schools should be co-educational," was defeated.

Arising from her Christian conviction came the great school expedition to the new Coventry Cathedral. An enthusiastic scribe wrote:

"The first school pilgrimage to Coventry by special train, taking about 470 from Cole Station straight to Coventry and back, was a remarkably inspiring experience for us all. From the gathering in the ruins of the old Cathedral for prayers led by an American pastor, to the cups of tea provided by the members of an International Conference, great friendliness was extended to us. We were particularly grateful to the Staff and parents who accompanied us and to Major Fraser for his efficient courier work on the day and to Miss Coles for the organisation of the party groups and leaders. The steady procession of extremely well-behaved boys and girls and the special police at all the crossings and the white-coated railway official, the Station Master greeting us in bowler hat, made an impressive sight. Everyone did exactly as told and British Railways were at their best. As the train came in dead on time, after a glorious summer day, Cole Station with all the gleaming car lights looked a veritable Piccadilly Circus. Coventry and Surrey newspapers, however, took more interest in this unique expedition than our Somerset local press. The letter in a Surrey paper was headed: 'Beeching at his best.'"

Margaret Carter as School Secretary had a different viewpoint: "I had to stay behind to 'mind the shop,' but I organised the whole trip. I went down with a bucket of whitewash early in the morning and marked out bays in the car park, so that everybody knew which coach they were to travel in. When the train arrived, everyone filed on to the train, and as the train departed I sank back exhausted. But it was a great experience for them."

Miss Chappell could look back on lighter moments.

"Among the incidents that occurred during my years at Sunny Hill - an occasional straying child or animal to chase, a professional burglar's visit (when the boarders did not, in Angela Brazil fashion, lock him in a grandfather clock until the police came), pleasant conversations with Teddy Boys in my drawing room and unpleasant conversations with trespassers in the grounds, night visitors to chase, confiscations of prospective dormitory feasts and more unpalatable literature, April First addicts to be outwitted, other practical jokers to be unmasked. I remember four particularly well: the incident of the 'time-bomb' about to explode in a laboratory, which proved to be myriads of flies buzzing away after swarming on the warmed West wall of the Day School and gently insinuating themselves through every crack and chink; a ray of light from a crack of the door under the stage on one dark winter night - not midnight burglars but four small girls in dressing gowns playing a silent game of cards by the light of their torches; the discovery of a shrouded, white rabbit, whose funeral had been forgotten in the excitement of nearing holidays; and the finding of a phial marked 'Arsenic poison', wrapped in a handkerchief in the music corridor which proved, after laboratory and dispensary testing, to be Syrup of Figs.

"Things have disappeared as mysteriously as things have been found. There is not much hidden romance in a 1900 school, but we need our wits about us. We expect exciting ammonites of all sizes close to the surface of our site. I knew where to find in the girls' gardens the vigorous opening polyanthuses which disappeared from the Head Gardener's rockery and my own trowel put down when I crossed the lawn back to the insistent telephone, but where did my cache of hidden treasure come from - a 2s. piece, 2 shillings, 10 sixpences, 3 threepenny bits and 1 penny - carefully buried near the school gate?

"The girl who once twisted the dessert spoon handles used her brilliant mind for a First Class in her degree, the girl who slept uncomfortably in a bath for a dare, is now a good teacher of Mathematics, the girl who downed the Staff by banging on the corrugated roof of the bicycle sheds is now a capable and selfless nurse."

Miss Chappell grew serious:

"We had tense experiences together, too - the polio epidemic of 1953, the bilharzia of Joan Brewster, the victimisation of Asian 'flu, a sudden run of appendicitis (five cases in a fortnight), the mental breakdown of a member of Staff and then of a Sixth Former, the great freeze up of 1961-62 [sic - in fact 1962-3].

"It was necessary for survival, and in the retention of a close link with the State system, to develop our academic strength. Our Advanced Level work has grown beyond recognition. During this period 73 girls have gone on to University and taken, or are taking, degrees in English, History, French, German, Dutch, Scandinavian languages, Psychology, Sociology, Mathematics, Aeronautical Engineering, Anatomy, Medicine, Dentistry, Pharmacy, Law, Divinity, Fine Art, Archaeology, Architecture, Physics, Botany, Zoology, Geography. Three girls have obtained First Class Honours and there have been several 2.1 degrees. Apart from our basic trainings - teaching and nursing, where there have been three gold medallists - we have sent girls on for Speech Therapy, Occupational Therapy, Radiology, Physiotherapy, Orthoptics, Psychiatry, Personnel Management, Art, Music, Institutional Management, Rural Science, Physical Education, Librarianship, Floristry, Horticulture and Agriculture."

Hers was a retirement full of well deserved tributes, and Miss Allen brought good news of its early days: "I have already visited Miss Chappell at Bird's Close. Mrs.Macaulay and I went over the day after the move and found a great state of activity and the house beginning to look like home. We were given a good cup of tea by Mrs. Barker and a warm welcome by Miss Chappell who, we thought, was already looking as though she had cast aside the chains of office and was ready for anything." But the end was not happy, as her secretary and fellow workaholic says. "I was so sad that when Miss Chappell suffered a stroke after her retirement she was resuscitated to a life without the use of her great intelligence." We prefer then to take our leave of her with her own verses on departing from the school:

SCHOOL OF THE HILLS
("Follow the Gleam")

Avalon and Sunny Hill
Gaze at one another still ...
Pilgrims there and pupils here
Seek for life's elixir rare ...
Eastwards Godminster's lost cell
Grew round site of Holy Well
Now instead of cross and crozier

~ Farewell to Miss Chappell ~

Poplars white and slender osier
Shimmering on a sunny day
Mark the ancient pilgrims' way ...
From the hillside south St. Maur
Hears the Benedictine lore
Stern and rigorous once in rule
Tempered gently to a school.
North Creech witnessed Celt and Roman,
Saxon thrall and English bowman
Strive and struggle at their shrine
To catch the glimmer of truth divine.
Evercreech, home of the boar,
Nature's plowman turning moor
Fertile for man's cultivation
From the waste and desolation.
Shepton's lynchett's curving lines,
Terraces for growing vines,
Hawk and hero, rook and swallow,
Haunting marlepit's rocky hollow,
Pitcombe's Rock and railway curve
All man's patient progress serve.
Tower in Coombe and Tower on Tor
Like the hills still skyward soar.
Drone of steam-saw drowns the church-bell,
Prophecy of coming death-knell.
If persists the fragmentation,
Work and worship's separation.
Look to the hills for inspiration.

ENID L. CHAPPELL

*   *   *

Right: Miss Cumberlege

Below: The Old Vicarage, formerly home to the Vicar of Pitcombe. It became a boarding house in January, 1968.

Chapter 20

The Dizzy Era Begins

The new Headmistress, Desirée Cumberlege, had been born in India, and arrived in September 1964 with all the right qualifications - Oxford M.A in English, Diploma of Education from the same University, and teaching experience in the south-east. She brought other less conventional gifts: her experience of South Africa, where she was senior English mistress in a Diocesan Girls' School in Grahamstown and in 1949 senior English mistress of Kingsmead College Johannesburg, where in 1956 she became Vice Principal. In South Africa she opposed the apartheid regime, officially started in 1948, through the Black Sash movement; its members, all women, were committed to keeping a record of the wrongs of the regime and protesting peacefully. The movement continued and gave evidence to the Truth and Reconciliation Commission. Another offering to the school was a Christian faith which was so strong that in the opinion of some it bordered on the fanatical, while to others "she allowed her faith to infiltrate her every thought, word and deed without compromise or personal affront to anyone." She was a member of a lay religious order whose members met in Bristol once a year, in silence. She was highly strung, and pushed herself mercilessly. Even her bedroom, it was reported, was knee deep in school papers on which she worked late at night. She made at least one staff appointment, that of the author, with a telephone call just before midnight. Another of her staff held that "in Miss Cumberlege's time the school was always in a state of uncertainty, since one could not predict her reactions." After her retirement she confided to a friend: 'You may not understand, but I never really fitted at Sunny Hill.' Yet she brought a great spirit of aspiration and enjoyment to the school.

"Dizzy," as she was known, loved her staff and girls and had an amazing knowledge of them. Wendy Coles said of her: "She knew every girl by name and her background and her problems. This was an outstanding knowledge and she was particularly concerned for the needy County boarders. I think of one who came to us at 11 years old from the Taunton area - a careworn little girl who had spent her life caring for her little brothers at home. This girl was loved by Desirée through her years at School and she went on, eventually, to become a happy wife and mother, bringing her children to see Desirée.

"I think of another girl who was raped before she came to Sunny Hill at the age of 11. Desirée nurtured her through her 6 years at Sunny Hill and loved her deeply. She too, is now very happily married and the mother of a lovely little boy. Desirée kept in touch with so many girls after they left school, because she cared about them."

One of her pupils, Alison Teale (Stibbe) said, "Often Diz was there when we didn't want her! But in retrospect, many of us can appreciate the responsibility she bore to clothe us with morality and some sense of propriety. Thus Diz could be found driving slowly past the Sunday crocodile as we dawdled by Sexey's School and up Lover's Lane. And her cry of "Three feet apart!" at socials and dances became a legend in her time."

✳　✳　✳

Under this very individual leadership the school continued to expand in numbers and in buildings.

There were more classrooms. In 1968 Miss Cumberlege reported: "To avoid what was clearly going to be severe overcrowding in 1969-70, we had to build three more classrooms. These constitute the Margaretha Language Centre and are a great joy to us. They are large, light, airy, and their furniture is designed to be mobile so that its use is flexible. Light stacking tables and brightly coloured chairs complement the lovely curtains."

During the second half of the sixties the boarding houses took the general pattern that was to last for the next quarter century. In 1966 the temporary arrangement of renting part of Hadspen House as boarding accommodation came to an end with the acquisition of Highcroft, officially opened in January, 1967. It was once Mr. Salisbury's house and weekly boarders had lived there under a subsequent owner, Mrs. Mees. When she moved, the school bought the house and remodelled the interior to house thirty-two girls. In about 1965 New House became the junior boarding house. Miss Cumberlege said: "When I first came here New House was a Senior House. I remember a young girl of 8 called Jane, walking downstairs with one older girl on either side of her, when she looked up to the two older girls and said: 'I'm too small for this school.' It was this that made me change New House to a Junior House." In January 1968 Pitcombe Old Vicarage was added to the boarding houses. Miss Cumberlege was characteristically enthusiastic about this "lively household, whose sense of humour I, for one, have greatly enjoyed. Now its extension is complete and the whole is ready for 55 girls. The rooms are light and bright; the curtains vivid and a pleasure to look at; there is a house mistress' flat and a small overnight sickroom as well as essentials such as showers and linen cupboards; there is one large double sitting-room and a smaller room for reading peacefully, as well as cellar space for practising the guitar without driving one's neighbour mad. There are twelve really beautiful study bedrooms." The house was dedicated in October 1968 with music provided by Old Vicarage guitarists and singers, and food and service provided by Old Vicarage girls and staff.

Miss Cumberlege also reported that "New House has absorbed the Cottage, thus creating two new dormitories. By this means the old Dorm. 7 (the big ward of Sanatorium days) has been released to form a games room complete with Ping-Pong and other tables and more Lebensraum for the hamsters."

In the summer of 1968 the Head said "We are still building but expect to call a temporary halt to this after the end of August 1968. Freeze, squeeze and the financial situation make this necessary." Yet in 1970 Highcroft had to be extended to house fifty-five girls. Miss Cumberlege then reported: "Necessary revision of plans made us late in starting and the builders had to dig through the rocky (and fossil-rich) hill side to begin operations. The design, and the gradually emerging finished article have reached the high standard we have come to expect from architect and builders - and our own putters of finishing touches, in the persons of the Bursar and Mrs. Baker. I have been especially delighted by the variety achieved within a very simple rectangular linking block. No one room is exactly like another and all possible use of views and light has been made."

Life in the boarding houses, as seen by a young teacher, Val Floyde, who joined the staff in 1963, had its ups and downs.

"The young members of staff were all resident, and at the beginning of each term had to root through the boarders' awful trunks, ticking items off against the clothes list, including four vests. One young lady from Uganda dutifully had four vests in her truck when she first came as a very little girl. The same four vests, which she never wore, were in her trunk when she left from the sixth form!

"We had at that time a wing of Hadspen as a boarding house. [This was before Highcroft.] In terrible snowy weather the buses were not running, and Miss Cumberlege decided that the girls at Hadspen had to come in to school. They would have to walk, and somebody would have to go and get them. She rang up a teacher living in Woodleaze to say 'You will walk to Hadspen (about a mile) and walk back to school (almost two miles) through the snow with a crocodile of girls. You will arrive in school by 9 o'clock.' It was totally unreasonable, and needless to say they did not get there. Miss Cumberlege had no idea of the practicalities of such things.

"On Saturday nights we attended the girls' entertainments because we had to. We probably enjoyed them in the end, but it was for the girls' sake, not our own. The younger girls certainly enjoyed themselves, but the seniors may not have done more than pretend to enjoy themselves for the sake of Miss Chappell or Miss Cumberlege. The houses used to take it in turns to put on plays or provide other entertainment. As other activities increased and more girls went home for the weekend, these weekend entertainments ceased. There were few exeats in Miss Chappell's time. The distinction between day girl and boarder houses disappeared imperceptibly, and the importance of colour houses decreased as boarders were grouped according to the new boarding houses, Highcroft, Old Vicarage and Old House, rather than by colour houses within Old House."

In fact day girl houses had already ceased to submit annual reports to The Gleam by the late sixties. Each boarding house was supplied with a sitting room, and the former colour house Cosies ('hardly cosy', as one girl commented) began to be used for such activities as "a full-scale Ping-Pong tournament in Red House cosy."

✻　　✻　　✻

So much for a staff view. Pupils saw things a little differently. Miriam Mead came into New House in 1965. The Prospectus claimed that it was a place where new girls "have the opportunity of finding their feet for a term or two, and where it is possible to make more special provision for the younger girls." Miriam chiefly remembers "Miss Peavitt and being locked in the laundry cupboard for talking after lights out; Miss Collier as Deputy Housemistress who terrified us all and who made us get up, get dressed, and strip and make our beds several times for the same crime." There were good things in New House too, like the Pets' Corner, where Miriam's second hamster lived, and there was scrambling down the railway embankment for an illegal visit to Pitcombe Shop.

Eleven year old Shirley Knapman also reports a strict regime, in some doggerel published in The Gleam:

> Our dorm is a cold dorm
> But we have great fun.
> We stay awake and talk at night,
> But our work is always done.

The matron staff are very strict,
They always shout at us.
Because of this dear Matron looks
At us in great disgust.

Leaving New House for Old House, a girl found Spartan conditions still like those of the forties: ice in the washbasins in winter, needing her sleeping bag under blankets to keep warm, staying in bed until after the silent reading bell, bath once a week, hair wash once a fortnight. She learned that loos were known as 'uncs', and that wicker laundry baskets labelled 'Thick Knickers' were for clothes to be washed by Mrs Thick. Mrs Thick had worked at the School for 64 years and died during Miriam's time at the school, at the age of 94. Rose Elliott, incidentally, was another very long-serving member of the domestic staff at the time, having worked for 50 years at Sunny Hill. The list of school uniform items which staff had to check included not only the four vests mentioned above, but two berets, three pairs of gloves, all different, and two dozen handkerchiefs. Summer dresses were measured in case they were too short or too long. Sunday best changed at this time from the 'Sunday sack' to a skirt, nylon blouse and cardigan. Mufti was restricted to a party dress and one skirt and blouse. Naturally older girls smuggled in extra items, and swapped with each other.

Sundays were specially memorable. Marion Corkill surveyed the school week in rhyme, ending:

On Sunday, bliss and heaven,
In bed till half past eight,
And Pitcombe Church, then dinner,
A service here at eight. Then BED.

Some were woken early to walk to Communion at Pitcombe or Shepton Montague. The weekly 3d. collection money came out of the termly allowance of 13s.6d. The afternoon walk in crocodile continued despite Miss Chappell's earlier decision, and there was tea with cakes, when early arrivals reserved their favourite by marking it with a finger. Afterwards girls might sit above the hockey pitch listening to Pick of the Pops (and on one occasion hearing music from the Pilton Festival), amid the smell of new mown grass, before evening service in the Assembly Hall. There Miriam remembers "feeling very homesick, watching fabulous sunsets and singing 'The day thou gavest'."

Food looms large in people's memories. Val Floyde, who came in Miss Chappell's time, gives the staff view: "At lunch staff sat at the end of each table and served food to about 16 girls. This was all right until the day for Irish stew - what the girls called 'bone stew'. Trying to separate and apportion nine bones and a little bit of meat between 16 people was not easy. You could never go for seconds until Miss Chappell's table had gone for seconds. If they were very hungry, there were no seconds for anyone else anyway! That was the one advantage of being on Miss Chappell's table, something the kids hated. You would have good conversation but could not get on with your lunch." Miriam Mead recalls that the best food was chocolate sponge pudding, and that in the French dining room "you always got bigger portions." She also thinks of queuing for the twice weekly fruit bags, of currant buns at break on Tuesday and Thursday, of picking apples in the orchard on the way to Highcroft, and of illegally toasting marshmallows in the Chapel in Old House, where the proper activities were Bible study and a singing group.

*　　*　　*

Academically the school progressed well under Miss Cumberlege. In 1966 girls won ten university places, and achieved a 72% pass rate at Advanced Level and one of 70.6% at Ordinary Level. Jenny Brown's Open Scholarship awarded by Manchester University was the intellectual highlight of 1967. She was the first pupil in the school's history to win an open scholarship. Her subjects were Mathematics and Physics and she hoped to become a nuclear physicist.

The following year the Headmistress wrote: "This year has been singularly enjoyable partly because, though much happened, it never seemed seriously to interrupt the steady flow of the school's work, as the very good 'A' and 'O' Level results proved." That year the 'steady flow' was helped when the Old Girls gave a clock programmed to ring a bell to mark the end of lessons. It was in memory of Miss Jane Thompson, a much loved and humorous personality of the early days of Sunny Hill whose feeling for law and order, for method and organisation was thus aptly commemorated.

Mary Walker, sitting in L IV B, evidently found it all too much:

> Teacher's voice went droning on,
> And I could feel how strong the sun
> Was lighting all the world outside,
> I left my thoughts to drift and glide. ...

It is interesting to learn from the prospectus what a full curriculum was on offer, with an extracurricular programme. There were two forms in each year. The subjects were: Scripture, English, History, Geography, Biology, Zoology, Botany, Chemistry, Physics, Mathematics, Greek, Latin, French, German, Art, Craft and Architecture, Aural Training and Singing, Gymnastics, Games and Dancing, Domestic Science, with Instrumental Music and Elocution as optional extras. Music, Art and Pottery could be taken at O and A level.

"There is a General VI parallel to the Academic VI where girls stay on for one or more years, with or without the incentive of an external examination.

"Once a week, the ordinary timetable gives way to free activity during the afternoon to stimulate or develop a range of interests. This includes field work, madrigals, recorders, dramatics, library work, needlework, embroidery, bookbinding, etc. There are also clubs including judo and ballroom dancing clubs, and inter-school discussions. Lectures, visits to plays and concerts are frequent occurrences. The School has its own wireless installations and television set, cine projector, film strip projector, epidiascope and electric kiln. The library is a centre of activity and has a fiction bay. The School also runs its own annual magazine, and encourages dramatic productions, supervised or spontaneous. There is a School Orchestra and lively choral work is done. This includes joint Oratorio performances with King's School, Bruton."

From 1966 the Art Department was run by Tony and Pam Watkins, who stayed until retirement. At first Mr Watkins taught one day a week in Sexey's, but soon found more than enough work in our school. He and Mrs Watkins produced some splendid stage sets in their early years, with the help of their senior students, and Tony continued with his own painting, having a picture accepted for the Royal Academy Summer Exhibition.

Ambitious musical projects were undertaken at this time. In 1965/6 Sunny Hill and King's took part in performances of Handel's 'Dettingen Te Deum' and Faure's 'Requiem Mass.' The school orchestra joined with Sexey's for two concerts. A joint Madrigals Society sang three anthems, including Handel's 'Zadok the Priest' at the King's School Christmas concert. At Corpus Christi they sang a concert performance of Gilbert and Sullivan's 'Trial by Jury.' The following year it was Verdi's 'Requiem' in Wells and 'The Mikado.' Then came Benjamin Britten's 'St Nicholas Cantata' and the musical 'Oliver'. Meanwhile the Bruton Subscription Concerts had musicians of the calibre of Jack Brymer (clarinet) and Cecil Aronowitz (viola), John Noble (baritone) and the 'Opera for All' company's performance of 'Rigoletto,' all in the same season.

Drama in the early sixties was a matter of joint performances with Sexey's and King's schools. In 1966 the plays were Bolt's 'A Man for All Seasons' (with King's) and Shakespeare's 'A Midsummer Night's Dream' (with Sexey's). In 1967 after a five year interval the school put on its own play once more, 'The Old Man of the Mountain' by Norman Nicholson. Sunny Hill girls still took part in Sexey's production of 'Macbeth': Ruth Iliff as Lady Macbeth and June Laing as the Gentlewoman. In 1970 Shaw's 'Arms and the Man' was again a joint production with Sexey's.

*　*　*

Some of Miss Floyde's anecdotes about field trips are too good to omit.

"Field trips with John Howe were memorable. Miss Cumberlege once wanted to come and see what we did on our field trips to Kingsbridge. John slept in the games room, virtually under the table! I had a room to myself, which I had to surrender to Miss Cumberlege when she came. I slept on a sofa in the sitting room. In my room was a very large chest of drawers, part of which John used to keep his belongings in. When Miss Cumberlege discovered my dirty socks and his dirty socks together in the same drawer ... John commented, 'Did she not realise how little bootees are made?' Miss Cumberlege had serious doubts about our field trips after that!

"Miss Chappell did not want the girls to wear trousers on field trips. She thought they should wear decent skirts, or even school uniform. John said that he did not feel he could walk up steep banks behind them when they were wearing skirts, so they were allowed their trousers. We were, however, told that we had to take the girls to church on Sunday, and for that they must wear school uniform.

"Wendy [Coles] and Miss Cumberlege once came to Kilve, where we had a special 4 day programme to prepare the less able pupils for O levels. Having spent days teaching the girls about rock pool life, and how the creatures in the pools were not snails, we had Wendy come down and immediately fall into a rock pool - the girls to their credit managed not to laugh - and then Miss Cumberlege came and said 'Oh what charming little snails!' Collapse of all concerned!

One day we took the Lower Fifths to Exmoor for a combined Geography and Biology trip. John took a party one way and I took a party the other. We agreed to meet at a certain time at the bus. I arrived with my party and we sat in the bus ... and sat in the bus ... and sat in the bus. There was no sign of John and his little party. We were particularly worried because one of the girls was diabetic. Two hours later he arrived. He had taken the wrong map!"

*　*　*

Religious activities, as one would expect, received the Head's full support. The sixties were a difficult time. As Wendy Coles observed, "It was an achievement to weather the 60s as a Headmistress, for young people and students were really in revolt then." Desirée had to admit in 1966, "This past year has been 'a winter of our discontent,' reflecting the confusion around us expressed in newspapers, articles and books." Yet there had been a varied stream of speakers at the Sunday evening service, and two Confirmations in 1965. Miss Cumberlege knew the courage it took to stand for one's faith in that decade. "I think that those coming forward for Confirmation today do so knowing that they are in a minority and this makes the choice a real one."

A year later she looked back and wrote:

"This has been a lively year of debate, and of the beginning of a range of new activities. Shepton Montague Church, rebuilt after the fire, with a plain, beautifully shaped east end created by blocking in the old Chancel Arch, a gay church, was rededicated on 15th December 1966, and now the senior members of the school walk to Matins there on certain Sundays each month. The Confirmation Service took place on 19th November 1966 of a group of fifteen girls who had understood something of the seriousness and hope inherent in that Sacrament. Sunday services have been very varied and the Sunday Club has given much to them by its singing. Geoffrey Beaumont [the composer of jazz-influenced church music] shook us up, thoroughly and beneficially, by making everybody SING as I have not heard the school sing before or since."

In 1969 churchgoing was made voluntary for the sixth form.

Fiona Gray [L VI C] clearly imbibed something of the faith that Desirée held so strongly:

Was it because I had been dreaming
As I lay slumbering in my bed?
Or maybe I was worried
About where my life would lead.
I could not find the answer
That puzzled my troubled mind.
But as I journeyed onward
Silent prayer revealed the truth.

* * *

The Staff at this period still had the time and energy to put on a pantomime for the school. In 1966 a staff concert was announced. The girls dutifully filed in and sat respectfully. Mrs. Palmer (for over 20 years a music teacher who could play anything she was asked on the piano, and latterly Old Vicarage house mistress - a gentle soul) flexed her fingers and began with a delightful rendering of the 'Sugar Plum Fairy.' "The curtains swept back, and with a flutter of gossamer wings, in floated the most lovely fairy we had ever seen. 'My name is Twinkle,' she confided charmingly. Of course it was really Miss Coles cunningly disguised."

"All was now revealed - Mrs. Biddick had been up to her tricks again and for the rest of the afternoon the true nature of the staff came out in the frolics, gaiety and frivolity of that most poignant of stories, 'Cinderella.' In the leading roles, Miss Haskell gave a heart-rending performance as the lovely Cinders, and Mrs. Olive was the dashing young Prince. The hooligan element could not be left out, and Mrs. Hudson and Miss Read filled their parts admirably. Finally, a daring characterisation of Dandini was given by Miss Cumberlege herself."

(Mrs Hudson was about to leave after ten years as a scholarly and effective Head of English. Her daughters and granddaughter attended the school. She was once heard to say "I've got all the 'Sons and Lovers' I need." She later returned to the staff and retired in 1973. Miss Read first came to Sunny Hill in the Forties to teach the juniors, and returned in the early Fifties. She was told once by the Head: "Stop stirring up trouble amongst the young staff." She stood up for the younger teachers, feeling that the regime was too restrictive and that they should be able to get away.)

In 1970 it was Jack and the Beanstalk when the staff acted with the Sixth Form and Form I. The flavour may be gathered from these lyrics:

> We are Sunny Hill girls,
> The purest you have seen,
> Going up to Sunny Hill,
> Following the Gleam,
> Trying to be ladylike whatever may befall,
> Down the road to Bruton and up the road to Cole.
>
> We are modern schoolgirls
> Never even vexed
> By that complicated
> Grown up mystery of sex.

We have learnt the mammal; we know what it's all about,
And it's no more interesting than the housefly or the sprout.

We are Sunny Hill girls
Growing up apace,
Learning that discretion
Must go with a pretty face.
And when we are in the world, we'll use that self control
That we learnt once at Bruton and on the road to Cole.

Mrs. Monks, the Head of Modern Languages for twenty-three years, seems to have avoided pantomime appearances. She left in 1967. Miss Cumberlege wrote of the affection girls had for her: "It was noticeable how, at every Reunion, she and Miss Haskell were always surrounded by Old Girls who wanted to talk about careers, families, jobs, all the exciting things they had done or hadn't done."

As Mrs Monks left, Miss Sue Slade arrived to teach PE. The tradition of long-serving members of the teaching staff continues.

Not so long after the deaths of Sir Arthur and Lady Hobhouse came the loss of another distinguished Governor. Brigadier Arnold de Lerisson Cazenove, C.B.E., D.S.O., M.V.O., D.L., J.P. died on 2nd April 1969 after a lifetime of service, in the Army, to the Diocese, as Chairman of more than one school's governing body, and as Chairman of Bruton's Finance Committee.

On July 4th 1970 a marquee was used for Speech Day for the first time. It was erected on the hockey pitch below the terrace. Miss Coles issued the order: 'Clothes are banned from all form rooms.'

The 1975 Pageant included girls in the school uniform of different periods

Chapter 21

Change Without Decay

During the years from 1970 to 1976 the school lost, by retirement or death, more than its fair share of long serving and well loved friends and workers. It is worth reading what others said of them, both for their own sakes and because we get a flavour of the school which they influenced.

Miss Brierley retired in 1970 after nineteen years at the school. Val Floyde says: "She taught Classics and epitomised spinster school teachers - tall, very scholarly with a wonderful mind, but not quite knowing what was going on. The girls could eat oranges in the back of her lessons and she would not notice. She did not understand teen age girls! She was a stickler for detail. She lived in the Lodge and used to empty her teapot in the washbasin!" According to Anthea Cox "She was called The Dinosaur. She rode a motor scooter, and would take Miss Carter, her particular friend, on the pillion." The author's sister did teaching practice under her. "She did not teach me about teaching method. There was no 'method' in her day, I suppose. She was kind and nice. The girls listened to her. She kept herself a bit aloof from me - just a different generation." In the words of someone who did A level Latin 'she was the sweetest of them all.'

On 17th October 1971 Miss A.K. Daniel M.B.E., J.P., Chairman of Governors 1963 - 1971, died peacefully in her sleep, having only just retired from the chair. Her energy and concern for the school since the forties have been shown in our narrative. The new Chairman was Major Fraser, who served until his retirement to Norfolk two years later. He was a colourful personality, with a distinctively military style of speech. He in turn was succeeded in 1973 by Paul Hobhouse, grandson of the Founder.

In 1972 Miss Haskell retired, having devoted almost the whole of her teaching life to Sunny Hill. Anthea Cox has this impression of her: "I remember listening on Miss Haskell's radio to programmes like 'The Glums (Take It From Here).' She was known as Hack. She had her hair swept back in a strict, matronly bun. She was nice but very strict. When we went back to Old Girls' Day a few years ago we asked her how she could have been so awful, and she replied, with those big eyes of hers, 'Awful? I don't know what you mean!'" Glenis Perry remembers "We were all terrified of her. She was however the most brilliant teacher that you could wish for. She is a lady with a tremendous sense of humour and even though we were so terrified we could still recognise the great kindness and concern for us that went with Miss Haskell who never seems to age."

That same year Mr. Leslie also retired after sixteen years at Sunny hill. Some of his many talents were revealed in an interview. He had written two symphonies, two string quartets, two piano quintets, a piano trio, and various songs and piano pieces (including two sonatas). He had worked as a journalist in Rome during the war, where he was briefly imprisoned as a spy. He had studied singing there, including a six-month period under Tito Gobbi. He had also written a novel. Val Floyde says: "Louis Leslie was really an engineer, with a Cambridge degree. Although he was no doubt a great musician, he had little idea about teaching method. The girls used to sit and knit in his lessons. He would bribe girls to listen to his records by promising that they could bring their own records to play afterwards. He was a lovely man. At Christmas parties he was the person that the juniors all wanted to take. He was like a grandfather to them."

It was in 1972 that Jane Townley Wells, Headmistress of Sunny Hill School 1929-1950, died at the age of 87.

A School Caretaker can have a great influence on school life. Mr W.P.T. Farrow died in April 1973 after 16 years' service. According to Val Floyde: "Mr and Mrs Farrow, the caretakers, were wonderful real Lancashire people. The school was known as Mrs Farrow's mosque, because she made quite sure that if you had dirty shoes you took them off before coming in through the door. Anyone caught making a mess was in trouble with Mrs Farrow. Mr Farrow was a real poppet, a favourite with the children, particularly the juniors. He used to talk to them and tell them how to behave. They would really appreciate his telling them that, he said, when they got a bit older and knew what life was like." Miss Cumberlege wrote: "Few of us knew how much time he spent making shelves, adapting lockers, experimenting with floor seals, patching linoleum, all for the school's good."

That same year Mrs Hudson, whom we met in a staff pantomime, retired. She had begun her connection with the school very many years before by helping out. She taught Latin, even to the O level candidates, sitting up all night over unseens. Later she joined the staff full time, until she left to lecture in Bath. She returned to be Head of English for fifteen years. The Head called her "a mainstay of the school." In her final year she was Senior Mistress, helping Miss Coles the Deputy Head.

Miss Read, the staff pantomime actress who stood up for the younger staff, left in 1974 after running the Prep. Department for twenty two years. She had come to Sunny Hill in the forties, and returned in 1952 after a spell in Minehead. "Whenever you saw Miss Read walking along, darting not far from her, and often around her and eagerly chattering, would be members of Form II - 'her' special form." She was "known far and wide, beyond the boundaries of Sunny Hill, and many a 10-year-old has been brought here especially 'to get her into Miss Read's class.'"

In 1975 Mrs. M. Robinson retired as Head of the Modern Language Department. She had taught modem languages for seventeen years and arranged and accompanied girls on innumerable visits to France and Germany, not to mention entertaining large numbers from time to time in her own handsome house.

Mrs Clare Palmer, the pianist of the staff pantomime, retired that year after 27 years at Sunny Hill. "An accompanist unparalleled," said Miss Cumberlege.

Mrs South, another fine pianist, arrived as a part time teacher two years after Mrs Palmer, and retired after 12 years in a full time capacity in 1976. Her husband, also a professional concert pianist, had taught at King's before coming to Sunny Hill part time.

In 1976 Colonel Stuart, the School's first full-time Bursar, and a respected figure in the district, retired. The steady flow of new buildings during his twelve years bore witness to his ability. Colonel and Mrs. Stuart knew nearly every girl by name and the Bursar had his special workers who helped in the garden for great occasions. He took part in R. N. L. I. fund-raising activities, the Pet Show, School Dances and functions, driving girls half way across Somerset at night to visit other Schools and going to call on the hamsters at New House. He returned from retirement to organise a big appeal a year or two later.

*   *   *

Colonel Stuart's skills were needed as the school continued to grow. In 1972 there were 541 pupils, 256 boarders and 285 day girls. Marshalling everyone into the hall for morning assembly became an exercise in ingenuity for the games staff. In 1971 the field south of New House was purchased. In 1972-73 the kitchens were modernised and a cafeteria system introduced for meals.

Meanwhile, girls enjoyed the Highcroft extension begun in 1970. The old building, which held twenty-nine girls, was extended and joined on to the barn across the yard to form a much larger house for over fifty girls, plus a flat for the house mistress. The girls found that from their dormitory window they had an excellent view of the building site, "but unfortunately the builders had an excellent view of us too, so we had to be careful to draw the curtains when we changed after school at four o'clock."

The builders could not quite keep to schedule. "When we arrived in September after the summer holidays expecting to find our new house all ready, we found that only the dorms were completed; so for the first ten or so days of the term we had to wash in old tin cans and the like!" The opening ceremony took place on January 7th.

In 1974 Sunfield House (now the Bursar's Office) and the Orchard were bought by the school, and the New House cottages were extended.

On October 1st 1974 two new junior classrooms were officially opened to make a block of three situated conveniently near New House. "It is also a delight to see the grounds grow even more beautiful under the skilful direction of Mr. Biesheuval." The Old Gym that the juniors vacated became the Music Centre, which, "for that purpose, has at least the merit of being detached from the rest of the school."

In 1975 the old girls presented the school with a memorial to Miss Wells, a miniature language laboratory of "three record-player-and-headphone sets, a wireless and several dozen cassettes." But a larger project was the creation of the Sixth Form Centre in what were once Old House 'cosies.' The rooms were some of the classrooms of the original school building, long since made into common rooms for boarders and had, for years, to serve also as overflow dining rooms. The conversion was all done in the very short Easter Holiday, and efforts to raise the £4000 included a Sponsored Walk on the land around Alfred's Tower, which we shall return to later. Miss Cumberlege described the new Centre: "One long carpeted room equipped with comfortable chairs, coffee tables, coffee bar and television, offering warm colours and the atmosphere of a quiet hotel lounge, and another, rather more spartan, furnished with tables and chairs for concentrated essay writing." Old House was given in return "a common room that can merit the term Cosy and a small television room as well" upstairs.

In 1976 in spite of inflation, new building continued. Two new classrooms and a room to house the language laboratory were added to the Modern Languages block, and were in use in September. Four of the grass tennis Courts were converted into hard courts, making seven in all, and a solar heating system was installed at the swimming pool. Lastly New House was further extended to give the juniors a little more space and to provide additional laundry facilities.

*　*　*

Life in a boarding house in the seventies was vividly evoked by a piece in The Gleam by Sally-Ann Woodward, of U IV L:

"Messily and untidily the 'judy-box' curtain hangs in a vain attempt to cover the shoes, slippers, boots, fallen coats and dressing gowns. Round the corner there are untidy beds, rumpled and wrinkled, where people have 'sat down and not straightened' when they have flown out on some vital mission. Shelves are overcrowded, books and paper lie on the floor. All the dressing table tops, except those belonging to the extremely tidy and practical girl in the corner, are scattered with talc tins and toys. School books stand in ugly piles on chairs.

"Later the scene is changed. Noise erupts through the doorway. A girl is sprawled on a bed reading a 'mag' that has been passed around for at least a week. It is torn and crumpled yet still interesting. Many kinds of noises can be heard: singing and guitar-plucking, whispering and gossiping, secrets passing, the click of a pen, the thudding together of the reader's heels as she lies on her stomach with her knees bent and feet swinging above her, in contrast to the clinking of two parts of a steel ring someone is trying to piece together, whilst humming to herself in tune with the guitars. Down the passage is heard the fury of a member of staff who has caught two or three villains red-handed.

"Someone enters the dorm. She crosses to her bed, lifts up her pillow, and takes out a piece of tuck. Under that pillow are letters, photos, a squelchy tube of hand-cream, a pair of socks and a few assorted crayons and pencils.

"Then the semi-silence is broken by a shout: 'Oh! Table laying!' Next moment, after the crazy stamping and thudding of feet and the squeak, eight times, of the floorboard by the door, the dorm is left in silence. Looking around it is not surprising we are bottom in tidiness, but at least we enjoy our school (home?) life."

Occasionally Minutes of house staff meetings make interesting reading. Girls could enjoy simple pleasures, even when celebrating a coming of age. "June 14th 1971: E. Alexander's 18th Birthday had been a great success, and very simple. Games were played e.g. musical parcel, musical chairs etc. Very simple refreshments, but very attractive. Mrs Norman [housemistress] had been very happy with the whole affair at Highcroft." In relations with the opposite sex, a balance had always to be struck between freedom and restraint. Sometimes the house staff advocated more freedom: "March 10th. Shopping in Bruton and Walks: Upper VI had to go in threes for walks which meant that very often the third girl was the gooseberry and it was embarrassing and unpleasant and often meant walking alone at a distance, while the other two had boy friends. As they were allowed to shop inBruton in twos might they not walk in twos?" The head mistress rejected the request. As for visits by boys: "April 21st 1975: Upper VI would meet their boy friends in their own houses, in Cosies with other members of the House present in the Cosy too. Old

House would not be used as a central meeting place. Boys would use the Staff Loo when visiting VIth Form Centre."

Boarding houses, not Colour Houses, were now competing in music and drama. They did not always take competitions seriously, as this account of Wayside's 'Cinderella' in 1975 shows: "At the beginning of Spring term we were asked to produce a play to enter the House Drama competition, but we didn't really bother to do anything about it until a few weeks before the competition. How we finally managed to produce a play I really don't know. At that time it didn't seem as if we were going to get anywhere. There were thirteen of us in the house. Some didn't want to do it at all, and a few others only volunteered to work behind the stage. We had no producer, no director or anything, and as a result the play was most unorganised. Later we lost some people, some were absent and some wanted to back out, so the whole thing nearly collapsed. But then we came to our senses and thought we wouldn't give up after all the troubles we'd gone through. By then, there wasn't much time left. The rehearsals continued, we were all sick and tired of the play... it nearly drove us crazy. During the play the tape-recorder went wrong, and we kept forgetting our parts - even the curtains didn't close at the right time! To no one's surprise we came last in the competition."

Claudia came from the USA to spend the year 1974-5 in Bruton. "I prepared myself for the strictest discipline imaginable and for a rigorous athletics programme. Happily, neither turned out to be so severe as I had dreaded. In spite of the more obvious differences between Sunny Hill and my school in the States, some things will never change. Girls still complain about the food and the favourite conversation pieces still seem to be staff and sex - not that the two form an association in the schoolgirl's mind."

One Lower Sixth former, Grace Kitto, expressed well what it was like to be sixteen:

> I am an ungainly mass of tangled emotions
> I am a lump in my throat which I cannot swallow
> I am my red and bloated face
> I am a blurred picture magnified in places
> By a blob of salty water.
> I am conscious only of one huge throbbing feeling
> I am I, I, I, continually.
> I can see no one through this large wall
> Which is me, self-pitying
> I am tarred and feathered by hairs and tears

I am nausea rising in my stomach
I am ever-welling tears in my nose, eyes, mouth
I am my wobbling voice
Aching for self-control
And dignity.

*   *   *

Despite these hidden emotions, the academic and cultural life of the school flourished. In 1972 Carolyn Vincent gained a place at St. Hilda's College, Oxford, while still in the second-year Sixth. 1975 was an academically successful year with pass rates of over 70% at both A and O levels, and the daughter of one of the staff, Carol Harrison, won a place at St. Anne's College, Oxford, to read mathematics.

Drama flourished with joint Sunny Hill/Sexey's productions. In 1971 they were 'The Miracle Worker' (about Helen Keller and Annie Sullivan) and 'Gaslight'. In 1973 'The Playboy of the Western World' was a brave venture. "Lisa Penny as Pegeen Mike had beautifully mastered the Irish accent and intonation. Most of the male parts were adequately if not memorably filled." Sunny Hill itself staged 'The Devil's Disciple' and 'Hans, the Witch and the Goblin' that same year; in 1975 'A Midsummer Night's Dream' and in 1975/6 'The Boy with a Cart' and 'A Phoenix too frequent' by Christopher Fry, verse plays seen as "quite different from anything previously attempted."

Music also flourished. There was a joint Sunny Hill - King's Madrigal Group which sang Vivaldi's 'Gloria' in 1971, and in 1973 'Carmina Burana' and 'The Gondoliers' were performed. A scribe observed, in less than perfect English: "The tradition of Sunny Hill/King's societies seems to involve 'extra activities' other than singing, but this year the emotional maturity of the singers (!) has proved much more stable owing to less emotional involvements."

In 1973 the School Orchestra, having been dormant for a few years, at last developed into a vigorous enthusiastic body of musicians, under the guidance of Mr. Beadle, with violins, cellos, double bass, piano, flutes, clarinets, bassoon, trumpet, timpani. On Speech Day they played a movement from Beethoven's Seventh Symphony, an 'Intermezzo' by Bizet, and 'Carnival Parade' for 2 cellos and piano, composed by pupils Sarah James and Caroline Beadle. A Second Orchestra was also formed.

In 1975 a House Music Competition was launched, and the South Cup and the Palmer Shield presented.

Of 1976 it was reported: "It has been a good year for music awards, five cups being won at the Bath Festival, and the general level of academic achievement has remained high with an 84.7% pass at A level and a 74.3% pass at O level. Within the school there have been many other extracurricular activities – productions of opera and plays, concerts, fund-raising activities, visits abroad, visits to theatres and much else."

But lest we think that all was scholarship and high culture, here are some misconceptions revealed around this time:

> Mary did not come to see Philip a lot because he had his country to rule. He would come on odd weekends.
>
> The stitch is chiefly used on seams for knight wear.
>
> I am very sorry about the blobbs and smudges of ink on my prep, but my pen miss behaved.
>
> Nous sommes une douzaine d'oeufs.
>
> On use of words: That bowl of flowers she had on the table was most loquacious.
>
> 'Loquacious' is a word I don't know. 'Eloquent' is just as bad.
>
> And some Lit Crit: I enjoy Wilfred Owen's poems greatly, but not in the sense that I want to read them.
>
> De la Mare talks more as though he already could be dead, but he probably is not.
>
> I would like to see what sort of a person Rosamund really was, not just the book's idea of her.

*   *   *

At ten minutes to four on a hot Wednesday afternoon it is very quiet up by the swimming pool. The water is a deep blue and there are no disturbing ripples on its shining surface. But suddenly, barely a few minutes after the bell has rung, there are shouts and scuffles on the other side of the closed door. Soon cheers go up as Miss Prideaux comes into view, the door is unlocked and flung open wide. In less than five minutes the pool is no longer calm and peaceful but is a mass of small breakers and glistening white foam. Girls are shrieking at the tops of their voices as someone comes up behind them and 'cruelly' pushes them in. For half an hour they race against each other, dive, swim under water, and carry on many other noisy pursuits. All too soon the whistle is blown and there is a shout of "Everybody out or you'll be late for prep!" In a few minutes the pool is calm again as the waves die down to ripples and finally disappear leaving a blue sheet like glass; very little to show for the havoc of five minutes earlier.

Rosemary Thomas, L IV B

Leisure activities apart from swimming were numerous, with a Young Farmers Club, Jazz Club, Guide Troop, Bridge Club, Chess Club (with 30 members), Sixth Form Union, and Judo Club taught by 'a third dan black belt'.

The sponsored walk mentioned above was reported by Imogen Watson, III H, under the title 'I felt like dropping dead.'

"We came to the last check point where Mrs Helps and Miss Szwarnowski were waiting for us. I felt very tired at that time but they said it was not much further and it was all along a road, so we pressed on. They also said that it was only one and a half miles!

"After we had lost sight of the car, our feet seemed to ache even more and every step was a great strain. As well as being very tired, very hungry and slightly wet it was getting hotter. The road just passed under our feet as if we were walking on a conveyor belt and we did not seem to get any nearer to King Alfred's Tower. Instead of its being one and a half miles it felt like five and at the end, before we saw King Alfred's Tower I felt like despairing and just dropping dead where I was, but we saw it: KING ALFRED'S TOWER! I don't think I have ever felt so glad to see it and then I seemed to have lots more energy."

One feels that the great walkers of Sunny Hill's first years would have looked pityingly on their successors.

Serious sportswomen plied their craft to good effect. In 1976, for example the school beat Millfield in one match. Mandy Patten gained a place in the First Junior County Hockey XI, as well as being selected as Reserve for the South West of England team. Sarah Matthews also played for the Junior County XI and Sheridan Ryles and Gillian Matheson represented Somerset in the South Western Schools' Athletics Championships.

*　　*　　*

Some of these activities happened without the Headmistress. In the summer of 1972 it was announced that Miss Cumberlege was required, on doctor's orders, to take six months complete rest. Those who were aware that she had for too long been burning the candle at both ends, scarcely allowing herself time off during the holidays, were thankful that such a decision had been made for her. She stayed with Dr. Marion Asthenia, receiving psychiatric treatment. Wendy Coles took her place as acting Head. According to Wendy's sister she did not enjoy the experience, but the school flourished under her temporary leadership.

Fortunately Miss Cumberlege was back at the helm for the celebration of the school's seventy-fifth anniversary, for which Mrs. Biddick wrote and produced a pageant, closely based on that of 1950, and Mr. Welling composed his new setting of 'The Gleam.' Girls and staff from the French and German schools with whom Sunny Hill exchanges visits were present. The long connection (just over twenty-five years) with Leer was most generously marked by the District and Town Councils of Leer from whom Frau Meyer brought greetings and a present of 1500 German marks - about £250.

*   *   *

Maintenance Staff

Chapter 22

"Is that school Sunny Hill still going?"

Desirée Cumberlege's last few years saw continuing growth in many ways, including the beginning of a new series of buildings, the first permanent buildings to be erected since the gymnasium block in 1961 and the staff cottages in 1966-70. Other buildings had been extended and adapted, or existing buildings bought, but these were brand new. Many would agree that they were also the first buildings since the original 1900 day school designed to look pleasant in their surroundings. I refer to the Music School (1979), Cumberlege House (1982), the Science Building (1983), Hobhouse (1985), and Thomson (1989). These carefully planned buildings were all put up within eleven years and paid for without the need for any special appeal. It was a considerable achievement, and a tribute to the stewardship of the Governors and of the Bursar, Commander John Calderwood.

We shall look more closely at these buildings in due course. Meanwhile, let us take up the story in 1977. The school's success in hockey that year was so exceptional that it earned first mention in Eileen Olive's survey of the year.

"Our best ever 1st XI won all their matches, won the County 1st XI tournament without conceding a single goal and represented Somerset in the West of England tournament. There they played the best 1st XIs from seven counties coming 2nd by only one point to Cheltenham Ladies College, who represented Gloucestershire. Mandy Patten captained the West of England team, and both she and Sarah Matthews played regularly for the Junior Somerset and West of England 1st XIs. Miss Szwarnowski gave a trophy for a Junior Tennis Championship and Jill and Janet Northover a cup for a Senior Tennis Championship; Michele Sims and her parents gave a cup for Junior Swimming.

"In a determination to see that the school's present high standard on the hockey field should be maintained, if not exceeded, the school hockey pitch has been given an all-weather surface at a rumoured cost of £27,000. It was with some alarm that we saw bulldozers reduce it to a sea of mud in the spring, but by the end of the summer it looked very smart, providing eight more hard courts."

In the classrooms, too, things were going well, with a 73% pass rate at '0' level and 79.4% at A level. Fiona Tremethick obtained grade A in three modern languages at A level, and Alison Teale A grades in all nine of the subjects she entered for at O level. Mrs Richards, grand-daughter of William Knight, co-founder of the school, provided (and still provides) the William Knight Prize for Science; Mrs Godeseth gave a shield for junior Cookery; Caroline Lennard-Payne gave a cup for Greek. These and the new sporting trophies indicate a striving for ever greater heights.

The usual multitude of activities continued. The Speech and Drama Department presented 'Olde Tyme Music Hall' and various other groups sang and played in concerts, skied, trudged over Exmoor, visited London and Art galleries, entered verse-speaking competitions, worked in homes for the handicapped and the elderly, visited theatres, including Stratford, walked round the Hardy country and the Welsh Folk Museum, entertained German friends from Leer, entered Bath Festival competitions and acted in a Staff pantomime. A Fete raised £1,000 for Wells Cathedral and a Sponsored Walk raised another thousand for solar panels to heat the swimming pool. One walker put her recollections into rhyme (I use the word loosely):

> We couldn't find the starting place
> Which made some cheerfully cross!
> Fancy that! before we'd started
> We'd managed to get lost!
>
> Then we, the misdirected group,
> Slogged up the valley sides
> And at the top we reached a fence-
> And instead of left turned right.
>
> A hundred or so trustful girls
> The four of us led astray.
> What a lot of visitors
> The farmers had that day!

Onto this happy and successful scene burst the ominous news that Somerset County Council, for political reasons, was no longer going to send girls to the school,

Above: Music School

Left: Charlie Biesheuvel and JT; Right: Jean Thomson at speed

but was going to provide the boarding they needed by expanding Sexey's. Paul Hobhouse at Speech Day regretted that Sunny Hill's connection with the County, which had been a happy and harmonious one, would come to an end in 1979. The Governors hoped to be able to offer some free and assisted places to girls living in the district, and a fund was launched for the purpose, but Miss Cumberlege warned newly appointed staff in 1978 that numbers would decrease and staff would have to be made redundant. Fortunately she was too pessimistic.

＊　　＊　　＊

The school showed no signs of retrenchment. Improvements to the site continued; in 1978 the Jubilee Changing Rooms came into use, and Coburn field was scalped and re-laid for the sake of better drainage. Musical life flourished. In Bath the Junior Choir won the Hambledon Shield for School Choirs Under 12, and Nicola Neill won the Cup for the Piano Solo, 13 and Under 14 class. Several girls took leading parts in Sexey's production of 'The Bartered Bride', and several more joined in the Choir and Orchestra for King's Corpus Christi Concerts in June in a performance of Handel's 'Dixit Dominus' and Bruckner's 'Te Deum'. Earlier in the year many girls had taken part in the inaugural concert of the Bruton Choral Society, when a performance of Brahms' 'Requiem' was given in Bruton Church. The School Opera 'Cinderella in Salerno' was notable for excellent sets and lighting by Tony Watkins and Greg Newman. O level results improved on the previous year. A Sixth Form Bursary was established. And a new Music School was planned, prompting an ode to the old one by a music teacher, Lindsey Thorne. This old music school was none other than the hut welcomed so gladly in 1919.

> ... Desks and chairs and instruments
> And posters all around.
> A grand piano at one end,
> A store-room too, we found.
>
> But gradually as time went by
> Some other things we saw-
> - Like rising damp and falling damp -
> - A gently sloping floor.
>
> We never knew quite what to wear
> A coat and scarf – or not?

At 9 a.m. 'twas freezing cold,
At 4 'twas steaming hot!

The piano that we used in there
Annoyed us quite a lot,
Sometimes the keys would sound
And sometimes they would not.

But most of all, we shall recall
From days so blithe and gay,
The way the large hole in the roof
Grew larger every day!

In the early evening of Saturday, 9th December 1978, Miss Cumberlege unlocked the New Music School, built on the site of the old orchard, with a silver key. The opening concert was given by two choirs, an orchestra and a wind band, with a staff trio and audience participation. The main hall, well designed practice rooms and staff teaching rooms were much admired. School music was advancing: at the Bath Festival the Senior Choir won the Howell's School Trophy for the first time; the Junior Choir won the Hawesley Herriott Shield; Alison Churchouse and Rachel Golledge won the Sainsbury Trophy in a pianoforte duet class, and Alicia Jelly won four different cups in various recorder classes. The only misjudgement in the design of the Music School was the flat roof, which soon leaked and had to be replaced with a pitch roof at great expense.

Meanwhile the stage in the School Hall was given new curtains - green velvet and grey - and two canvas backdrops on rollers; and the stage lighting was overhauled and adjusted. Eileen Olive reported "The swimming pool has become less of a commando training exercise ground by the fitting of an oil-fired booster heater to augment the solar heating which seemed somewhat inadequate in the absence of Sol."

*　　*　　*

At about this time a Physics teacher was moving into the area and in search of a job.

'I walked into Sunny Hill by the wrong door, was taken down the covered way by someone very nice, was shown into the office. Fred Metcalf [the Secretary] looked up and said, as only she could: "Yeah, what do you want?" I stood there very humbly and said "I was just coming to see if there were any jobs. I'm a physics teacher."

Whereupon Diz emerged from a nearby filing cabinet and said "Come with me!" She took me into her little rabbit-hutch of a room where we had a long conversation. She spoke with enthusiasm and authority about the aims of the school, academic and spiritual. It so happened that Mike Garvey, the current Physics teacher, had told her that very morning that he was retiring. I must say that one thing that really attracted me to the school was that while Diz and I were talking, at 4.30 or 5 p.m., there was the sound of children playing under her window. At the end of 45 minutes Diz said "I shall bear you in mind. Keep an eye on the newspaper."

"When the post was advertised I applied, and came for interview with several other applicants. After a first interview in Wendy's sitting room, quite early in the morning, I was shown into the staff room and left there for hours. My first impression of that staff room was that it was a Dickensian counting house, with Wendy standing at the high desk overseeing everyone. One almost expected the teachers to have those white cuffs to protect their sleeves from the desks! I learned afterwards that Sue Slade had come in and after looking me up and down had told other staff members: 'She'll sort us all out!' I was taken to lunch, and was impressed by the liver and onions! After lunch I was so fed up with waiting that I volunteered to help Mike Garvey with a Sixth Form practical lesson, and had to fend off the girls' question 'Excuse me, can you tell me why you are here?' I was eventually interviewed at about 4 p.m. and offered the job. I have to say that no interview day since I was responsible has been like that!"

This was, as the perceptive reader will have divined, Judy Wade, who stayed at the school for 19 years as Head of Physics, Deputy Head and the school's last Headmistress before the office was abolished in favour of that of Principal.

*　　*　　*

In previous chapters we have enjoyed the recollections of Old Girls and gained insight into school life through them. We have now the immediate reflections of a Sixth Former, Peggy Harris, when about to leave after six years.

"4.45 p.m. Wednesday 15th September 1971 trouble struck Sunny Hill, a small devil arrived - me! Now, in less than a week, after six years of fun, trouble, laughter, tears and great learning, a changed person will be leaving. The trouble with being a miniature blonde devil-in-disguise is that although you learn a great deal at an establishment such as Sunny Hill, you always learn the hard way.

"Third Form was a great year; there was the school to explore and, even more fun, many more staff. I also learnt that it was no fun to break one's leg or to badly bruise one's backbone. Lower Fourth was, in a way, even more enjoyable. We found out that Males existed, and only a mile down the road. I'm sure the staff that took us on a day trip to London deserved a medal for keeping us all alive, let alone all in one group!

"In the Fifth Years I began to realise that to pass exams you must not doodle, write letters or tell jokes during lesson or prep time. We were told that we were now seniors and we had to set a good example. Yet, in these two years most of us got ourselves into mischief and thereby into trouble. We have all at some time stood outside Miss Cumberlege's office with rattling knees and clammy palms; all of us have come out alive and a good deal maturer than when we went in.

"My last year - the Lower Sixth - has been most enjoyable. It has sunk home that even the staff are human; they treat us more as equals, but we maintain the appropriate degree of respect. Many a time I have been filled with rage, declaring just what I thought of Sunny Hill, but now my views are changing. The most important years of my short life have been here, and I have learned the basic ideals of life. It will be good to be free of Sunny Hill, yet these last six years will always be with me. They have launched me on my voyage of life, and I have many happy memories of the school."

Another pupil who stayed on to become Head Girl adds her feelings:

"The first assembly was quite horrific, all those bright eyes staring at me - it certainly made me sit up straight and I felt I must look awake even if I was still spiritually curled up in bed. I soon found myself quite unaffected by all those faces at my feet, but what caused me great amusement was the attitude of the new girls of the school. We were 'persons to be avoided at all times and when encountered to be treated with extreme caution'. Doors were flung open before me, beaming faces met me everywhere, and I soon acquired little friends who would greet me with a cheeky 'hello' every time we met."

*   *   *

Miss Cumberlege was to retire in 1980, and she could characterise her final year as 'golden.' The A level pass rate reached 80%. Fiona Stock had a place at St. Hugh's, Oxford, Clare Eales-White was going to Girton, Cambridge and Alison Nisbet to St. Hilda's, Oxford. Would-be engineers were going to Imperial College, London. Chris Welling, the Director of Music, and Eileen Olive put on a version of Mozart's 'Magic Flute,' called 'The Golden Flute' with some excellent singers. Mrs Preller staged 'The Children's Crusade' with a cast of 80. ("She screamed frantically at us, despaired over us, and almost gave up hope of ever producing the play," said one actress.)

Girls sang and played for King's annual Corpus Christi Concert, which included Bach's 'Magnificat', Dvorak's 'Te Deum' and Elgar's 'Coronation Ode' of 1911. Seven cups were won at the festival in Bath. The Junior Chamber Choir sang Evensong at Wells Cathedral most movingly. On this high note Chris Welling left. In the Autumn an exhibition was mounted in Bath of art produced at Sunny Hill, which won very high praise. Sport also flourished with places gained by several girls in the Junior Somerset Hockey XI and Netball teams, and many others winning Lifesaving awards for swimming. One of the more light-hearted attempts by the staff to make noteworthy her final year was the pantomime, 'Little Bo-Peep,' written and directed by Mrs Biddick, in which "Miss Cumberlege made a most elegant and benevolent Queen of Conviland." On Speech Day a performance was given in the marquee of 'Alice in Cumberland', an entertainment specially written and directed by Mrs Biddick to mark Miss Cumberlege's retirement. It was full of wit and good humour and no one seemed to enjoy the parodies of Miss Cumberlege's well-known traits and idiosyncrasies more than the Headmistress herself. Almost a third of the school was involved in one way or another.

Casting something of a cloud over Miss Cumberlege's final term was the controversy over a house mistress. The Western Gazette, North and East Somerset Edition, 11th July 1980, carried the headline: 'Sacked Bruton Teacher Forgives.' The report began, "Sacked house-mistress Miss Heather Papworth does not blame the governors or complaining parents for her dismissal from Bruton School for Girls after she conducted spare time Bible Classes. 'It was an unfortunate sequence of events which got out of hand. They all got caught up in something they didn't want to start,' she said on Wednesday. If anyone was to blame it was religious sects such as the Moonies which had given Christianity a bad name. The Chairman of Governors, Mr Paul Hobhouse, had asked her to stop the classes but she had refused, said Miss Papworth. He had later asked her to resign and she had refused and then been dismissed.

"Mr Hobhouse refused to comment."

Someone who has known the school from outside for many years has given her impression of the matter: "It was at the time when there was unbalanced charismatic activity. A pupil had gone home and told her mother what had been said at a meeting, and the mother went to Malcolm Widdecombe, a charismatic clergyman from 'Pip and J' in Bristol, who really had no right to interfere. His fame got the matter national publicity. I think he did untold damage to Sunny Hill." My own memory is of lunch time meetings in classrooms with drawn curtains, accusations that the local Vicar was not a Christian, one girl being withdrawn from the school, and the work of commending the Christian faith in a reasonable way over the next year or two being extremely difficult.

*　　*　　*

Jean Thomson taught at a prep school at a salary of £40 a term before going up to Oxford. Her real teaching career began at Roedean, followed by a post as Head of History at Wimbledon County School, and then the first of three Headships. At only 35 she became Head of Richmond County Grammar School, and then of the Royal Masonic School for Girls.

Her arrival in Bruton is best told in her own words.

"When I first saw the School advertised in the Times Educational Supplement as Bruton School for Girls, I wondered if there was still a school in Bruton called Sunny Hill. When I lived in Wimbledon as a girl, opposite me there lived a family called Blair. Katherine's father was evacuated to Frome, and they all left in a great hurry. Katherine wrote to me that they had settled in Frome, and she had been entered for a lovely school nearby called Sunny Hill. [She stayed at the school from 1940-44.] I can remember thinking 'Doesn't that sound lovely, a school in the country called Sunny Hill.' When I applied to Bruton School for Girls and came down, Marjorie Parkin, the Secretary, met me at the station. I asked 'Is that school Sunny Hill still going?' She said 'That's the place you have applied to be Head of!'

"They had advertised for someone under 50. I hesitated for a long time, because I was going to be 50 just as I would have started. I thought 'They won't be interested.' But then I thought 'Put the application in and see what happens.' [One of the Governors] had been put out of action by being kicked by a cow, and was unable to get to the Governors' meeting. He always maintained that if he had been there I would never have been appointed, so I owed my appointment to the cow that kicked him!"

Charlie Biesheuvel has his own memory of Jean Thomson's arrival, which throws light on his warm good nature as well as hers. His words are reproduced as he spoke them. "I always had to fetch the VIPs from the car park when there was anything special on. When Miss Thomson came for her last interview I walked with her from the car park to the front door. She had never seen me before. We walked over the gravel drive, and that was all. She didn't know my name. She knew I was the Head Gardener - that I might have said. I had a heart attack two or three days later, and the very first letter I had in hospital was from Miss Thomson, a complete stranger who had never seen me before. From that day onward, nobody must say anything ever …. I love the woman!"

We shall let Jean Thomson introduce another new arrival.

"After being appointed I came to a tea party organised by Dizzy to meet the staff, in what was later the Lower Sixth common room in Old House. I carefully memorised names of heads of departments and their subjects. The next day I had to come back to the school for the appointment of a new Director of Music - Jonathan Palmer. I always felt he was worth it. Wasn't it fun? As far as music was concerned, the place just hummed. I know he could be awkward, but it was worth it."

* * *

Jonathan and Barbara Palmer with Barbara Jenkinson
in the school hall

Chapter 23

The Gavel Disappears

Jean Thomson may be small in stature, like Edith Radford and Enid Chappell (who died in Miss Thomson's first term aged 78), but like them she was not to be pushed around. Unlike her four predecessors she had previous experience as Headmistress. For her first year she lived in the traditional Head's flat at the far end of Old House. There she had dormitories above her, the Dining Room the other side of her kitchen door and the school waiting room in the dining room next door. She claims that she would not have got to know the School so well in that first year if she had not been really within it.

She soon came to see some of the school's strengths: "As a community it was local, whether the girls were of Service families a bit further afield, in naval bases, Yeovilton, Warminster, or really local girls whose families have been tilling the soil for generations, and who did the same themselves before and after school hours; and I always felt that this was a wonderful experience for the boarders, because they were coming into a living community which was at one with its surroundings. For many of them that is a very valuable thing, when coming from abroad they were very rootless themselves. The School's integrity was very stabilising.

"There has always been a tradition that a good proportion of pupils at Sunny Hill have been assisted with fees. This is really the very essence of the School. It is this, as much as anything else, that attracted me to it: it was wonderfully mixed, and you did not have to be wealthy to be there. It means that you can teach good values; you are valued for what you are and for what you can contribute personally, not for what your bank balance is. Sunny Hill would not be the same school if it ever became exclusively a posh fee-paying establishment."

The school also recognised Miss Thomson's qualities. John Howe says, "Jean Thomson is one of the best speakers I have heard. She has a wicked sense of humour and her addresses at memorial services have been masterly. She has the same kind of astuteness that Miss Chappell had." Eileen Olive agrees, pointing to her "gentle manner, quick wit and keen interest in all that goes on."

In the interests of honesty it must be admitted that Miss Thomson had, in many people's estimation, one serious drawback - her dog, Robbie. The Headmistress' Office at that time was tiny. It is now used as a stationery cupboard. Its advantage was that it was in the heart of the school, and both Jean Thomson and Judy Wade resisted suggestions that they should move away from the centre to quieter surroundings. The size of the room meant that visitors were uncomfortably close to Robbie, knowing that when the time came to leave, Robbie would attack their legs, particularly if they were men. One person who visited Miss Thomson regularly had to buy chocolate drops every week and make her escape while Robbie was eating them.

* * *

A new boarding and study house for the Upper Sixth was being built at the Bruton end of the car park, with a link to Sunfield, the Bursar's domain. A handsome redbrick building, designed by Mrs P.A. Lea, ARIBA, B.Arch., partner in the firm of Messrs Vallis and Associates, and built by Messrs Neill and Wolff Developments Ltd, it had study bedrooms for 33 boarders, a study room with 32 built-in desks for day girls, a social area with kitchen, a coaching room and a house mistress's flat and office. The Topping Out ceremony was on 16th Dec. 1980. Completed at a cost of $\frac{1}{4}$ million pounds, in June 1981, it was opened by Miss Cumberlege on Speech Day, and named in her honour Cumberlege House; girls occupied it the following September. This left the Sixth Form Centre in Old House as the sole preserve of the Lower Sixth.

The new building was part of the trend towards treating VI formers more like students. The first occupants expressed modified rapture. Tamsin Haggett wrote in the March after moving in: "We moved in expecting perfection, and began to discover the disadvantages. The plumbing, heating and electricity have been temperamental. For a few days the hot water pumping system went haywire. Then we had a heavy dose of weather and the electricity went off; so did the heating. We left for Christmas before the electricity was restored. On our first night back in January it went off again.

"All the same, Cumberlege House is the school's current showpiece, so we were invaded by hordes of governors, influential persons, prospective parents and, above all, rival bursars struggling to keep up in the one-upmanship stakes. It was a real luxury to have a colour TV and we watched more or less what we liked. Although it's not the ideal home we expected, Cumberlege House is a great asset for Sunnyhill. I feel it has prepared us well for university or college life."

Tracey Bright, giving a Canadian's view of Sunny Hill, wrote: "I was not long in

Above: Cumberlege House, the Upper Sixth house, opened 1981

Below: Science building, opened 1983, seen beyond the 1961 building

realizing that on Thursday evenings at 7.25 p.m. a metamorphosis took place. Cumberlege House had ground to a halt. The reason? That highly cultivated product of the BBC - Top of the Pops. I must commend the invaluable service rendered us by the toaster and kettle. I really could not comprehend the panic that would ensue if either of these appliances were to break down, as orders for hot buttered toast and black coffee are placed to the unfortunate person standing nearest the kettle or toaster." She summed up the atmosphere as "a little friendly insanity".

Meanwhile, Jean Thomson broke with tradition and chose to live in Wayside. She remembers: "I used to love Wayside. It was delightful, because you could do your night walks round the school with the dog very conveniently. You could see Old House, you could see Cumberlege, and yet you were just that little bit apart."

* * *

Several small but significant changes came with the new Head. Sixth formers no longer wore school uniform. They were restricted to skirts and comfortable shoes rather than jeans and stilettos, and in most years they showed good sense about their dress. Handwriting as a time-tabled subject in the First Year went out. The first computer, a Commodore, was purchased, and staff volunteers were taught programming by Greg Newman. He had already been taking bus loads of girls after normal school down to the army computer at Blandford to teach them computing, and this novelty had impressed prospective parents. Black and white television sets in the girls' rooms were replaced by colour. The school even acquired a video recorder. House mistresses' meeting minutes in September 1982 noted the ominous fact that table napkins were not being used. They were to be discontinued. O tempora! o mores!

Jean Thomson, herself a person of strong and disciplined Christian faith, felt that some compulsory services were so unpopular as to be counterproductive. She says: "Sunday evening service in the School hall was a strong tradition but the hall was bad for listening in for long, and on Sunday evening it was always cold. The girls really resented the evening service. Those who had been out for the weekend had to come back for it. As for the boarders who had been to church in the morning, the last thing they wanted was another dose of the same medicine. I decided to drop it. When Cumberlege opened, and the Upper Sixth Form girls were beginning to see themselves as apart from the rest of the School, they were allowed to go to the 8 a.m. Communion in Bruton, and not to the later morning service."

At this time girls ceased going to church at Shepton Montague. Shepton, rebuilt after a fire, was a lovely church, but the under-pew heating pipes were a hazard, and children used to come back with burned legs which Sister had to dress.

Other traditions happily continued unchanged or modified. Instead of compulsory crocodiles, Miss Thomson says, "I used to take any girls who would come with me, often New House children, on Sunday afternoon walks. We used to go down and over the top and down again into Pitcombe, that hill where all the badgers are. I kept up the very pleasant tradition of reading to the young ones after tea on Sundays. I read 'The Borrowers' (very successful!), 'The Wind in the Willows,' 'The Secret Garden,' 'Narnia' books and others. The girls were much less sophisticated than they would have you think. They used to love coming over to my sitting room, bringing their knitting and sewing. I can remember one little 7 year old, whom we had taken in so young because her sister was coming and her parents were being posted abroad. She had clothes which were unmarked, and name tapes to sew on. She would try to poke the needle through, and was very independent; she would not accept help."

There were socials for the boarders, when boys were imported from King's. They were very heavily infiltrated by house mistresses and Headmistress. There was Sunday afternoon visiting by boys, which rotated round the boarding houses, with Ann Nash, housemistress of Old House, from her window keeping an eye on departures and arrivals. School Dances went psychedelic.

*　*　*

Winnie Besly retired, having taught Chemistry for 22 years. She organised the Subscription Concerts, accompanied girls to King's Madrigal Society, sang in choirs, and tramped over the Mendips with many years of Upper Fourths. Charlie Biesheuval 'retired' after 29 years as Head Gardener. He is still working in the grounds nearly 20 years later.

Advances were made in several fields. Sue Slade and Verity White opened out the variety of sports when they started Cross Country with Mrs Cath Longman and field athletics events like putting the shot and throwing the javelin. In 1981 Jonathan Palmer hired Wells Cathedral and put on a concert including his own large scale composition, 'The Five Joys of the Virgin Mary,' for female voices, brass and organ. The opera 'Hansel and Gretel' with Sunny Hill pupils taking part featured in the Subscription Concert programme, and the Middle School Choir won a shield in Bath for the fourth successive year. The English and Drama departments produced 'The Hobbit', revived the Debating Society, and trained a Public Speaking team which won the district final.

In 1982 the Chamber Choir performed on BBC 'Let the People Sing', and at festivals in the Albert Hall and in Tours, France. The Public Speaking team won the West Country Regional Finals. Louise Ball won the 1500 metres at the County Sports and represented Somerset in the South-west Championships. Two girls won places at Oxford and one was given British Aerospace sponsorship to Manchester. Benjamin Britten's 'Noye's Fludde' was a major achievement. Over 100 girls took part in three performances including one in St John's Church, Glastonbury. The Modern Languages Department staged a French Evening with extracts from Anouilh's 'Antigone,' food and wine, songs and sketches. Decorations for the Sixth Form Dance grew more ambitious in the hall and long corridor. The school joined BAYS [British Association of Young Scientists] and actively supported its meetings. There were ski trips, cruises, and a journey to Egypt.

In 1983 the school play was Lorca's 'The House of Bernarda Alba.' Fewer girls than usual were involved, but the performance, with set designed and built by Tony Watkins, had a claustrophobic intensity which made it, for the present writer, the most moving of all Elspeth Preller's excellent productions. The Chamber Choir broadcast again. The first Post O level Fortnight offered Fifth Formers a programme of lectures, expeditions and study skills training. Former pupil Alison Nisbet was awarded a first in PPE in Oxford with the highest marks for a woman. The first of a series of biennial Classics Evenings, which involved almost every girl who learned a classical subject, was a logistical nightmare for the staff but was enjoyed by a full house of parents and long remembered by the girls who took part.

* * *

And in 1983 the Science Building was opened. It was Jean Thomson's suggestion and was readily accepted by John Calderwood the Bursar, who had "trained the Head well not to demand things until the money was in the bank," and by the Governors who "were very open minded and ready to follow advice about what was needed. When we built the Science Block, science was the coming thing; and we had Angela Dixon, who was a scientist, on the Governing Body."

As Judy Wade recalls, science facilities had been good, but not ideal. "When I came to the school the labs were very cold. My first winter I was standing in Marks and Spencer's holding up thermal underwear and saying 'That would be just right for Sunny Hill,' only to turn and find one of the pupils standing beside me. I have never been so cold at work as I was that first winter. The labs, which were built in the Fifties, were split between buildings. They were well designed, and compared with those in other schools were more flexible, without fixed benches. The workmanship in the lab furniture is beautiful, and this at a time when the school

Wendy Coles, Speech Day

was very tightly constrained financially. Before the 1983 Building went up, the sciences were split apart: the Biology lab was downstairs in the main building, where the craft room is now, and the Chemistry lab upstairs, while the Physics lab was in a different building."

Mrs Wade was not altogether happy either with the equipment she inherited. A previous Physics teacher, Mr Stobbs, was "a real character. He was a do-it-yourself addict and smoked a pipe. This meant that he had an abundant supply of tobacco tins and lighter fuel tins, which he used with great ingenuity to make physics apparatus. Much of this was in the Physics department when I arrived, and I immediately threw out some of the high tension electrical apparatus, fearing it might be dangerous. But other pieces of equipment are still in service, and Mr Stobbs' home made demonstration gold leaf electroscope is the best I have ever used."

A new building was therefore much to be desired. Whenever a new building has been planned for the school, those who are to use it have been consulted. Their advice may not always have been followed, but architects have not been allowed to indulge in flights of fancy. Judy Wade took time out to study in York. She deliberately did her Master's Degree on Teaching Spaces for Science, and the knowledge was very useful in planning the Science block. "We were able to have a simply planned building which is both cheaper and more effective than other, more lavish looking labs. They work very well."

And that was the end of the wooden hut and its two classrooms with no soundproofing between, which stood near where the Science Building now is.

*   *   *

That same year two notable members of staff, out of fifty regular teachers, retired. Diana Biddick, Head of History, had great physical presence, rapid speech, and a tremendous work rate. Lean and severe, but with the interests of the school at heart, she did not accept trite answers or poor study habits. As Senior Mistress she acted as go-between for the staff to the Head or Deputy. She wrote pantomimes, and there was gentle irony in her ode to Sunny Hill's coerced charity in days long gone: 'Food sale in the form rooms, Guide Dogs for the Blind, Pennies down the covered way, OOh, aren't children kind.'

The seismic shock, however, was the retirement of Wendy Coles. She had taught briefly at Swansea High School, but otherwise her entire working life from 1948 had been devoted to Sunny Hill. We have noted her appointment as Deputy Head in 1962. Recognising her first 21 years at the school, Miss Cumberlege said in 1969:

> "Miss Coles has comforted, encouraged or spoken appropriately stern words to more girls than we could possibly count, and ably seconded by Miss Haskell, copes with time tables and organisation of the day school from fetes to the public exams. It is hard to imagine the School without 'Aunty Wendy' and numbers of Old Girls who come back to see her, as well as present girls who rely on her for help, have reason, as I have, to be grateful for the genuine attention she gives to the needs of all and each and for her readiness to put her own wishes aside for the benefit of Sunny Hill."

John Howe's first impression of Wendy was when he joined a joint Geography - Biology Field Trip to Swanage. Wendy insisted that he could not stay in the same Youth Hostel as the girls. She herself also went elsewhere for a bed, because with her bad back she needed to sleep on a door, which the Youth Hostel could not provide. She had always been delicate from childhood. John's first sight of Miss Coles was standing outside the Youth Hostel wearing an enormous Panama hat, an aertex blouse which she seemed to wear for the whole week, a voluminous skirt, open toed sandals and ankle socks. He says: " That moment is indelibly fixed in my memory. Wendy must have been quite young [she was 38]. She was bouncy in those days. She was amazingly enthusiastic about flowers, and about them she and I became in a sense soul-mates. She was very good on field work trips, great fun to be with. She was so kind and very unworldly, and people could not help being swept along with her enthusiasm."

Her twin sister saw another side: "Her bedroom in school for years was a very small room opposite the surgery. In her later years at school she had a sitting room, and a loo of her own; before that she had shared the same loo as the girls. She had a teddy bear called Very (he was very bare!). A Roman Catholic ex-nun on the staff got hold of Very and dressed him beautifully. He even had a handkerchief with a teddy bear embroidered on it, and a chocolate teddy bear in his trouser pocket.

Very was very special to Wendy."

According to John Howe, "She to a large extent ran the school, because Miss Chappell, who was a brilliant woman, in many ways did not really know what was going on, or if she knew, preferred to turn a blind eye." The gavel with which she banged for attention in the staff room deserves a place in any school museum. Her hand-written daily notices kept the school running, and at exam time filled the staff room walls. Changes were added in red ink, and changes to the changes were in green. She made the school timetable by hand, and hand-wrote each teacher's timetable, until her sister, returning 'from the sticks of Africa' as she put it, told her she should use the photocopier. Judy Wade says: "Wendy's time-tabling was miraculous, when you think that there were more than 600 girls in the school and only four labs. She must have been a brilliant, if eccentric, time-tabler. She started with people's hairdressing appointments!"

A strong Christian faith kept her going despite difficulties. For the last fifteen years she would come home from school and cry because of her feet, which were so deformed with arthritis as to be unrecognisable as feet. She bore this, like the cancer after her retirement, with courage, and continued to think first of others. The farewell entertainment, 'Wendy in Always Always Sunny Land', given shortly before her last Speech Day, showed the real love in which she was held.

*　　*　　*

Jean Thomson can tell some interesting tales.

"Wendy appeared in my bedroom at the far end of Old House at about 2.30 in the morning in her red dressing gown and said, 'There's a man on the top corridor. He has got into the medical room and he is taking all his clothes off! I think you had better come. I have alerted Ann Nash, and she is bringing Tinker.' So, under the protection of a Skye Terrier and a Toy Poodle we accosted this man. He was clearly suffering delusions. He thought he was contaminated with nuclear fallout, which was why he was taking all his clothes off. Having summoned the police, we went along with this to humour him. I thought we had better have the Nurse on the scene, so we got Dawn to come as front person. We provided him with plastic bags and nuclear-free blankets until the police arrived and took him off. The girls never knew it had happened. We knew that no word had got out because it did not even come back through Christopher, the hairdresser, who was the source of all gossip in Bruton!

"We had girls who ran away. I remember one I picked up in the lane on the way down to Shepton. She had a suitcase with a blanket in it, and a teddy bear and some sweets, and other useless things. She was very low because her parents had been posted by the army to Belgium, and she had no bedroom that she could visualise. She did not even know where Belgium was; so I took her back to Wayside, gave her drinks and sweets and things, and we looked at maps. We saw that there really was a place called Belgium, and it was quite near. She became a lot happier and settled in after that.

"We had hilarious times where we were snowed in at Christmas. We had no electricity, but the kitchen staff cooked a full Christmas dinner for all the boarders. We ate by candlelight, and afterwards went down to the Hall for carols by candlelight, by which time we were completely snowed in. Subsequently we had no water and no telephones. The school could be very cold. None of the windows fitted properly.

"Another time all the services went on strike. We were without water, without telephones, without post. The Bursar got the water supply restored by providing good hot meals around the clock for the workmen, in the canteen. A water main had burst, and they were not repairing mains during the strike, but they then saw to it that we had water."

✻　✻　✻

Judy Wade was appointed Deputy and John Howe Senior Master. The gavel disappeared.

Miss Elspeth Preller. now Mrs Richards, was responsible for drama of the highest order.

Chapter 24

Music, Live and Frozen

We wondered where school musical achievements could go after the concert in Wells Cathedral and BBC broadcasts. The answer soon came with concerts in March 1984 by the Chamber Choir in Sherborne Abbey and Clifton Cathedral, the very ambitious programme including Britten's 'Missa Brevis' and Poulenc's 'Litanies' but most memorably 'Trois Petites Liturgies' by Olivier Messiaen, which had never been sung by a school choir before. It required a large string orchestra, and soloists on piano, celesta, ondes martinot (an early electronic instrument) and percussion. The only ondes martinot in the country came, with its owner and player John Morton, and the whole experience was unforgettable.

An innovation was the Christmas Concert, a large-scale and light-hearted entertainment by the serious musicians of the school but also by a staff choir and overwhelmingly by the Christmas Chorus consisting, to quote Heather Goodhand, of 'absolutely anyone who can emit any type of sound from their throats and who are willing to give up a few of their lunch hours.' This annual event became immediately popular and eased the pressure for the Junior and Senior Carol Services in St Mary's, Bruton, to become concerts, and they remained the joyful but restrained celebrations of Christ's birth by school and parents which they were always meant to be.

Broadcasting continued, with another Daily Service and an appearance in a broadcast designed to show what high standards of music can be achieved in a non-specialist school.

The Chamber Choir included Britten's 'Ceremony of Carols' in one concert in a local church in December 1983. Peter Maxwell Davies' children's opera, 'Cinderella' was given in February 1984 by the Upper and Lower Fourths. The school orchestra and Chamber Choir joined King's orchestra and Concert Band for the first time in many years for a successful concert in December 1984.

Over the next couple of years Jonathan Palmer composed a musical, 'Bombshells,' with book and lyrics by Martin Dimery. It was produced in the spring term 1987.

Set in a wartime munitions factory, it provided many solo parts for girls, a girls' chorus, and a few male roles for contrast. Linda Sharvell-Martin, the dance teacher, choreographed, and Elspeth Preller produced. Performers and audience alike were aware of being part of a very special occasion.

Musically this was an exciting time to be part of Bruton School for Girls.

*   *   *

Architecture has been called 'frozen music,' and another fine building went up, stimulating the Domestic Science and Drama departments to even greater things. Miss Thomson in 1985 broke the news to the Old Girls thus: "I have to confess that we had had to sacrifice one of the monuments of the past: you will no longer see the old gymnasium hut as you enter by the front gate. On the site rises a new building which will afford two cookery rooms, a needlework room, a drama studio and a uniform store." The building was opened on Speech Day, June 29th 1985 by Lady Ryder of Warsaw, better known as Sue Ryder.

As well as bringing an end to the gymnasium hut, with its bicycle racks in the undergrowth behind, ideal for surreptitious smokers, the new building meant a farewell to the large cookery room in the day-school building, with its old-fashioned oven built into the wall, as well as some slightly more modern equipment. (For a 1937 classroom it had not been very modern. In 1946 a prospective parent was horrified that girls were taught to iron with old-fashioned flat irons, something she had not seen for about 20 years.) A pupil, Alison Neill, called it cramped and totally inadequate. Her main memories of the old room "were of always managing to tip dirty water over the edges of the bowl, invariably down my skirt and into my shoes, as I carried the bowl from my unit to the sink." The old domestic science room became the Head's study, with a small office for the Head's secretary, connecting with the school office, and a reception area for visitors. That antiquated oven has been preserved as a feature of the waiting room.

The new building at last provided a memorial to the Hobhouse family which has been vital to the school from the beginning, and is known simply as Hobhouse. Apart from the teaching rooms it provides offices and some storage space for the domestic science and drama departments.

The drama studio became the power house of much good work under Elspeth Preller, and provided a smaller space for performances for which the hall and its stage were not appropriate. Theatre Studies were added to the list of A level courses available, and became a popular choice. Recitals of literature on various themes were given from time to time ('An Evening with Jane Austen,' for example), and

parents and friends crowded in on Speech Day for a varied dramatic programme. One particularly memorable performance in Hobhouse was of 'Green Silk is Thicker than Water,' an original play by the Head of English, Caroline Drennan, which was later taken to the Edinburgh Festival Fringe. Other fine offerings included Metamorphosis, the play by Birkoff from Kafka's horrific short story, and on a different level 'Daisy Pulls it Off.'.

Meanwhile drama continued also in other places. 'As You Like It,' funny and touching, with delightful scenery, was acted in the Hall in 1983. T.S. Eliot's 'Murder in the Cathedral,' an ambitious choice, was produced in Bruton Parish Church in November 1984, with Rachael Kay as Thomas Becket. The Gleam reviewer rightly praised the chorus for "absolute clarity of diction, variations in tone and pace, excellent use of small groups and contrasting individual voices."

The opening of Hobhouse coincided with changes in the Bruton area parishes. Twelve churches were now served by three, sometimes only two, clergy. There was no longer a Vicar of Pitcombe, and so the one ordained member of the school staff was appointed school chaplain. Sunday morning services in Hobhouse now alternated with visits to Pitcombe church, those in Hobhouse being more popular with the boarders, partly because they had less far to go. Miss Thomson had been struck by the instinctive hush that the drama studio had imposed on audiences, and chose it as the best place for boarders' worship. An electronic organ was bought, but a music group organised by assistant house mistresses made a frequent welcome alternative. Services used an Anglican framework, within which boarder volunteers contributed music and drama, and once or twice even took over the whole service.

Experiments with other meeting places confirmed Miss Thomson's wise choice. After some time visits to Pitcombe church ceased, when that church chose to cater only for the traditionally inclined, and youngsters no longer felt at home there. Bruton parish church was always welcoming, but it became clear that to descend upon that church in large numbers three or four times a term inevitably disrupted the worship of the regular congregation and hindered its normal life. It seemed best to worship in the school. Indeed, changing patterns of boarding meant that there were fewer weekends when any boarders were in school, and fewer boarders there on any given weekend.

* * *

As more was offered to pupils in many ways, competition for the available time grew more acute. The Gleam reports on the following visits and trips during three years in the mid Eighties: Overseas: two skiing holidays, a Classics Italy tour, a French Exchange, a Guardian trip to France, an Egypt tour. In England: History trips to Bath and South Wales, twice each, Geography trips to Corfe, the Mendips, Exmoor, Bristol and North Devon, Economics trips to London (twice) and Taunton, Classics trips to Cirencester, Fishbourne and Bath, Art trip to the Tate Gallery, English trip to Hardy country, Social Biology trip to Bagborough Farm, Junior trips to Shepton Mallet, Farleigh Hungerford Castle, the American Museum, Swanage, Brownsea Island and the Roman Baths.

Apart from such trips as these, most extracurricular activities had to be fitted into the school day because, with the closure of the railway in the Sixties, day girls came to rely more and more on the school buses, which left the rather inadequate car park at various times between 4 and 4.30 p.m. For teaching staff, one of the less popular duties was the supervision of the car park until the last bus had gone and the last girl was safely away. In the Eighties only male staff were considered able to do this duty. The car park was inadequate in three respects: there was no one-way system; there was no shelter from the rain; and the surface was as the bulldozers had left it. All these, fortunately, are now largely rectified, but wrong-headed advice from the local authority postponed the introduction of a one way system far too long. It is a matter of great thankfulness that despite the suicidal rule-breaking of girls who ran across the path of cars and coaches to their waiting parents or swarmed out to coaches still in motion, no one was injured. Before mobile phones were common, the wait for a coach that may or may not have broken down (usually it had) was an interesting exercise in suspense.

After a successful French Evening, and the regular Classics Evenings, a German Evening was held in March 1986, with more than 100 staff and girls taking part. Mrs Brenda Bolton was the prime mover in a pleasant occasion.

Some of the activities fighting for time were inspired by Felicity Redmond-Lyon, who from the moment she took up the job of staff member responsible for charities brought a new proactive imagination to the post. There were already several charitable activities. Each form chose its preferred charity (animals were more popular than humans) and organised a fund-raising event for it if they wished. The annual Pet Show began in 1971 and raises money for the People's Dispensary for Sick Animals. It is a good social occasion for Juniors and their parents, and adds grey hairs to whoever is called upon to judge these cherished animals. In addition to such events, Mrs Redmond-Lyon organised, for example, a Summer Fayre (horrid spelling, great occasion) in 1985 in aid of Ethiopian famine victims, and £2,000 was raised. Next year the school undertook to sponsor two children at the Good Will Village in South India, and a Third World Lunch was instituted, when pupils and staff could opt for rice and vegetables instead of a full school lunch, with the money saved going to help sponsor the children. A mini-fete in the Hall raised the rest. An annual visit by a representative of the Good Will Village to speak to the junior year kept interest alive after the initial enthusiasm.

Two other members of staff, Sue Bamping and Cath Longman, encouraged girls to be active in conservation. From 1984 they worked on two projects with the recently formed East Somerset Young Conservationists, the East Somerset railway at Cranmore and a pond site at the Bath and West Show ground, helping with surveying of plants and clearing work. They also helped with surveying rivers for pollution by counting the various types of invertebrates found there. Junior girls undertook a six month project studying a hedgerow on Trendle Hill at Gant's Mill Farm, and won first place in their class at the Bath and West Show. Their representatives were presented to Princess Anne.

When Cath Longman died in 1993 after a protracted illness courageously fought and bravely borne, her memorial in the school was the conservation area with pond near the lower school gate, below the Music School.

Conservation was not her only enthusiasm. As we have seen, she helped the games staff to introduce serious athletics in addition to tennis, swimming and team games. Lethal-looking javelins flew across Coburn and girls trained in a range of track and field events. Alison Pitt in UV took a wry look at it: "Athletics is REAL fun! The longer distances are OK, unless you get harpooned by the girl in front's spikes - accidentally. The 400m sprint is the worst. By the time you get half way round you're shattered, and this gives your nearest rival the excuse of her 'poor tired legs' uncontrollably swinging sideways to perform acupuncture on your calves." Mrs Longman's speciality was cross-country running, although she herself was by now very lame. In 1985 the first Inter-House Cross-country competition was held, with over 100 runners. Tanya Harris in Form III saw the event like this:

"BANG. You're off. Only two miles of muddy grassland and about 70 other people to beat. That's quite enough for a beginner and great fun once you get started. The hills are the worst and trudging up a two mile hill is not something to look forward to. The greatest obstacles are the mud and the rivers. The worst is over when you're on the way down the hill. Just a quick slosh through the river then a good old trudge through the mud brings you home to the best part - the finish."

*　　*　　*

As the roles taken by women changed, so the old career choices of nursing, teaching or 'home life' noted by Miss Radford against her pupils' names in the early years of the century were hopelessly inadequate, and Letitia Holt was giving much time to individual careers interviews, as well as arranging weekly talks by visiting experts. Miss Menon of the National Advisory Centre for Careers for Women came each year to lecture, and to meet Lower 6th girls individually. In 1986-7 Chris Davidson became Careers Advisor to the middle school, as choices for the newly-introduced GCSE exam had to be made, affecting later career possibilities. That year two Sixth Form conferences were held, one promoted by the Industrial Society, and the other by the Chaplain. The managers in the 'Challenge for Management' conference explained their personal backgrounds, reported by Kimberley Pledger like this: "Nearly half of them lived with their boyfriends, had five A levels and engineering degrees, and had undoubtedly feminist attitudes. Were these essential ingredients of success?" The second conference, entitled 'Career, Vocation, Fulfilment' brought a surgeon, a teacher, a dentist, a solicitor, a general practitioner, a deaconess and a nurse to speak, each from experience, on reconciling the various demands made on her as a working woman.

*　　*　　*

Three important members of the school community retired in 1986. Connie Harrison taught in the Art department for 23 years. The pottery and decorative needlework which the girls produced under her gentle guidance was of excellent quality and for long adorned the dining hall walls, but it is for her own character that she will be most remembered. She lived by her convictions and inspired great affection among her pupils.

Joan Waller taught in the English department for 24 years, and was joint Head of Department with Eileen Olive for 13 years. Her husband Rex was Deputy Head of Sexey's, and they still live and are active in Bruton. Mrs Waller is particularly enthusiastic about English literature, and has returned to the school to judge public speaking competitions and to encourage the speaking and writing of poetry.

Paul Hobhouse, Chairman of Governors, announced his own retirement on Speech Day. With his going the Hobhouse name, but not the line, fades from the history of the school. The Hon Victoria Jolliffe, the next Chairman but one, is the founder's great granddaughter.

The Honourable Mrs Prudence Louisa (Toodie) Fortescue took over from Paul Hobhouse. Jean Thomson sums her up like this: "Mrs Fortescue was tremendously reliable. You knew exactly where you were with her. She was very sound, very hardworking. Before she became Chairman she was a most useful Governor; she would always be there, and she was really aware of what was going on." John Howe, speaking as a teacher, said privately: "She was the person who opened up the Governing Body to us." In his public tribute after her early death in March 1992 at the age of 66, he told this story:

> "I first met Mrs Fortescue, when Miss Chappell was Headmistress, at a staff leavers' party. I was a new member of staff trying hard to present a very low profile at a table in the corner of the Hall. 'Hullo' she said with projection that Mrs Preller would appreciate. 'Miss Coles tells me you're new - I'm a new girl on the Governors - can we be new together!'
>
> "As you can imagine that was the end of my low key, low profile evening as Toodie set about gaining a staff's eye view of the School and its workings.
>
> "At that time most of the Governors were seldom seen but working hard in the background and rarely had direct contact with Staff or girls . This was not Mrs Fortescue's style. She constantly showed a determination to be well informed about how all members of our School Community were thinking and also - importantly - feeling. Her directness and obvious concern for the well being of all members of Sunny Hill had a way of disarming people, who opened to her in a fashion that a softly, softly approach might never have achieved. On many occasions, I remember her breaking away from the line of Governors going to lunch to put her tray down beside a junior girl and to enquire of the startled child what she thought of the school

lunches and how was her work going. Children are perceptive and you could see the quick realisation that here was someone who did want an honest answer, and did not always expect to hear a comfortable one.

"My lasting memory of Toodie will be of a larger than life lady, bending to say thank you to a very nervous little Jl who has given her flowers on Speech Day. Each year she unfailingly put the little girl at her ease and acknowledged the small service she had done her."

The following July Jean Thomson retired after seven years as the school's Headmistress. The Gleam carried the reminiscences of two girls whose school career began and ended with hers.

* * *

Frances Jose remembered as the biggest step "the move from tiny toilets and miniature milk bottles into the Third Year, and thus 'Big School.' Then the arduous development of friendships began. Upper Fifth (O level year) drifted past as a sort of nightmare. Lower Sixth - Gone is the bottle green, the restricting armour in A-line form. Everyone becomes transformed in their trendiest togs. However, after about two days the 'What shall I wear today? Oh this'll do' routine sets in. Then comes the Sixth Form Dance. Suddenly the whole of the Lower Sixth live, sleep, eat, drink and breathe ... MONEY. Discussions about theme, the backdrop, clothes and men (well OK, boys) begin. Eventually enough money is scraped together; the decorations are hung, and 160 odd girls and about 25 'odd' boys troop into the hall and 'boogey on down.' All too soon Upper Sixth arrives and with it the realisation that school doesn't go on for ever. You feel an excitement and determination to succeed, with the self-confidence that Sunny Hill has given you."

Alison Neill's memories included the first one of "being crushed up against the front of the stage sitting cross-legged in my new uniform; everything and everyone seemed very big - but even then, on my first day, I felt part of something and was aware of the happy atmosphere Sunny Hill has. Even now as I sit above all the little new girls who look totally overawed as I once did, I still feel the same warmth, and it is with sadness that I leave. During my seven years I have seen quite a few staff come and go. I would be lying if I said I liked them all. However, I found as I progressed up the school that the staff really were concerned with my welfare and that they wanted the best for me, even though sometimes I wished that they had gone about it a different way. I have enjoyed my seven years. The School could not have given me a firmer base on which to build in future years."

Three Swedish girls spent four weeks in Old House in 1985, and give their own view of the school:

"It took us quite a while to get used to the rules which have surrounded us here. Some of them, such as the one about not wearing shorts in the dining room, do seem rather peculiar from our point of view. Clothing rules do not exist in Sweden.

"Another great difference between our schools and yours is the relationship between teachers and pupils. We always use first names when we talk to them, and our entire attitude to our teachers is much more informal. This makes us feel like companions working together to reach a common target, but it doesn't make us lose our respect towards them.

"One thing that really is a great advantage to you is that there are so few pupils during the lessons. That gives each pupil opportunity to ask and get personal assistance from the teacher."

Yet in 1990 three other Swedish visitors judged: "The relations between teachers and students are much more friendly here than in our schools." Quot homines, tot sententiae (Opinions differ!).

*   *   *

Maurice and Doreen Vincent and their team of cleaners

Left: Mrs Judy Wade; Right: Miss Ann Nash, the Miss Marples of Old House

Below: The kitchen staff are an essential part of the school

Chapter 25

Judy Wade Takes Over

Miss Cumberlege once took Judy Wade to task because one of her form, a girl who never found it easy to look smart, was wearing her socks drooping around her ankles. Judy apologised, and said that she had not noticed. "That," Miss Cumberlege said severely, "is why I am Headmistress and you are not!"

Whether Mrs Wade became more observant, or Miss Cumberlege's criterion for Headmistress quality was inadequate, is for others to judge. The fact is that Judy Wade became the sixth Headmistress of the school.

She did not apply to be Head. She saw the difficulties, being modest enough to think that she might not be given the job, and proud enough to think that if she did not get it, it would be difficult to work with the new Head, who would know that she had applied. She thought, in fact, that she would stay one year to see the new Head settled, before applying for another post. Mrs Wade takes up the story: "There had already been two rounds of interviews, and the Governors had probably almost reached a decision, when they invited me to drinks. One of the Governors turned to me and said 'Would you like the job?' and I replied 'Yes, please!' There was a flurry of activity before the offer was officially made to me and I officially accepted."

One of the other candidates said later, "I went to Sunny Hill for interview, and afterwards said to my wife who was waiting outside, 'I don't know why they are advertising for a Head. They've got one there.'"

Before her appointment was announced, Mrs Cath Longman asked her, as Deputy Head, "When will the white smoke appear at the chimney?" She made a noncommittal answer. When soon afterwards the announcement was made, Cath said to her, "My goodness, I wouldn't mind playing poker with you!"

*　　*　　*

Mrs Wade was delighted to be offered the job because she loved the school, but the fact that she was Head did not fully come home to her until one day in the dining hall a girl broke a glass. Judy went to the servery and said "Do you think somebody could give me a dustpan and brush?" Immediately there was consternation, and someone insisted "I'll do that." Judy thought "Why are they behaving like that? Oh! I'm the Head!" People recognised that there was not much 'side' about her.

One of the advantages of being promoted to the headship from within the school was that she did not need a year to get to know the staff's needs. The disadvantage was that having taught alongside most of the staff there she had to mark out her change of status deliberately, but tactfully. One simple way was by totally changing the layout of the room for her first staff meeting as Head, to mark the change of leader.

There was not much of substance that she wanted to change. She had worked closely with Miss Thomson and was glad to feel that after her retirement she could still call upon her experience and advice if need be. While continuing to be friendly to all, she could no longer have special friends among the staff; that would suggest favouritism. Judy recalls: "One member of staff asked me when my appointment was announced, 'When do we have to start calling you Mrs Wade?' I said 'When you feel it right.' But none of them did. I remained 'Judy' to the staff, although most of the new teachers did me the courtesy of addressing me as Mrs Wade until I invited them to be less formal." It was indicative of her approach that her office door remained open unless she had a visitor or interview.

Having been a non-resident deputy head, she found that now she learned a great deal that no one who is not resident in a boarding school can know. She says, "It is a different world. When I was first appointed Head, Ann Nash, the Senior Housemistress, asked me what I wished the House Mistresses' meeting to discuss. I replied 'Anything except knickers and eggs!' Ann Nash and Fiona Gilchrist may have been old-fashioned house mistresses, but they had a real concern for the children, and set extraordinary standards of behaviour and tolerance of other people. Jean Thomson and I both called Ann Nash 'Miss Marples'. She would sit in her room knitting, and would know, how I could never work out, exactly what was going on at the other end of the House. For her last couple of years she hardly moved from her room, but she still knew all about everyone."

Once a group of Fourth Year girls from Old House had been to Bath and had come back with some cider. They were caught, and the Head was called to confront them alongside Miss Nash. Miss Nash had her suspicions that other misdemeanours had been perpetrated on her night off, but she did not know what. Head and House Mistress sat on high chairs, and gained the psychological advantage by having the girls sit on the floor. They were a kind of double act, and the conversation went like this:

"So you brought cider back from Bath. Did you really go into an off licence and buy it?"

"Oh no! We gave the money to this tramp, and he bought it for us."

"Well, while you are here, we shall talk about the other things that have been going wrong over the past few weeks. Who is going to start telling us about it?"

"You mean about the King's boys?"

"Oh! Er ... yes, about the King's boys."

"You mean about the getting out?"

"Yes, about getting out at night."

"Well, we went down to meet them on the bridge."

"And what time was this?"

"About 2 o'clock."

"And I suppose, being chivalrous boys they left you to come up the hill by yourselves."

"Oh no, they saw us back to school."

"And abandoned you on the doorstep?"

"Oh no, they came upstairs."

"Up the red stairs?" (In shocked tones - the red stairs were forbidden)

"Yes, because we had to go to our dorms, you see."

"So you took them into your dorms?"

"Yes, we had to, you see."

"Why did you have to?"

"We had to get the kettle. We were going to make them a drink."

"So these boys were in the dorms when other girls were asleep?"

"Yes ... (The implications dawn) ... oh, yeees."

"So where did you go to make your drink?"

"The prep huts. We had left the window open."

"So what did you do in the prep room?"

"We just had the radio on, and had choc-o-mix."

"And then what?"

"They went home, and we went back to bed."

By this time Miss Nash was convinced that she would be sacked, and when they met next day Mrs Wade teased her a bit. To her anxious promises that such a thing would never happen again, the Head said: "There is one thing that really worries me. How are we going to prevent the Bursar finding out that King's have been drinking our choc-o-mix?"

Miss Nash said of those times, "We laughed and we cried, but we laughed more than we cried."

As Mrs Wade was the first Head to be appointed from within the school, so Mrs Catherine Millar was the first to come in as Deputy Head from outside. The balance between new blood and inside knowledge was thus maintained. Mrs Millar brought with her a great love of music, literature and the arts, and an enthusiasm for the computer, which around this time was becoming a really useful tool for school administration and record keeping.

The exams to be organised now included the new GCSE with its course work, taken for the first time in 1988. Victoria Bunyard, one of the guinea pigs, told it like it was, in what was apparently an address to John Howe as Geography teacher:

"They say you can't fail GCSE Sir,

So, we all did our course work, Sir.

We wrote about developments, quarries, tourism and industry,

We wrote about Blaenafon and coal mining, Sir.

We wrote, Sir, about virtually everything we could think of,

Or invented something.

We, Sir, were assessed on writing results,

We were assessed on designing experiments -

We were even assessed on carrying empty test tubes.

In fact, Sir, we were assessed on virtually everything YOU could think of.

We went to our lessons, Sir, we learned our work.

You taught us well, Sir.

And came that fateful day,

When we entered the exam room,

We read the instructions, we headed the paper, we commenced battle.

Did I say you taught us well, Sir?

You did, Sir, to the best of your abilities;

It was a pity the board got it wrong.

Grid references which do not exist, Sir,

Maths questions which were not on any syllabus, Sir.

So we did our exams, Sir.

We worked till all hours, drinking coffee by the gallon.

We sat our papers, Sir.

We threw them about a bit and used them for paper darts, Sir.

We even mopped up spilt coffee with them, Sir.

And we still couldn't actually fail them, Sir.

Well, not all of them anyway."

Victoria in fact passed eight subjects with grades A-C, and the overall rate was 80.3%.

After the exams were over, Fifth Formers were offered work experience, instead of the more light-hearted post-exams week of the previous years. Letitia Holt had been busy since early in the year arranging placements related to girls' chosen careers, and over 80 girls, supervised by 15 members of staff, were briefed, shown to their place of work and visited on the job. They worked with travel agents, beauty parlours, TV and newspapers, solicitors, chemists, accountants, vets, hospitals, and many more. Many girls realised for the first time what real work was, and many were confirmed in their choice of career. Almost all found it a valuable experience. So began a regular annual event, and it was good in later years to find how willing employers were to accept another girl from the school, having once found out the calibre of the students.

No sooner had Miss Holt taken on this burden than another was added, the care of the library. The previous librarian, Mrs Eileen Olive, joint Head of English, retired in 1988. She is a lady of formidable intellect, definite views and forceful personality, Hockey Captain at Cambridge, producer of school plays, pantomimes and operas, and for many years editor of The Gleam. Her pithy Gleam reviews of each school year have been the unacknowledged source of much in this history.

At the same time Miss Hazel Ford retired after 20 years as Head of Religious Studies. She saw the subject through difficult years when the emphasis of the syllabus changed and pupils lost the old certainties. She fought resolutely for the position of the subject as she fought her increasingly crippling arthritis. Less sympathetic girls used to take advantage of her good nature to play pranks. One such girl confesses: "In Scripture lessons we used to pretend to Miss Ford that there was a dip in the classroom floor, and as any of us passed the spot we would bend our knees. We had a model mouse which we used to throw across the classroom, and then climb on the tables and scream as if it were a real one."

*　　*　　*

The library over which Eileen Olive presided was upstairs in the day school, a well laid out and much loved and used room with excellent views, but the time had come for the last new building of the century to be built to house the school library, along with four English classrooms, a departmental book store, tutorial rooms, and the Design and Technology department below. The architect was Mrs Pamela Lea. This new building, like most of the other school buildings on the sloping school site, was designed to make a virtue of necessity. Set between the road to the lower school gate and the Coburn playing field, its upper floor is entered from the road, and the smaller lower floor from the Coburn side. There is no connecting staircase between the two floors, as there is in the science building which also has entrances at two levels, so the Design and Technology department feels like, and is, a separate entity.

To make way for the new building, the last of the shabby old huts was dismantled. This was where Hazel Ford used to teach, and had gas heaters strung up on the ceiling. The atmosphere at the end of a lesson was terrible. The windows would be running with water, and the girls would come out with scarves and mufflers, almost asphyxiated.

The new library retains as much of the furnishings of the old as possible. It has wooden window seats from which the view of the playing field is a delightful constant distraction from study. A computer system was installed to hold the catalogue and deal with borrowings.

Jean Thomson was invited back to school on June 29th 1989 to open the building and was told that it was to be called Thomson. She said later, "It was quite overwhelming to have a building named after me, but it could not be a building closer to my heart. I just hope books will go on holding their own against CD Roms." Just before the Autumn Term she arrived back in school with a bronze hippo, which she said would look ideal on the octagonal table in the centre of the library. It is a beautiful piece of sculpture, and now it is polished, because nobody can resist touching it.

*   *   *

The new building left the way open for reorganisation in the day school. The staff moved upstairs and the old staff room was restored to two History classrooms, which soon sported a plaque proclaiming 'History Department.' The image-makers were arriving. Meanwhile the staff, accustomed to a cramped, two-level room with the Deputy Head's desk, big brother-like, overlooking the lower level, a coffee machine lovingly tended by the Caretaker, Maurice Vincent, to well beyond its natural life span, and a small flight of steps from which the staff-room demagogue could urge the staff to mutiny, found themselves with two large rooms, the ex-library as a sitting room with kitchenette, and the ex-Geography room as a workroom. Meanwhile the Geography department relocated up the next flight of stairs, taking over an old laboratory and adjoining classrooms. The staff area also had space for a Deputy Head's office, a Senior Master's office, pigeon holes for giving in prep, and a smoking room for the small but determined band of addicts.

As staff cleared their desks ready for the move, some after many years, bets were taken on the date of the lowest stratum of papers on the Senior Master's desk.

The change in rooms was in most ways a great benefit, but it did mean that staff were no longer thrown so closely together. The Deputy Head and Senior Master became more separate, and for the first time the phrase 'senior management' was heard, though never from the Head. This change fitted the spirit of the times, but older members of staff feared lest the family atmosphere of shared endeavour which has always been part of the school be lost.

* * *

In January 1990 came the dreadful day of the great gales. After huddling in the Hall passing the time with a sing-sing, girls had to hang together in lines to reach their buses. Colin Watkins, at the top of the covered way, organised a line to get girls across between the stairs and Old House, because they could not stand up in the wind. Windows in the Hall blew in. A member of staff escaped serious injury by inches when a great shard of glass fell from a skylight onto a flight of stairs. A tree near Wayside fell, but fortunately in the other direction. One wing of New House was evacuated when the school was advised by an expert that the big tree nearby would fall in that direction. Mrs Wade says, "The only time I have literally seen the earth move was under that tree!" Next day the expert changed his mind, and so the other wing had to be evacuated. The girls were puzzled, and had to content themselves by thinking that the wind had changed direction!

Mrs Wade says, "It was when I heard on the radio that night of the tragic death of a schoolgirl in another girls' school, St. Brandon's, Clevedon, that I fully realised how fortunate we had been to avoid injuries or worse. After a day of coping in practical ways with all the dangers, my knees turned to jelly at the thought of what might have happened to us."

Some prospective parents, who had an appointment to see the Head the morning after the worst gale, came to find trees down, and children huddled in overcoats in labs trying to keep warm with Bunsen burners because there was no electricity. The Head met them, wearing wellingtons, sweater and trousers, and looked at them in amazement."You are here?" They explained, "We couldn't get through on the phone to cancel the appointment." She said "I am very happy to show you round, but things are not exactly normal!" Despite everything, the children looked perfectly happy. Going into Old House, where there were fifty girls and no power, the parents commented "It is not very tidy." Their daughters did come to the school!

* * *

Building continued, though on a more modest scale, with new wings added to two of the boarding houses, Old Vicarage and Highcroft. These were officially opened on 18th May 1991, and were designed to provide separate working space so that boarders did not have to return to school to do prep. It made the Houses more self-contained and homely. Mrs Wade had noticed on arrival at the school that "the boarders felt secure on their own territory, and welcomed me with confidence into their home, in a way that my street-wise pupils in a day school had not. Sunny Hill girls did not feel the need to try out a new teacher. The confidence built up by boarding is incredible."

It may be interesting to read some of Mrs Wade's other thoughts on boarding in general: "It was good to see how, if a girl came into the school with an arrogant manner, the other girls would, without bullying or nastiness, gently smooth down the sharp corners and enable the new girl to mellow and fit in. I was sensitive to the problems that could arise if a girl, particularly a boarder, should tend to grow away from the customs and manners of her family, but normally her parents were quite aware of this and had chosen the school because they felt that this was the way to give their daughter the best start they could. Girls naturally divide into boarders and day girls, but the rule against boarders going back to their House during the day was one attempt to minimise the division. Perhaps the increase in weekly boarding and the introduction of 'sleepovers' for day girls will further diminish the distinction. My first prospective parent began the conversation in my room by saying, 'I was a pupil here.' 'How nice,' I said, 'you enjoyed it so much that you want your daughter to come here?' 'No, I hated it,' she replied. 'Tell me how it has changed!' The reason there is a backlash against boarding now is that the people who are making their views heard were themselves at school in the Fifties and Sixties, and cannot realise how boarding has changed."

The new prep rooms allowed boarders to do their work when they chose, and released the period after school for an unprecedented range of new activities, co-ordinated by Dorian Wood, many suggested by the girls themselves. They included football, flower arranging, bird watching, bridge, electronics, cookery (conventional and Roman), origami, woodwork and play reading.

Another of Mr Wood's innovations was "Green Jelly." This is a short news sheet with information about events and people in the school, which has been produced with more or less regularity since. The whimsical title refers to a former Head's alleged banning of green jelly from the school dining room on the grounds that it would make the pupils hyperactive, or, according to others, that it was an aphrodisiac.

Meanwhile activities undertaken as part of the Duke of Edinburgh's Award scheme grew even more varied, with karate, fencing, and canoeing added to the expeditions and other challenges. Elizabeth Boon won the school's first Gold award in 1990 and Claire Coulthard the second in 1991.

* * *

Several farewells were said in the early Nineties to people who had served the school for a number of years and had made a particular mark.

Commander John Calderwood, retired in 1991 after 15 years. He ran a tight ship financially, which meant that his decisions were not always popular with staff who wanted money for this or that, but, as Mrs Wade says: "Under John Calderwood as Bursar the school put aside a certain amount of money each year, and only when enough had been accumulated would they proceed with the next building project. It was not always so. One Speech Day in the past nearly had to be cancelled for lack of funds, but went ahead in the end. At the end of one year, in Ian Stuart's time, the surplus was just £1 - a real Mr Micawber situation. Parents would often ask how the fees could be so low, and I would answer that we had no debts and owned all our own buildings. This meant that we weathered the period of high interest rates in the mid Eighties when other schools who had borrowed heavily to expand were in deep trouble." Indeed several West Country independent schools actually closed during this period.

Mrs Alison Smerdon, who succeeded Mrs Olive as Head of English and Gleam editor, left for a part time post, having taught in Bruton since 1977. Like Mrs Olive, her annual reports have clearly set out the events worth recording in this story.

Ann Nash, who has already appeared in this chapter, retired in 1992 after 12 years in Old House. She inspired great affection and, when needed, not a little fear. An ebullient character.

Richard Harley left at the same time after 15 years as Head of Modern Languages to concentrate on fruit farming. A loveable teddy-bear of a man, he penned verses with kindly wit, and impersonated Goon Show characters with relish. A pupil remembers "his relaxed but gently disciplined style of teaching." He could occasionally even be punctual.

Jonathan Palmer left in 1992 after 12 years at Bruton. His achievements in music have been well enough described. It is typical that he left for Bermuda with no firm plans, and there did supply teaching and became cathedral organist.

Sadly, 1992 was the year when the Chairman of Governors, Toodie Fortescue, and former Headmistress Desirée Cumberlege died.

* * *

Above: Through all upheavals, the work in the classroom goes on

Below: The library in Thomson building overlooks Coburn playing field

Chapter 26

Pressures Mount

For some years the government had been subjecting the world of education to one initiative after another, in the quest for higher standards and a better educated population - or was it a better trained work-force? We have already noted the introduction of GCSE, the General Certificate of Secondary Education, to replace GCE (General Certificate of Education) Ordinary Levels, and CSE (Certificate of Secondary Education, which had been designed for less academic pupils). Although there was supposed to be no 'pass' or 'fail' in the new exams, for practical purposes grades A to C were regarded as a pass, and by that yardstick the school scored a 96% pass rate in 1996. There were those who complained that GCSE did not stretch abler children and did not provide a good foundation for A Level teaching, but at A Level too there was a gradual improvement, with a school pass rate of 92.3% in 1993 and 95.7% in 1996. GCSE did, however, entail considerable time and expense to introduce in the school.

The next major innovation was the National Curriculum. When first mooted, it appeared that this would be a fairly small core of knowledge and skills which every child in the country should be expected to possess, and as such would scarcely affect a school like Bruton school for girls, since all girls would take it in their stride. After dreary months of committees and reams of jargon-ridden reports, it became clear that those in charge were proposing to prescribe a large percentage of what should be taught in schools, and to leave little time for any subjects that were not in the National Curriculum, and little choice among the topics that were to be taught in, for example, History. The National Curriculum was not to be compulsory for Independent Schools, but it would be a foolish school which disregarded it, if only for the sake of pupils who had to move from one school to another and would be expected to know what the Curriculum required.

It was, I think, Jean Thomson who once remarked in a staff meeting that trends in education went like a pendulum, and that the school usually managed to catch the trend as it swung back. Fortunately a swing back did begin quite soon in response to widespread protests. The proportion of school time taken up by the National

Curriculum was reduced somewhat, and the school, always committed to education rather than mere training, was able to retain its own breadth of syllabus including, for example, Latin.

Once again, much time and expense were needed in order to comply with the new demands.

Testing at newly designated Key Stages followed not long afterwards, and the school felt it wise to fall in with this, too, if only to be able to show parents and prospective parents the high standards which were being achieved.

A final change, which fell heavily upon Bruton School for Girls, was New Labour's undertaking to abolish the system of Assisted Places at Independent Schools. Mrs Wade has described the school's make-up like this: "Sunny Hill has non-fee-paying scholarship girls as well as fee-payers, and contains a wonderful mix of farmers' children, girls from overseas, boarders and day girls, who are all good for each other, and produce a community that is delightfully normal. The children are privileged, not because their parents have money, but in two ways: first, they are of above average intelligence, which is a natural gift and not something to be stuck-up about, and secondly, they have parents who have gone out of their way to find the school, thus showing how much they care for their children." The school, standing by its policy of providing a first class education to those who can benefit from it, regardless of income, had embraced the Assisted Places Scheme when it was introduced, and a considerable proportion of the pupils were now relying on it. The imminent end of the scheme concentrated the minds of the Governors wonderfully, and the complete reorganisation of the school in 1997 was their response. More about that in due course.

One legacy of the Thatcher years has been a culture of competition, sometimes competition to reach the top, often simply to survive. Schools in the maintained sector were encouraged to tout for custom, and began to issue prospectuses and to advertise their achievements in the hope of attracting pupils and being judged successful. Independent schools had to look to their laurels. Dorian Wood, camera always at hand for a good picture, made sure that some at any rate of the school's achievements and activities were regularly reported in the local press. Traditionally the best advertisements for the school have been the girls themselves. Prospective parents have been shown round the school by senior girls, and have been able to ask them for an honest assessment of the school. This remains the case, but other methods of getting the message across are now needed in addition. The Financial Times did the school no harm when one year, balancing exam results, fees and other factors, it judged it best in the region. We live in a Lewis Carroll world where you have to run fast to stay in the same place.

*   *   *

The work of the Deputy Head included organisation as well as pastoral responsibilities, and in 1992 Mrs Ann Napier arrived to share the burden with Mrs Millar, taking over the pastoral side. She had been a house parent in Millfield School, and also, with her husband, had run a restaurant. She knew the practical side of her subject, Business Studies. She arrived like the new broom of the proverb.

Among the early projects was the enrichment of boarding life. The time after lessons was filled with clubs and activities, with members of staff pressed to share their enthusiasms and expertise. Weekends were themed, with an Australian weekend inspired by the assistant house mistresses from Oz, or a Murder Weekend. Girls visited an animal sanctuary regularly.

It is undoubtedly mere coincidence that a fantasy appeared in the Gleam at the end of that year, which included the following:

> "Mrs Spode, the Headmistress, was in Scunthorpe at the annual G.S.A. meeting and the offenders were to be dealt with by the new deputy, Mrs Nuclear. ... There would be tears and flying geraniums at least.
>
> "'WELL, WHAT HAVE YOU GOT TO SAY FOR YOURSELVES?' A brief moment of silence, then
>
> "THUNK! The calendar shivered on its hook. That must have been the Bavarian Crimson.
>
> "'THIS IS JUST NOT GOOD ENOUGH.'" And so forth.

Another project was the campaign against bullying, with senior girls nominated and trained to listen to those who felt they were victims of bullying. It was well publicised and quite effective. The Childline telephone number had for some time been prominently displayed for any who felt ill used at school, and the Rector of Bruton was appointed as an outside adult to whom such girls could turn in confidence. A shocking and harrowing case featured on the television programme 'That's Life' had made all boarding schools very careful to avoid any hint of ill treatment either by staff or other pupils, and despite the happy atmosphere and girls' mutual support which are such a feature of the school's life, official safeguards had to be in place.

*   *   *

The Lower Sixth were consulted about their Centre in Old House, which occupied the original school of 1900. On their recommendation, the work room was enlarged and refurbished with individual work spaces for each day girl, and the now smaller leisure area redecorated and re-equipped. A new changing room was provided, complete with vanity units. The whole project was finished for the Summer Term of 1994.

Two Lower Sixth Formers, Sarah Davis and Jessica Harbron, recommended Sixth Form life to the Fifth Year:

"When you first start the Sixth Form in September you really notice how different it is from the rest of the school. There is no form room and instead there is a centre with a TV, stereo and kitchen which is an ideal place to unwind and relax on a bean bag with a mug of tea. And yes, we do even watch 'Neighbours' from time to time. Also, next door is a study room for the day girls where you have your own private desk to plaster with your favourite Adonis and Keanu piccies.

"There are several responsibilities that as a Lower Sixth you are expected to carry out. For example 'Zone Management.' It sounds boring, we know, but all it involves is half an hour walking the school corridors. This duty enables you to keep in touch with the rest of the school and you don't feel so detached from the lower years.

"Lessons are also very different in the Sixth Form. They are immediately a lot more enjoyable and fulfilling as you are doing subjects you've chosen to do and the other people in the group have chosen them too. Classes are also much smaller; for example our largest class is English with six people!

"Extra Sixth Form privileges involve:
1. Rugby (hey girls! you get to see Mr Wood in his shorts!)
2. Going to Bruton at lunch time (to pursue social activities!!)
3. Using Crush Hall door (Hmm! Wow!)
4. Wearing mufti (for free!). Sadly you will no longer be able to wear your school uniform!"

The mention of 'wearing mufti for free' refers to 'Mufti Day' when girls were allowed to wear non uniform clothes in return for a small donation to charity. A few members of staff could usually be found donning school uniform for that day, in a reciprocal gesture.

A rugby team had indeed been formed under Dorian Wood's coaching, and in 1994 reported a triumphant season with victories over Wells Blue School, Leweston and Chew Valley.

Head Girl Katy Dean was a persuasive advocate of Sixth Form life:

"Some people leave Sunny Hill in order to go to a mixed school and such people often ask those who stay, with a concerned look, 'Do you have a life?!' Just because you remain at a girls' school doesn't have to mean that you become a man-hating, antisocial feminist! Some of my best friends are ex-King's boys met during my Sixth Form - to my surprise there are decent King's boys behind the arrogant few you meet in Fourth Year socials. The House Staff and Mrs Napier genuinely tried to make our weekends good fun organising balls, concerts, dinner parties, trips to neighbouring school balls. And of course with UVIth come the trips to the Blue Boar and Brian the friendly barman. Day girls and Boarders alike developed an interesting and varied social circle."

Such attitudes and the new facilities for Sixth Formers made the step to a 'Bruton College' for Sixth Form girls a logical one.

*   *   *

Old Vicarage suffered a major fire during the 1994 summer holidays. Although rumours flew wildly - I was told by an acquaintance that the school had burned down - the fire was quickly spotted by Julia Lindley and reported to the fire service. Smoke damage was extensive, but on January 13th 1995 the same Julia Lindley was able to reopen the beautifully redecorated house.

A safe fire was regularly lit on Bonfire Night. As one observer said, "Very Sunny Hill is how girls managed to enjoy themselves at the November 5th bonfire with only a sparkler each. Recently David Collyer (the Bursar) and Jigger (Colonel Foster, Estates Bursar) have organised a fireworks display." In 1995 Helen Fifield of 2W showed how real the enjoyment was.

"The Sixth Form served out the supper. There were beef burgers, hot-dogs, chips, baked beans, onions and salad, a terrific selection which was very popular. To finish we were handed round chocolate brownies - if we could manage them!

"At 7.45 we all piled out in warm clothing to go to the cow field behind New House. A large bonfire was lit and we watched as the fire spread and sent off smoke. The warmth and glow of the bonfire was lovely. After being told to stand back, we watched some fireworks go off. They were noisy and colourful. There were Catherine Wheels and rockets which sometimes took us by surprise. We lit our sparklers and watched them sparkle until they died out. As they reached the bottom of the sticks, we wrote our names with them. Hot chocolate and doughnuts were offered round and were met with joyful faces. It was soon all over and we went back to our houses."

*   *   *

Death, who 'lays his icy hand on kings', took in October 1993 Wendy Coles, who gave 35 years to the school and, particularly during her years as Deputy Head, was an enormous influence on every member of it. Jean Thomson wrote: "Certain it is, that so long as the School shall flourish, it will draw inspiration from her spirit which it so firmly enshrined in its heart."

The following January Paul Hobhouse died. He had been a Governor since 1972 and eventually followed his father and grandfather as Chairman. With his death the Hobhouse name, as already mentioned, is no longer to be found among the Governors, although it remains on the school's lips as a handsome building.

In the autumn of 1993 came the untimely death of Cath Longman. Some of her work has already been mentioned. Let us mention one more moment. She and her husband Raymond collected much needed supplies for a Romanian orphanage, and themselves drove a lorry to deliver them. Mrs Longman, calm and apparently unemotional, gave a brief account of their epic errand of mercy in school assembly. It was only when she came to say a prayer for the children in Romania that her voice broke, and she apologised that emotion had overcome her. It was a rare glimpse of the feeling within her.

Retirement robbed the school of a number of faithful and valued people. Fay Griffiths, who claimed to have told only one mathematical joke in thirty years, went in 1994, after 20 years in the school, to warmer climes in Spain. Tony and Pam Watkins slid away from the Art department and the school eschewing fuss and farewells. Pam had kept the plight of prisoners of conscience in the minds of the staff; one characteristic remark of Tony's spoke volumes: at a staff meeting the Head had announced the enlargement of the Art department by one extra room. She said "I hope you are pleased, Mr Watkins." Tony stretched back in his chair and just said "Well ..."

In 1995 Colin Watkins, Head of Science for 12 years, retired to his bees and many other interests. When the author proposed to walk the length of Hadrian's Wall, Colin wrote him 'The Watkins Guide to the Wall' full of quaint and useful tips. For a Physics Evening, he caused a scratch choir to sing Newton's First Law of Thermodynamics in Latin to an Anglican chant. At the same time Felicity Redmond-Lyon, whose timetable was at one time adjusted so that she could feed the goat, retired and bought a share in a canal boat. Her enlivening of the charities has been mentioned. One of the maintenance staff once told the author that he had been under a sink doing repair work during a Physics lesson taught by Felicity, and had himself been fascinated by it. Mrs Liz Langdon, whose French classroom once had a notice on the door saying 'Close the door or you will let the love out,' retired to give a year, with her husband's blessing, to teaching in a school in Nigeria.

Unhappily, a virus left Mrs Catherine Millar slightly paralysed and unable to continue as Deputy Head in 1995, and she and her dog Lotte retired to Bunbury, the picturesque retreat near the school whose name shows Catherine's humour and literary bent.

There are some who maintain that the most important person in a school is the Caretaker. Maurice Vincent with his wife Doreen held that post for twenty two years. He was always ready with some home-made solution to a problem, using as often as not recycled materials. His drawings of horses delighted the pony-mad among the girls, and although he could blow his top, he and his 'ladies' were normally a cheerful and efficient bunch. Their hideout below stairs in the day school could be entered only by those privileged with an invitation, and was a place of banter and laughter.

*   *   *

Despite the pressures of work, the dizzy round of educational trips, theatre visits, lectures, Duke of Edinburgh Award activities, Guides and Brownie Guides, Ski trips, sports, conferences, Classics Evenings, concerts, carol services, drama clubs. foreign exchanges, a Sixth Form Culture Club and more, continued unchecked. School plays included a delightful 'Midsummer Night's Dream,' a suitably confusing 'Comedy of Errors,' and a chilling 'The Crucible' - that scream echoes in the memory still - without mentioning junior drama. Under the new Director of Music, Mrs Joan German, and Mrs Preller (who married the Rector of Bruton to general delight and became Mrs Richards), 'The Boy Friend' and 'My Fair Lady' were staged. The Bursar proved to be a deft performer on the drum kit in these and many other performances. 'The Boy Friend,' though a slight piece, was charmingly sung and acted, and girls may have felt a special sympathy for the leading female characters in their search for the ideal boyfriend. 'My Fair Lady' is more substantial, and Arabella Neville-Rolfe made a fittingly infuriating Professor Higgins, while we were treated to two Elizas on different nights. Barbara Jenkinson, one of the longest serving staff members, continued her good work with junior musicians and staged such pieces as Ocean World and later Yanomamo.

Individuals brought credit to the school in athletics and music. Tommy Kemp and Helen and Nicola Fifield, while remaining very modest, achieved great things in cross-country running. Laura Trayhurn, whose lovely voice had often been heard with enjoyment in school, broadcast in the final of the Radio 2 Choir Girl of the Year competition in 1997.

* * *

So many problems, so many achievements, so many retirements and deaths, must be balanced with the fresh views of two girls new to the school.

"On my first day I felt worried about what type of work we would be doing and if the work was going to be really hard and if I was stuck would the teacher help me or just send me away or shout at me?

"When I got to the J block it was time to go inside. Then we went to Assembly and everyone gave me a warm welcome to Sunny Hill. All my worries gradually went away after the first few days and I felt more welcome every day. Then I began to get more friendly with the girls who went there as well and that made the lessons more easy to cope with and I am now settled and very happy at Sunny Hill."

That was by A-non-E-Mouse. Shona Henderson tells a similar tale.

"My first thought was Help! There were about 50 or 60 people on the bus so you could imagine how I felt.

"My thoughts about my first day were not very good but I was telling myself that it would get better and believe me it did.

"When I was walking down with my sister I didn't think the school would be this big, it was like an enormous maze. In the junior block everybody in the upper classes was talking eagerly but I just couldn't think of anything to say. At break I found that everybody was friendly so we all got on well. It seemed a long time till lunch.

"I am sure that everyone has had this feeling, it is: School dinners, Yuck or Yummy?

"When we did go to lunch, I was surprised - they were alright!!! We all sat on one table with twelve seats. It was good.

"In the afternoon we went round the school looking at things. Now all my feelings of fear and worry have gone, I am glad. I think the school is better as you go on even if the work does get a lot harder. When I got home I told my Mum that it was great."

To quote Frank MacCourt: 'Tis.

* * *

Chapter 27

One Hundred Not Out

Sunny Hill may not have produced its first Prime Minister yet, but a single issue of the Old Girls' Association News Sheet (1998) reveals some of the extraordinary variety of lives and careers of which education at the school has formed a perhaps important part. It seems fairest to present a small selection in alphabetical order, as the News Sheet does.

The Revd. Zena D. Attwood (1954-61) was engaged in Parish Ministry in Canada. She took on a third congregation at the beginning of 1997 and in August of that year, with her two sons in their early twenties, began studies towards a Doctor of Ministry degree at McMaster University at Hamilton, Ontario, while continuing her full time parish work.

Three who were at the school in the eighties were treading contrasting paths. Sian Bamping was working in Inverness during the winter, and from Easter time worked on a hotel barge on the Caledonian Canal, travelling up from Inverness to Fort William. Annalese Banbury was in her third year at university studying European Marketing, and spending that particular year in France, at IUT Valence, south of Lyon. Annabelle Hitchcock who had just got married and moved to Troon, was working for a company of economic strategy consultants in Glasgow.

Daphne Boothby, née House (1942-48) was a busy sculptor, putting on exhibitions and designing and making trophies in bronze and marble for the professional World Wind-Surfing Association to be presented in Brazil, while her son worked freelance for French television and her daughter for 'Next.'

Among those who came to Sunny Hill in 1978, Alison Chilcott (1978-82) was a Police Officer stationed at Minehead, acting as a Community Beat Officer for an area on Exmoor; Emma Collins, nee Hanscomb (1978-87) was doing up their newly bought flat in west London while working for an exhibition company, doing the PR for four different shows including one in the food industry; and Sarah Davies (1978-85) left Perkins Diesel Engines after eight years, to set up her own business, 'Turquoise,' specialising in hand-crafted silver and gold jewellery and creative wedding items.

Liz Davis née Tait (1963-70) had been teaching at Greenwich Community College for 20 years and still loved teaching mature students who were going on to university. She was also doing research, interviewing children and parents in families where a parent had a drug or alcohol problem. She also worked with four primary schools, on a project to help families and school to work together.

Two had taken early retirement from teaching, and had embarked on new ventures. Valerie Lane (1955-63) began training as a Reader in the Church of England, while SusanTincello née Elmes (1942-49) bought a lathe in 1989 and set up a one woman wood-turning business which had taken over her life.

This brief and probably unrepresentative survey has space for two more reports. Fiona Woodward (1980-88) was in Ecuador, running an Ecotourism Lodge in the Haquipucuna reserve, where 4,000 hectares of mainly primary forest supports a vast variety of birds, butterflies, mammals and plants. She provided trail walking, bird watching and swimming in the rivers for visitors from Ecuador and beyond, so helping the local people. By contrast, Gaby Yateman (1987-94) took an English degree and went to serve voluntarily with a church in a tough area of Nottingham, with high unemployment, many underprivileged children and single parents, and found the work very rewarding.

The list could have been extended almost ad infinitum, and no family news has been included. Old Girls report with pride their children's and grandchildren's achievements, as well as stories of heroic endurance of suffering and loss. Some look back from a serene retirement on a full and worthwhile life. Others would agree with one Old Girl's question: "Retirement - what's that?" The picture that emerges is of much enterprise and achievement, much unselfish work for good causes and suffering people, much delight in family life, and a considerable devotion to the friends made at Sunny Hill. Henry Hobhouse, William Knight and Edith Radford would be amazed at the opportunities open to women today, but they would find satisfaction that the school they founded had continued for so long to instil the values they held important.

* * *

Meanwhile in Bruton there were major changes. Judy Wade had been asked to stay as headmistress until the year 2001, in order to lead the school's celebrations of its centenary, and in return for agreeing to this had been granted a term's sabbatical leave to recharge her batteries for the extra years beyond normal retiring age. She chose to take the period from half term in the spring term to half term in the summer term, so that she could be back to finish off the school year.

Soon after her return, which was welcomed by girls and staff alike, a meeting of all school employees was rather mysteriously called after school one day. All assembled in a darkened school hall, and were treated to a series of speeches by the Chairman of the Governors, by another governor whom most of those present did not know, and by the Headmistress. The first two speeches had begun by insisting that the governors had confidence in the future of the school. This naturally made the hearers apprehensive, since they had up to that point not doubted that the school would survive. This insistence was followed by hints of a major reorganisation. When the Headmistress stood up to speak, the staff hoped for some of the reassurance and explanation that their long and trusting relationship with her led them to expect. They were disappointed, because she seemed to be under some constraint, almost like a cadre mouthing the party line. The Bursar then showed a number of neatly prepared overhead projector transparencies which explained in detail how the school was to become three separate institutions, Sunny Hill Prep School for the under 11s, Bruton School for Girls up to GCSE, and Bruton College to replace the Sixth Form. The abolition of forms and their replacement by all-age groupings was also to be part of the plan, and the changes would take place at the end of 1997.

One at least of the proposed changes was generally welcomed. Miss Radford had pioneered the idea of a junior school, and organic developments over the years made this further step to a separate Prep School a logical one. There was pleasure that the name Sunny Hill had once again some official status, although, despite misgivings from at least the time of Brigadier Cazenove whether the name was a liability to the school, it remained and remains the most widely used name for the whole school in the locality.

There were misgivings about the Sixth Form College as proposed, partly because it would entail the destruction of the happiest of the boarding houses, Highcroft. There was, however, much to be said for treating the Upper and Lower Sixth as a unit.

The change from forms to 'vertical' groups was discussed with some anxiety. There was a fear that new girls would be overwhelmed by the presence in their group of bouncy girls from years 9 or 10. In fact, although a young girl stayed away from school for just this reason, the efforts of the staff have made the scheme work.

What caused most disquiet, however, was the emphasis in the Bursar's presentation on 'command structures' which seemed more suitable to the army, or perhaps big business, than to a community of self-motivated, loyal and responsible people such as the school staff. It was also noticed that administrative or 'management' posts were increasing, with salary implications for the school -

effectively for the parents. There also seemed to be an undue emphasis on marketing and image creation, rather than on substance, that is, on the happy and respectful relationships between all the members of the school, adults and pupils, and the care for individual pupils that helped even the weakest to reach unexpected heights of achievement.

One or two of the audience may have noticed that the new plans made no mention of the ideals which had inspired the school hitherto, whose fruits are exemplified in the lives of old girls noted above. These ideals included a (non-sectarian) religious outlook, repeatedly emphasised by the founder, Henry Hobhouse, and reinforced by each Headmistress from Edith Radford to Judy Wade, an emphasis on service, and a determination that the school should serve families in the neighbourhood, even those without the means to pay large fees, by charging as little as possible and providing the best and happiest education possible with that little. (See the speech by Henry Hobhouse on the school's coming of age in 1921 and elsewhere.)

*   *   *

The following school year saw further developments. The major event of the autumn term was the non-appearance and then resignation, or unexpected retirement, of the Headmistress. A local newspaper report the following May included this: "Former principal Julie [sic] Wade resigned eight months ago allegedly following a clash with the governors." In the absence of firm information, parents and others were left to wonder whether her sabbatical leave was used by others in the school to make changes that left the post of Headmistress virtually untenable.

The governors did provide a farewell party where in the presence of staff of all sections of the school tributes were paid to her 19 years of excellent and devoted work as Head of Science, Deputy Head and Head. Your humble scribe sang a gently satirical song referring to his own recent retirement as well as that of Miss Holt and the Head:

> Now Letitia has retired, and Judy quit;
> Losing one may be misfortune, I admit;
> Losing both within a year
> Looks like carelessness, I fear,
> But I'm out of it, and all is for the best. ....
>
> Now a trinity's gestating for the school,
> And they're following a (maybe) golden rule.

Spring surprise upon surprise,
When in doubt, reorganise.
But I'm sure we'll find that all is for the best.

For the best, for the best,
For the B.E.S.T. best,
For the best, for the best
In the best of possible worlds.

This little squib, which in any normal circumstances would have been cause for at most a bit of tut-tutting by the decision makers and gentle amusement by the staff, and was indeed graciously accepted by the Chairman of Governors in that spirit, proved to arouse considerable anger in one of those most closely associated with the changes in the school, and extreme joy among a wide spectrum of staff members. This suggested that there were passions and resentments about the changes which could not normally find a safe outlet. Enquiries about life in the school during that and the following term brought different responses, none of them reassuring. A Sixth Former said that she concentrated on her work and tried to ignore the rest. Office staff were evasive. Teaching staff said that they were being asked to give way to every whim of the girls and their parents, and at the same time to achieve record exam results; the governors, teachers claimed, were deaf to all suggestions, or reacted with threats; morale, they all agreed, was very low.

* * *

Meanwhile a new Headmistress was sought, and the Sixth Formers were being invited to prepare the rest of the school for the coming changes. The post of Head was not advertised, presumably because the governors already knew the ideal person for the job, and invited her to accept it. She was Mrs Lesley Watson, the young and attractive recently married Deputy Head of Benenden School, known most widely as the place where Princess Anne was a pupil. Among changes explained by the Sixth Form was to be the abolition of the four Colour Houses, Red, Blue, Brown and Yellow, which had been part of the school since 1911, and their replacement by four Colour Halls, Red, Blue, Purple and Gold, each made up of several of the new all-age groupings. One teacher, in cynical mood, suggested that the change from Houses to Halls was in order to cut off the school from its traditions as far as possible.

One cosmetic change was to call Mrs Watson Principal, not Headmistress. A change of more substance had been to take the opportunity of Mrs Wade's last summer holiday to move the Head's office from its central position near the school office, staff room and assembly hall to splendid isolation in Old House. It was returning, in fact, to somewhere very near Miss Radford's original quarters, but in her day that was at the centre of the school. Previous heads had chosen not to move away from the hub of things, but Mrs Watson was not given the choice.

She was, one imagines, given a full and honest account of the governors' plans for the future direction and style of the school, and came to carry out those plans. During her first weeks she seems to have built up a good relationship with staff and pupils. By the last day of her first term, which was given over to inter-Hall competitions, she seemed quite at home in the assembly hall, and fully accepted by the girls, as she announced competition results.

When, however, the old girls gathered at the school in the summer term, it was to hear that the school photograph had been taken the previous day, without Mrs Watson. Her unexplained absence from a formal occasion produced unease. She did not come to explain the new arrangement of the school to the old girls, that job being left to the Deputy Head. The following Friday the Western Daily Press reported the worries of parents:

"One parent said last night: 'A number of us telephoned to find out what was going on, but were fobbed off with an excuse that she was in discussions with the governors. We were offered no real explanation as to why she had left her duties and given no indication when or if she would return. It is obviously a very worrying situation when the head of a school is not at her desk during a crucial part of the term.'"

That edition contained an attempted reassurance:

"Bursar David Collyer said yesterday: 'She and the governors are discussing their respective visions for the school. Mrs Watson has not been sacked and has not left the school.' No one from the governors would comment last night." The following day's edition announced, under the headline, "New blow for girls' school as head quits": "HEADMISTRESS Lesley Watson has become the latest member of staff to leave an exclusive West girls' school - after just four months in the job. Shocked staff at Bruton school for girls in Somerset were given the news yesterday afternoon, as the 590 pupils left for their half term holiday."

Staff members were not only shocked, but bewildered. They felt that they were being kept in the dark, and at the same time were forbidden to talk about events at the school, even to their husbands or wives. They could not understand how a Principal who had been head-hunted by the governors and appointed to carry out their policy, could so soon leave because of "differences of view over the future direction and style of the school, at a time of great change and development" particularly since the governors themselves acknowledged that since her arrival on January 1 1998 "she has demonstrated energy, enthusiasm, commitment and professional skills at the school." She has since become Headmistress elsewhere.

An influential group of parents, including a lawyer, made their feelings known to the staff and the other parents, since they found that they could get no satisfaction from the governors. One governor, recently appointed to maintain liaison with the staff, resigned. The governors were faced with finding yet another Principal.

*   *   *

Ann Napier guided the school through the interregnum, and managed the difficult Speech Day skilfully by getting senior girls to give the traditional Head's review of the past year. There was, however, an uneasy feeling to that Speech Day.

Not until the arrival in April 1999 of Mrs Barbara C. Bates could everyone relax in the knowledge that, in the words of one who met her, "a feisty lady" was in permanent charge, someone with sympathy for the aims of the school, a clear vision for the future, and the strength to realise the vision despite opposition. Mrs Bates was previously Academic Deputy Head at James Allen's Girls School, Dulwich, with a London BA in Philosophy and History of Art and an MA in Education. She is a member of the Institute of Managers and Institute of Directors. Her husband Dr. David Bates heads a Life Sciences department in London.

In June 1999 she wrote to parents setting out changes to be made in the next academic year. These included a nine-period day, more teaching time for GCSE and A level, an A level History of Art course, more German and Information Technology, and the replacement of Needlework by Textiles.

Mrs Bates made it her intention to review the recent changes in the school set-up, with outside help, during her first two terms. She concluded that the new scheme was top-heavy on management, and implemented changes.

There would be two Vice-Principals, each teaching 12 periods a week, a V-P Academic, to whom Heads of Department would be answerable, and a V-P Pastoral. In future there would be no Director of the Sixth Form (Bruton College) or Director of School. The vertical tutor system was to stay, but 'Bruton College' was to be 'brought back into the fold'. The Prep School was still called Sunny Hill, but was quite definitely a department of the school. To the Old Girls Mrs Bates confided that not all the changes were new. "We are returning to some of those sound, tried and tested traditions which outlive the fads and fashions of education policies." In fact, such is her respect for history and tradition that she plans a centenary corridor in Old House, to be decorated with memorabilia from the first hundred years.

Boarding House arrangements brought the younger girls into Old House, the 5ths into Old Vicarage, while the 6ths stayed in Highcroft.

Coinciding with this review, there were big changes in the governing body. The Chairman, the Hon Mrs Victoria Jolliffe, resigned in January 2000, ending 100 years of the Hobhouse family's representation on the governing body; and Count Charles de Salis retired at the same time. The Revd Matthew Persson took over as Chairman. The Bursar, David Collyer, also left in January 2000.

The school uniform changed to a more substantial kilt and a school blazer.

League tables published in November 1999 rated Bruton School for Girls the top school in Somerset. New building work began to make a Centenary Fitness Suite, which is used not only for ballet, aerobics and dance, but also for meditation, and an Aerobics/Dance Studio.

* * *

Long serving staff who retired in July 1999 included two who taught in the Hobhouse building, Mrs Chris Patterson who ran Domestic Science and Mrs Elspeth Richards the head of Drama.

In the summer of 2000, along with Gill Brown, Sue Bamping and Olivia Bourne, all of whom taught at the school for a considerable time, the longest serving member of the present staff retired. Valerie Floyde served the school for 37 years. Readers will recall her tales of her early days at the School (Chapter 20). After all the changes that she has seen, particularly the upheavals since 1997, she will be reassured by words of the Principal in December 1999:

> "Much has changed since the inception of Sunny Hill but the basic aims remain - to provide a high quality of boarding and day schooling for girls and to provide subsidised education for girls from families of modest means. Bruton School for Girls has grown to match the demands of the twentieth century and will continue to rise to the challenges of the twenty first."

May Bruton School for Girls continue to be what it has been: above all a happy and co-operative community, relying perhaps too much on the unfailing goodwill of its staff, who are content to go beyond their allotted and paid duties for the sake of the girls. These girls enjoy the advantages of a very mixed community, with the daughters of local farmers and teachers mixing with those from wealthier families from Britain and overseas, hardly aware of the differences between them, and with boarders and day girls each bringing their own experiences, and each feeling they have the better part of the bargain.

*   *   *

A class of Confirmation candidates prepare to Follow the Gleam.
Also in the group are the four housemistresses at the time and the author

Appendix A

The School Song

II
Over the valley
In early summers
Over the mountain,
On human faces,
And all around me,
Moving to melody,
Floated the Gleam.

V
Down from the mountain
And over the level,
And streaming and shining on
Silent river,
Silvery willow,
Pasture and plowland,
...
Slided the Gleam -

VIII
And broader and brighter
The Gleam flying onward,
Wed to the melody,
Sang through the world;
...
For thro' the Magic
Of Him the Mighty,
Who taught me in childhood,
There on the border
Of boundless ocean,
And all but in Heaven
Hovers the Gleam.

IX
Not of the sunlight,
Not of the moonlight,
Not of the starlight!
O young Mariner,
Down to the haven,
Call your companions,
Launch your vessel,
And crowd your canvas,
And, ere it vanishes
Over the margin,
After it, follow it,
Follow The Gleam.

Extracts from Merlin and the Gleam, by Alfred Lord Tennyson, from the collection *Demeter and Other Poems*. The text is that of the Oxford edition, and differs slightly from that commonly sung.

Appendix B

The Arms of Bruton School for Girls (Sunny Hill School)

The School was granted Arms in 1960.

SHIELD: Per chevron Azure and Argent in chief a Sun in splendour Or and in base a Cross botony Vert.

CREST: On a Treath Or and Azure a Laurel Wreath proper enclosing an Estoile radiated Or.

MOTTO: FOLLOW THE GLEAM.

In ordinary language the blazon (heraldic description) means that the shield is divided chevron-wise, its upper part being blue and its lower white or silver. On the blue section is the sun surrounded by rays (in splendour) issuing, as it were, from behind the peak of the white portion of the shield, on which is portrayed a green cross, each of its limbs ending in three knobs (botony). The wreath on which the crest stands is the conventional representation of the torse, a twisted ribbon usually of the principal metal and colour of the shield, but in this case gold and blue. Proper mean "in natural colours" and an estoile radiated Or is, simply, a star surrounded by rays, all of gold.

Every emblem in this achievement of arms (as the whole heraldic composition is called) has meaning. The sun and the peak of the chevron have an obvious reference to the Sunny Hill which is the site of the school. The sun is shown setting behind the chevron which also represents the Glastonbury Tor, a well-known local landmark. The cross botony is from the Arms of the Abbey of Glastonbury. The star of the crest, taken directly from the crest of the Hobhouse family (with the permission of the former Chairman), who have served the School since 1900, may also be said to represent the "gleam" of the motto; and the laurel wreath, added for a difference - since no individual or corporation may have exactly the same crest as another - symbolises the honour which is to be won by those who "follow the gleam" faithfully. The motto indicates the dominance of Tennyson in a 1900 foundation - the gleam is the light of inner inspiration, and draws added meaning from the fact that the School also looks out upon the home of the Holy Grail in Glastonbury.

From the folder written by David Christie-Murray and first published 1964.

Appendix C

Chairmen of Governors

The Honourable Henry Hobhouse
(1900-31)
Mr. R. T. A. Hughes
(1931-36)
Sir Arthur Hobhouse
(1936- 63)
Miss A. K. Daniel
(1963-71)
Major H. M. Fraser
(1971-1973)
Paul Hobhouse Esquire
(1973-1986)
The Honourable Mrs Prudence Louisa (Toodie) Fortescue
(1986-92)
The Honourable Mrs Victoria Jolliffe
(1992-2000)
The Reverend Matthew Persson
(2000-   )

Appendix D

Headmistresses

Miss Edith Jane Radford
(1900-1929)
Miss Jane Townley Wells
(1929-1950)
Miss Enid Lorna Chappell
(1950-1964)
Miss Desiree Cumberlege
(1964-1980)
Miss Jean Thomson
(1980-1987)
Mrs Judith Wade
(1987-1997)

Principals

Mrs Lesley Watson
(1998)
Mrs Barbara Bates
(1999-   )

INDEX

~ Index ~